Spirit Dogs:

Life Between Lives

by

Susan Kelleher

Spirit Dogs: Life Between Lives
a novel

Copyright © 2005 Susan Kelleher
Published by Owl of Athene Press
PO Box 23683, Silverthorne CO 80498
www.spiritdogs.com

First Edition

Cover design by Rod Lawrence:
www. RodLawrence.com
Interior design by MacGraphics Services:
www.macgraphics.net

Library of Congress Control Number: 2004117318

13-digit ISBN: 978-0-9650495-2-3
10-digit ISBN: 0-9650495-2-3

Printed in the United States of America

Thanks

I extend sincere gratitude to all the people who read this novel, gave me feedback, and encouraged me: Trula Daugherty, Sandy Van Nest, Irene and Charlie Reifsnyder, my son Alex Ryan, Carol Occhipinti, John Bradley, Beverley Sutton, Mark Minter, Don Folgueras, Josie Quick, Captain Haggerty, Charlie Stewart-Fippin, Dr. Nancy Schenck, Lench Archuleta, Stephanie Goldman Meis, and Bob Reifsnyder. Thanks also to Gail Nalepa of Top Dog Show Supplies for her tremendous enthusiasm about both *Spirit Dogs: Heroes In Heaven* and this book, which she hasn't even read yet. Thanks to Sally Terroux for all she taught me about dogs in general and about canine aggression. She, along with Captain Haggerty, opened my eyes about genetic versus environmental aggression, because Sally asked me to write a series of articles for the *AKC Gazette* "Flat-Coated Retriever Breed Column" and for the Flat-Coated Retriever Society of America *Newsletter* on some concerns about signs of aggression emerging from this most lovely, gentle breed. For those articles I also interviewed and learned from Jeffrey Pepper, AKC Sporting Group Judge, and Joan Mason, Brenda Phillips, and Mary Ward, all Flat-Coat judges in the United Kingdom. Thanks to Tom Ryan, who remains a very special friend, for enhancing the "About The Author" section in the back of the book.

I thank the real Ivan for bringing this character to life as well as my Flat-Coated Retriever, Fiji, for watching me write this book and listening while I read it out loud to her and the cat. Such loyalty.

Thanks to Lewis Mehl-Madrona, MD, PhD for helping me discover The Spirit of Many Words, a fun-loving guide who never talks, in a Native American sweat lodge; Emily Dickinson in a guided meditation; and Lench, Yaqui Spiritual Elder, during a healing intensive in Arizona. All four contributed to the successful completion of this book.

I am grateful that renowned wildlife artist Rod Lawrence not only illustrated *Spirit Dogs: Heroes In Heaven* but designed the cover and paw prints for this book. His artistic genius has wowed me for over twenty years. Check out his artwork at www.RodLawrence.com. He has won many awards as a wildlife artist and has commissioned some very impressive dog portraits.

And an extra-special thanks to Emily. This manuscript wouldn't be what it is without your help.

Susan Metzger Kelleher

February, 2005

Introduction

While *Spirit Dogs: Life Between Lives* is thoroughly enjoyable to be read as pure entertainment, especially for those of us who are dog lovers, don't let the easy-to-read story fool you! Kelleher's warm tale of canine characters, derived from her extensive dog expertise, reveals profound spiritual truths. The author affectionately describes the evolutionary differences between various dog breeds in her informative and light-hearted tale, as she adds much more colorful detail to our thoughts on the afterlife. I can't think of a more delightful way to gain important spiritual insight than to give ourselves the pleasant opportunity to spend some time with *Spirit Dogs: Life Between Lives* as a metaphor for our own lives.

Stephanie Goldman Meis, MA, Reiki Master-Teacher
Therapeutic Spiritual Exploration
Highland Park, IL

From A Cat Lover

Dear Susan:

When I started reading *Spirit Dogs: Life Between Lives*, I didn't realize how difficult it would be for me to read about spirit dogs. I think it was therapeutic, because I kept stopping to cry about my cat, Mia. I miss her so much.

I used to say that she thought she was a dog, because she never acted aloof like cats are supposed to. She greeted me at the door every time I came home. She slept by me while I practiced violin, followed me around until I went to bed at night, was constantly either by my side or on me. She never held a grudge when I went out of town or took her to the vet. She always just adored me. We would joke about how I was being adored because she would pour herself into me and gaze up at me. She was so clingy that at times I would tell her that she needed to act more like a cat and quit being in my way all the time. Now I miss having her be a pain because she wanted my constant attention.

Reading about spirit dogs gives me hope that Mia is very alive as a cat spirit, exploring the role she played in my life. It has made me think of the lessons she taught me. It comforts me to think that every time I think I see her out of the corner of my eye, it may be her paying me a visit.

Josie Quick
Denver, CO

Chapter One

Ivan clenched his front paws over the edge of the tunnel. He peered into the whiteness of its depths and searched for an image of Sarah. His heart poured out to her. He searched every swirl of the cloudiness for her face, her hair, her body, even the glimpse of a hand, but saw only the opalescence. A whimper escaped from his nostrils as he paced around the tunnel's opening. He searched and whined, then sat down, swallowed, and decided to think. He replayed in his mind Boy's recent words to Sarah about it not being her time to remain in Heaven, that she would be going back to Earth, but it *was* time for *him* to be Boy's student in preparation for becoming a hero.

"A hero? Me?" he'd wanted to ask. "Why me? I'm happy just being Sarah's pet. Why do I need to become a hero? And just what do you mean by 'hero' anyway?" But, he thought to himself, *I didn't ask, did I? And now Sarah's gone, and I don't want to be here.* "Sarah!" he called down into the tunnel.

If only I'd pretended to be sick this morning, we wouldn't have gone down that icy highway to Denver for the herding competition. I could have faked a limp, and we would have stayed home. But no, I had to awaken her at 4:00 AM and lick her face till she got up. "Ohhhhhh," he moaned. "It's all my fault."

"It's not your fault at all, Ivan," said Boy. Ivan jumped. He'd forgotten that Boy was still here. "She'll be in a hospital for a couple weeks. When she goes home, her relatives will have put your bowls, toys, and leashes away."

Ivan felt small next to the handsome Collie, whose golden aura emanated for yards around him, actually encompassing Ivan himself. "But I could have prevented our going down to Denver this morning."

"This was meant to be," said Boy. "It's all part of the plan."

"Well, I think the plan stinks!" said Ivan.

"I understand how you feel, but you'll change your mind in time. As for the guilt you're feeling, herding dogs do that. I used to do it."

"What do you mean?"

"Herding dogs have guilt complexes. Terriers can't help but be feisty. Retrievers are overly-forgiving. It's part of our growth process."

"Huh?" asked Ivan.

"Come with me. I want you to meet some new arrivals." He walked away, and Ivan followed.

Boy stopped, turned to Ivan, and said, "You needed to learn guilt. You hadn't experienced it before. You'll recall more and more of your past lives as time goes on. You weren't a herding breed until this last life when you chose to be an Australian Shepherd. As I recall, you were a Labrador Retriever the time before, and, hmmm . . . ." He reflected a few moments. "Weren't you a Golden Retriever before that? And a Curly-Coated Retriever before that? A bit heavy in the retriever area. Do you recall?"

In a flash, Ivan viewed, as if on a movie screen, all the kinds of dogs he'd ever been. It was as if they marched right past him in a parade. He saw himself, among scores of others, as a guard dog for a Pharaoh in Egypt, a large working dog in the mountains of Tibet, a companion dog for an American Indian family, a sledding dog in Siberia, a short-lived dog bred for meat in China, a Labrador-mix all covered with skin sores in a biology laboratory, then as another mixed-breed who spent his entire life tied by a rope in his family's back yard, and as a series of retrievers—Chesapeake Bay, Labrador, Golden, Flat-Coated, Nova Scotia Duck Tolling, and Curly-Coated.

"The memories will become clearer with time," Boy said. "Now, we'll gather the next four or five arrivals. It's been determined that you will be a group leader this time. I'll facilitate the discussion to begin with. Then you'll take over."

I'll take over? Ivan wondered. *Why me?* Boy had already begun trotting back to the tunnel opening. *Guess I better hurry and follow him. I'll lead the group? I don't know how to lead a group.*

He looked around as he trotted after Boy. *This feels oddly familiar, this place,* he thought. *Feels like I've been here before, but how could that be? I've always lived with Sarah. Well, look at that—three more dogs. They look as bewildered as I feel.*

One dog was a glamorous, black Standard Poodle in a perfect show clip. A forlorn-looking, small, very thin, tricolored dog of mixed terrier-spaniel heritage sat shivering, his long ears tucked in close to his head. A few feet from him, a huge, white, thick-coated dog surveyed the scenes around her.

Soon, a brindle-colored American Staffordshire Terrier and an anxious-looking Lhasa Apso emerged from the tunnel's entrance. They peered around, unsure of where they were. Within moments, however, their faces softened.

Ivan stepped up to Boy. "Where are their owners?" he asked.

"Yours was an unusual occurrence," Boy explained. "Dogs seldom die along with their owners as Sarah almost did with you. It does happen on occasion, usually in car crashes like yours."

"Oh," said Ivan. *That makes sense,* he thought, trying to imagine what other circumstances would end the lives of both dog and owner at the same time. Hurricanes, bombings, tornadoes, and airplane crashes were all that came to mind, all unlikely events.

Boy approached the five dogs sitting around the tunnel. When they spotted him, reverent expressions came over their faces. Boy wagged his tail mildly in greeting. "Welcome," he said. "Welcome home." They wagged their tails in response. "Come with me," Boy said and walked toward an area between some woods and a lake. He found a clear, grassy spot and turned to face the group. Ivan stood at his side and listened, knowing he would soon be called upon to lead the discussion.

"I am Anubis, although most everyone calls me Boy," he said. "We've met before. Your memories of me may return shortly. This is Ivan, who will take over after I've spoken a bit longer. First, let's introduce ourselves and briefly state what job you just left, the primary humans in your life, the name they gave you, and how you died." He turned to the small, thin, tri-colored dog with the long ears.

Shivering so that his teeth chattered, the little dog asked, "M-m-m-m-me? You want me to go f-f-f-first?"

Boy nodded. "Please. You'll feel calmer very soon. You know that you're home now, don't you?"

The small dog peered around the area. Through his chattering teeth, he said, "W-w-well, I guess s-s-so. Th-th-th-that would be nice. I'm so c-c-cold."

"Why are you cold? What situation did you leave on Earth?"

"G-G-G-Greenland. An animal shelter. No heat. Before that with Helga, my mistress. She died. Her relatives didn't want me. Ohhhhh, Helga. I miss her so much. She loved me. She let me sleep with her, gave me bacon and warm milk . . . ." His voice choked up, and he could no longer talk. He shut his eyes and sobbed softly.

"What did she name you?" Boy asked.

"M-M-Murphy," said the little dog.

"Did you like the name? Did it suit you—the you inside?"

Murphy thought for a moment. "My Helga chose it. It must be a good name." He glanced up at Boy, who looked down on him kindly as a grandfather would upon a young grandson. This appeared to warm Murphy. His shivering subsided somewhat, and he went on with his story. "My j-job was to be a c-companion to Helga. She spent most of her time in a wheel chair. Her heart wasn't good. She didn't want to live in G-Greenland, but she had nowhere else to-to-to go. I listened to her when she felt like talking to someone, b-barked at the mailman, and bumped her with my n-nose when someone knocked at the door. She had lost her h-hearing." He nodded at Boy to signal that he was done.

"And your death. What happened?"

Murphy shivered for a moment, glanced around at his warm, heavenly surroundings, and sighed. "I died of exposure to the c-cold. And dehydration. No matter how th-thick or thin our coats were, we had to l-live outside at the shelter. Greenland must be the c-coldest place on Earth. The water was always f-frozen except first thing in the m-morning when they gave it to us. The dogs with thick coats seemed okay. I was c-c-cold all the time and only got colder. Today I just drifted away."

"Thank you, Murphy. You were very brave." Boy looked at the American Staffordshire Terrier, nodded at him, and said, "You're next."

The hefty dog puffed up his shoulders, and in a voice that resembled a growl, he said, "My name—it be Stealth." He stopped there. Ivan thought perhaps Stealth acted tough but was really quite shy. Stealth stared at the ground, and it was clear he had nothing more to say.

Boy gently urged him, "And your job. Would you tell us what your job was?"

Stealth looked quickly at Boy, then stared at the ground again. "Nah, nah. Nah, I really ain't up to it," he said.

"Okay," said Boy. "Maybe you'll feel like it later. Would you like to tell us who your humans were?"

Stealth shook his head "no."

"How you died?"

Stealth looked to the side, then mumbled softly, "I was shot with a gun." Immediately after saying these words, he grimaced and squeezed his eyes shut. Ivan felt adrenaline zing through his stomach. He realized he could actually feel Stealth's pain, even though he didn't know the details of the shooting, and was relieved when Boy moved on to the Poodle.

Ivan was eager to know whether the Poodle was male or female. With the fancy hair-do and puffy topknot, he couldn't tell. "Are you ready?" Boy asked.

The Poodle nodded, lifted his head, and spoke in a clear voice. "My name is Beauregard. I was a show champion and took Best of Breed ninety-seven times and Best In Show twenty-three times. I sired many champion puppies. I was loved by all." He lifted his nose into the air.

"Your job?" asked Boy.

"My job? Well, my job . . . . My job . . . ." He paused, then went on. "My job was to be the perfect show specimen of a Standard Poodle and to mate with champion bitches in order to pass along my splendid genes. Yes, that was my job." He nodded with finality.

"Your humans?"

"Ah, my word. There were so many. My co-owners, my handler, my groomer, my photographer, my exercise trainer, my kennel boy, my financial backer. All of them were my people."

"And your death."

Beauregard's teeth chattered momentarily. He took a deep breath. "They discovered a tumor on my leg. They removed my leg, but the cancer eventually spread to my lungs and my liver. My owners tried everything, but I became so weak I couldn't stand up. Just this morning, one of the vets came to our house. Steven, my favorite owner—with tears streaming down his face—held me and petted me, and the vet game me an injection. Now I'm here." He cleared his throat and swallowed hard.

Boy said, "Thank you," and turned to the large white dog. "And you, Madam?"

"I'm Jolly," she said sweetly and giggled. Her body was in perpetual motion. The wiggling either sped up or slowed down but never ceased altogether. "I was a lovable family pet. My mother was half Samoyed and half Golden Retriever, and my father was half Newfoundland and half Great Pyrenees. My job was to watch the four children—Jane, Jack, Joseph, and Jennifer. And their parents, John and Julie. I died at age twelve when my heart gave out." She looked at Boy for approval. He smiled at her and said, "Thank you."

To the Lhasa Apso, who sat with his flowing, brown and white coat hanging neatly around him, Boy asked, "And you? Would you like to share your story?"

The Lhasa Apso cleared his throat and began in a clipped, elegant style of speech. "My name is Carl. I was the canine companion of two psychoanalysts—Jungian analysts, to be precise. They named me after Carl Jung, the famous Swiss psychiatrist. My humans were Dora and Siegfried. We lived a quiet, sophisticated life in a superb condo near Central Park. My job was to greet analysands, to sit by their sides if they wanted me, and occasionally to cuddle into their laps if their emotional state needed calming. In addition, I served Dora and Siegfried by performing a variety of stunts they taught me through the use of positive reinforcement conditioning techniques. I also listened when they needed someone to talk to. I transitioned here to the other side when a loose mongrel in the park snatched me by the throat. Siegfried and Dora rushed me to the veterinarian, but it was too late. I'd lost too much blood."

Ivan was impressed with Carl's English and thought the little dog should be holding a book and wearing spectacles and a mortarboard. He seemed so intelligent.

"Thank you," said Boy. "And now Ivan."

Ivan jumped. He didn't expect to be called upon to share his story. *I thought I was the leader, not a participant like the others,* he thought.

Boy saw that Ivan was flustered. Gently, he said, "Ivan, recall that you just arrived, too. I'm sure they'd like to hear about your life."

Ivan pulled his thoughts together. *Gosh, I've been so busy listening to the others' stories, I haven't formulated my own.* Quickly, he thought of Sarah, how she'd named him, and all the services he'd performed for her. "Hi," he said and glanced at each of the other dogs nervously. "My name is Ivan. My human was Sarah. It was just the two of us. She taught high school literature and named me after one of the brothers in Dostoyevsky's *The Brothers Karamazov*, the Russian novel. I was a conformation show dog and competed in obedience, agility, and herding trials. My main job was to love Sarah and be her companion. She and I died in a car accident . . . except she didn't die for good. She's gone back to Earth." Ivan saw that the others listened intently to him.

"Very good," said Boy, speaking slowly and deliberately. "Now then, Murphy, Stealth, Beauregard, Jolly, Carl, and Ivan, you will be working together to sort through the events of this most recent life. You will help each other understand what each of you has learned and then figure out what you still need to learn in order to become what we call 'whole.' Once you become a 'whole dog,' you will step into the next level of existence, the place where I now exist and where you will all one day arrive. It is the Plane of Xoltl. Once you reach it, you will no longer need to go back to Earth. Your role, as is mine, will be to guide others along their paths of evolution. Ivan has been chosen as your leader, because he may have only one more incarnation on Earth. He will then arrive at the Plane of Xoltl, providing he fulfills his last mission. He can tell you more about that as he sees fit."

What? thought Ivan. *My last mission? What is that? To become a hero? I don't want to be a hero. This is all too much.*

"I suggest, Ivan, that you all agree upon a place to go by yourselves—to talk—somewhere that's away from the others." He scanned the entire area around them. "As you can see, you have many options. You may choose a field, a woods, the mountains, a desert, the snow fields, the ponds, or an indoor setting—whatever you all agree upon." He looked at Ivan and added, "It is important that you all agree. Otherwise, one or two of you may feel too uncomfortable to concentrate. I trust you can handle this." He gave Ivan an encouraging nod and began to turn away but stopped.

He took Ivan aside and said, "One thing more, Ivan. It's possible—common, actually—to take one's energy back to Earth for a short time now and then. New arrivals often feel the need to check in with their humans to make sure they're okay. This helps us feel better about leaving. Make sure they understand that they cannot re-enter their bodies. Only their essence—their energy—may travel back to Earth. Their humans will not be able to see them, but some humans can feel our presence—in its bare, energy form. Warn the travelers that most humans, when they feel their dog's presence, believe their minds are playing tricks on them. But it's real. Their dog's energy is, in fact, near them." Boy nodded and walked away. Ivan watched him, in his golden aura, float back toward the tunnel opening where two new dogs sat with puzzled expressions.

Ivan turned to his group. "Well," he said with a little tremor in his voice. "Where would we like to go?" A couple of the dogs glanced here and there, but no one spoke. They looked at Ivan. Ivan looked into each set of eyes and saw in them a reverence he didn't feel he deserved. "Well, how many of you would like to sit by that pond over there?" He glanced over his shoulder at a pond where retrievers fetched tennis balls that angels threw for them.

"Will they splash us?" asked Beauregard.

"Looks kind of cold to me," said Murphy as a shiver rippled through his body.

"I like it," Jolly said.

"Mmm," Stealth said, not committing one way or the other.

Carl said nothing but listened with interest to the others.

Ivan felt his chest tighten. He realized there was potential for conflict, and Boy had clearly said they must all agree. He looked over his shoulder to a small meadow near a woods where the sun shone on the grass. It looked warm and dry but was still outside. *I have no desire to be indoors,* he thought.

"I see a nice spot over there," he said and nodded his head toward it. "It's sunny and warm and appears to be dry." He started to walk in that direction, and the five dogs followed.

I love the warmth of the sun and the feel of this lush grass beneath my feet. He took a deep breath and felt his lungs expand with satisfaction. When he arrived at the exact spot, he turned and watched his group members form a semi-circle in front of him.

Stealth looked uneasy, as he crouched low in the grass, hunched up his shoulders, and glanced above and around himself. Carl took high steps as though he didn't like the feel of the grass. It was taller than his hocks. Beauregard sniffed at the grass with suspicion. Jolly padded right through it, glanced around, and wagged her tail. And Murphy lifted his face to the sun, basking in its warmth.

"This is lovely," said Murphy, and Jolly nodded.

"The grass is a bit tall," said Carl.

"Just what's in the grass?" asked Beauregard. "Ticks and fleas? I can't say I approve."

Stealth said nothing, but Ivan saw that his quick glances indicated fear of the wide-open space. Ivan's heart sank. *Well, where can we go?* he wondered. He began to feel some anger at Boy. *How is a newcomer like me supposed to know my way around here?*

"Well, I can see this won't work," he said.

"I like it a lot," said Jolly. "Why can't we stay here?"

"Me too. I love it," said Murphy. "The sun feels wonderful."

"Well, I'd like to find something else," said Beauregard. "I don't know that I can sit down here. The grass will get caught in my fur."

Carl just frowned, and Stealth had lain down and crouched as low as he could, trying to hide in the grass.

Ivan wanted to say, "Geez, you guys. This is the great outdoors. Dogs are supposed to enjoy this," but he didn't.

"How about over there in one of the living rooms?" Carl asked. "I see they're not all occupied by the Italian

Greyhounds." He stretched himself up onto his toes. "In fact, there's one in particular that has leather sofas, fine Oriental rugs, and a charming fire in the fireplace." They all looked at the room that Carl pointed at with his nose.

"The fire looks wonderful," said Murphy.

"It looks clean, very tastefully-appointed," said Beauregard.

"Cozy," said Jolly with a happy lilt in her voice.

I love the out-of-doors, the clean air, the breezes in the trees, and the birds singing, thought Ivan. "Stealth? What do you think?"

Stealth lifted his head and studied the room. He nodded as he looked into Ivan's eyes. "Yes. Safe. Warm. Mm. Me likes it."

Ivan sighed. *I can't imagine being cooped up indoors for hours, days, weeks—I don't know how long. I have no idea how to accomplish what Boy wants. I wish I could just be a member of a group and not a leader. This isn't much fun.* He thought, then, of Sarah and how she had made every situation pleasurable for him, whether it was showing in Conformation with words of praise or going for a walk in the woods or learning a new trick on a rainy Saturday. He felt a whimper welling up inside. *Maybe I should call Boy to take over,* he thought. Yet, when he thought about Boy's speech to Sarah during her brief visit here, Boy had told her that he was from a higher order of canines and had said, "Ivan is almost there. He'll be my student this time." This higher order of canines' role was to save a human life or to serve them in some heroic way. *Well, that's fine, but why the necessity of getting five dogs to agree on a place to have a discussion?*

"It looks very nice," said Jolly.

"Yes, it does," said Carl. They all trotted into the room and sniffed the couches, the chair, and the thick oval rug in front of the fireplace. Beauregard leaped onto a plush sofa, Murphy chose the oval rug, Stealth leaned against the side of a leather arm chair, Carl jumped onto the leather arm chair, and Jolly chose the other sofa.

Ivan stepped in front of the fireplace and opened his mouth to begin the session at the same time that Stealth slid down against the side of the chair and closed his eyes. Beauregard fell asleep instantly as did Murphy, Jolly, and Carl. Ivan thought, *Well, that's just great. This is not an easy job.* He marched in a small circle and pouted, then realized that he, too, felt sleepy. Murphy had taken up such a small part of the oval rug, Ivan lay down next to him and drifted off as well.

After they had snoozed awhile, the stirrings of one awakened another, then another, until they all stood and stretched at the same time. Ivan, as he awakened, realized with alarm that he was still in charge. Feeling his knees tremble a bit, he asked, "Would any of you like to go outside for awhile? I think we can find any number of activities out there. There are fields to run in, ponds to swim in, . . ." His throat tightened with guilt at avoiding a discussion.

"Where's the snow?" asked Jolly. "I would love to roll in some deep snow."

"I like it here," said Beauregard.

"Me too," said Stealth.

"Maybe a civilized walk in a park?" asked Carl.

"I'd like to sunbathe," said Murphy. "Is there a sunny beach?"

"Well, . . . um . . . ," Ivan stammered. "Maybe. I don't know for sure. Let's go look." He stepped from the luxurious living room out onto the grass. Murphy, Jolly, and Carl followed, sniffed the air, and gazed about them. "Oh, look, Jolly," said Ivan. "There's the snow—over there." He pointed with his snout in the direction of a shallow valley filled with deep snow and white-peaked mountains behind it. Although it was a fair distance, they could see a variety of Saint Bernards, Newfoundlands, Siberian Huskies, Malamutes, and Great Pyrenees strolling through chest-deep powder. Many of them plunged into small drifts and rolled around on their backs.

"Oh boy!" exclaimed Jolly. "May I go join those dogs?" Her whole body wagged.

"Of course," said Ivan. "But come back in about a half hour, okay?" *We'll have a discussion when she gets back,* he thought.

"Okay!" she said and trotted away.

Soon, Carl spotted a lovely park where a variety of well-groomed, pure-bred and mixed breed dogs strolled along paths and played under large shade trees. A paved path encircled a serene lake in the middle of the park. He headed in that direction. "I'll be back in a half hour, too," he assured Ivan.

Murphy headed for a sunny beach where gentle waves rolled leisurely onto sand dotted with multi-colored beach towels. Various short-haired dogs lay upon the towels, basking in the warmth. As Murphy ran at a fast trot, Ivan called to him, "Don't forget to come back in a half hour!" Murphy turned briefly and nodded his head without slowing down. Ivan watched him until he couldn't distinguish him from the others. He sighed hard to release the tightness in his core. "Whew," he said to himself. "This is hard work."

He glanced back at their living room to see Stealth and Beauregard stretched out in front of the fire, so he looked around for a field of grazing cows or sheep. He didn't see any at first, then finally located one behind their living room. He longed to stretch his legs, so he cantered around the living room and headed across a lawn toward the field. Once there, he galloped as fast as he could, circling small groups of cows and sheep that grazed undisturbed by Ivan and several others—a Belgian Tervuren, a Cardigan Welsh Corgi, and a Border Collie. Flying through the field at full speed, they made twists and turns, quick stops and about faces, then took off again, scooted around in small circles, then fell into a relaxed lope around the field. Ivan breathed hard and felt his blood course through his body. He felt so alive. He remembered feeling this good when he hiked with Sarah in the mountains, and she'd let him run off-leash along the forest trails.

Sarah. He slowed to a trot, then a walk. He stopped altogether, still panting, and lay down in the grass. His heart ached as he fell into a deep melancholy. He thought of her and imagined her sitting at her computer without him by her side. He felt very drawn to her and wished with all his might that he could join her for a few minutes. His sadness nearly overwhelmed him, when he remembered what Boy had said about going back to Earth. He could hear Boy's words in his head: "It is possible—common, actually—to take one's energy back to Earth for a short time now and then . . . ."

Ivan lifted his head. He felt ready to make a journey but wondered how to activate this. Boy hadn't instructed him in the mechanics. Instinctively, though, Ivan relaxed and imagined he was right there at Sarah's side. He smelled her and heard the "ticka ticka ticka" of the computer keys. He lay under her desk, touching her ankle, and felt her warmth. He looked up at her face and realized he was actually there. He sat up and leaned against her leg. She was concentrating on her computer screen and unconsciously reached to pet him. She looked down with a dreamy expression on her face, then pulled her hand back with a start. Her expression changed to fright. She glared at her leg, then lifted her eyes to gaze out the window. When she looked back down at him, she smiled and whispered, "Ivan? Is that you? Are you here?"

Ivan burned with love for her. He wiggled all over, leaped up, and licked her face, but she didn't seem to feel it. She didn't even touch her face to wipe the wetness away. Instead she looked down where he was but didn't make eye contact with him. "Oh, Ivan, I can feel you. You are here, aren't you?" Ivan put his front paws on her lap and snuggled into her belly, but she didn't stroke him, didn't seem to know where he was exactly. She looked around herself, searching.

Then he saw them—the cast on her other leg and one on her arm and the bandages on her face and neck. *Wow,* he thought. *She was very badly hurt. My poor Sarah.* He realized he'd lost all sense of time and didn't know how long it had been since they'd been in the car crash. It couldn't have been just this morning like it felt, or she wouldn't be home from the hospital. *Weeks, maybe. It feels like I died only a couple hours ago.*

"Oh, Ivan," Sarah said. "I miss you so much. You were the best dog in the world. Are you going to come back to me one day—as a new puppy? Huh? Are you? I'm count-ing on that." She grimaced with pain. "Oh boy, I'm not doing so great." She turned her chair a little but had to pick up the casted leg with her hands in order to move it.

Ivan thought he would go crazy. *How can she live with-out me? This is not fair. She needs me!* Just then the doorbell rang, and Sarah's mother and father came in with bags of food, a hot pizza, and some soda. Ivan sat back and watched while they fussed over Sarah, put away the groceries, and helped her up onto her crutches so she could walk into the other room. Sarah seemed to have forgotten Ivan. She sat at the dining table with her parents, and he heard her, as if in a long, misty tunnel, say, "The strangest thing happened. I thought I felt Ivan here with me . . . ," and Ivan found himself back in the field with the other herding dogs.

"Wait!" he said to himself. "I'm not done."

The Belgian Tervuren came trotting past. "Ahhhhh, you've just been visiting your human, haven't you? Don't worry. You can go back again—many times. At least for awhile." He kept trotting, then sped into a gallop. Ivan shook his head.

Oh my gosh. The group. How long have I been gone? He raced back through the field, across the lawn, and into the living room.

He expected to see Beauregard and Stealth still asleep and no one else there. Instead, the room was a commotion of wagging tails. Jolly took up the most space with her large body and feminine voice. "And everyone was home—Jane, Jack, Joseph, and Jennifer—the kids—and John and Julie too. John and Julie knew I was there. I heard them whisper to each other that it felt like I was. I was so happy!"

Beauregard, despite his attempt to be cool and collected, jabbered uncontrollably. "Steven could tell I was there, too! And Sheldon, Bruce, and Sally! I was so excited to see them. We were at Westminster . . . ."

Even Carl had lost his reserved demeanor and jumped up and down. "Dora and Siegfried were at home alone, and I know Dora could feel my presence. Oh boy! Oh boy! I can't wait to go back!"

Murphy sat with a wistful expression on his face. He listed to one side as though he were still leaning against his beloved Helga. "Helga is so peaceful. She's up here with us, and I'll get to spend more time with her. She can walk now and hear, too. She glows with happiness. She hugged me, held me. We love each other so much."

Stealth, on the other hand, looked disturbed and wasn't talking. Ivan wondered if he'd also gone back to visit his human. *Maybe he didn't. Maybe that's why he's so quiet.*

Ivan stepped into the living room. "Sounds like we all had a similar experience. Boy told me we could do this, but I was waiting till later to tell you about it."

"I was rolling in the snow over there," said Jolly, "and started thinking about being with the kids in the yard after a big snow storm. We used to play so much. And then all of a sudden, I was there with them."

"The same thing happened to me," said Murphy. "I was lying in the sun and thinking about Helga, wondering if she's warmer now, too. And before I knew it, I was in her lap. She's just over there in Human Heaven. We'll get to be together a lot, she said."

"Me too," said Carl. "Daydreaming turned into the real thing."

"Yes! Yes!" said Beauregard. "I was back at ringside with all my people."

"I had the same experience," said Ivan. "I spent some time with Sarah. She actually tried to pet me. She's a mess from the accident—has a cast on her leg and one on her arm and bandages on her head."

They all looked at Stealth. Carl asked, "Stealth, did you go back to Earth, too?"

"Yes sir, I did. I did." He looked at the ground, however, and wouldn't say more.

"Well, was it fun?" asked Jolly, wiggling. "Did you get to be with your favorite humans?"

Ivan cringed. Stealth just said, "Yes, ma'am, I did," but he wouldn't look at her.

"Well, tell us about it, Stealth," Jolly insisted. "We told you what happened to us."

"I'd just 'soon keep it private, missy," he huffed.

Jolly's wiggling slowed, and she looked at Ivan. "How often do we get to do that?" she asked.

"W—w—well, I'm not sure. More. I don't know how many times. Maybe until we don't need to anymore."

"I'll always want to go back. Every day," she said.

Ivan said, "Boy, when he told me about this, said 'now and then.' He said going back will help us feel better about leaving."

"That makes sense," said Carl.

Stealth turned his eyes to look up at Ivan but kept his head down. Ivan sensed that Stealth didn't want to go back again.

"I didn't want to leave in the first place," said Beauregard. "I liked my life, and I want to go back as often as I can."

"But, Beauregard, your body wasn't there, just your essence—your energy—your spirit," Ivan said as kindly as he could. "I didn't want to leave, either."

"I did," said Murphy. "I was miserable without Helga. And so cold. I was glad to die."

Jolly said, "Well, I sure didn't want to die. I wanted to stay with my family forever. And now I want to go back as many times as I can. I'll never feel good about leaving. Never." She stopped wiggling and sat with a pout on her face.

A heavy silence enveloped the group. No one spoke, and Ivan began to tense again. Boy had said that visits back to Earth would help them feel better about leaving, but Ivan saw that no one but Murphy seemed anything but frustrated. *So, what purpose did this serve?* Without thinking, he asked, "So, what good did going back do? Why are we able to do it?"

They all sat back on their haunches and looked at Ivan.

Murphy didn't hesitate. "It was good because I got to be with Helga. Because we're both in a better place."

For a moment, Ivan was annoyed with Murphy's answer. It was easy for him, because Helga had also died. Ivan wanted to hear from the others. He tried to meet the eyes of each, but they either looked down at the floor or up into the air, thinking. No one was coming up with a response, and Ivan felt the awkward silence descend upon them again. "You know," he said, "I think we've had a very long day, and maybe we should all go home and go to bed."

"Home?" asked Beauregard indignantly. "Where's home?"

Ivan winced at his own foolishness. He looked outside at all the play and work areas. Then he glanced around their living room. "I guess this room is our home now." With sleepy expressions, they all nodded. No one said a word but found their previous sleeping spots, curled up, and dozed off. Ivan's last thought before slumber was that, most likely, none of them would be able to understand how going back to Earth would help them until they'd done it a few more times. This thought resonated as truth, and he felt content knowing how he would begin tomorrow's discussion.

Chapter Two

Ivan awakened before the others the next morning and raised his head to study them. Most were snoring. Stealth lay with his chin on his front paws, ready to leap into action. *Poor guy,* Ivan thought. *His snore sounds more like a growl.* Carl lay in a loose half-circle snoring in a quiet, sophisticated manner. Jolly, in her feminine, childish way, lay on her side, barely snoring at all as her paws paddled through a dream. Murphy slept quietly curled into a snug ball next to Ivan in front of the fire. Ivan chuckled at Beauregard, who would have been humiliated to see himself. The fancy Poodle lay on his back on the sofa, rear legs spread apart, front paws flipped over, his jaw askew, and his tongue lolling out to one side. His snoring was sloppy, and drool ran down his cheeks.

Ivan gazed at each one with warmth, when a sudden swoosh of adrenaline surged through his chest. He thought, *Oh my gosh. We have so much to do. We have to figure out what we learned in this most recent life, the significant factors of previous lives, and identify what we still need to learn to become whole. Oh dear, oh dear. We haven't finished any of these assignments. Not one of them. I'm really bad at this. Why did Boy choose me? Someone else would be much better. Carl would be better. Murphy would be better.* His pulse quickened, his head became swimmy, and he felt sick to his stomach.

Maybe I should tell Boy to find another dog for this job. I don't want to become a hero. Ivan hurried out of the living room, and as he entered the sunlight, he felt small. In his heart, he felt inadequate. *I'm scared.* He searched the areas outside for Boy. "I'm not entirely sure I want to find him," he murmured to himself. He looked first toward the tunnel opening and saw a couple new dogs gazing about in wonder, but Boy wasn't there. He scanned the ponds, the fields, the woods, the living rooms, but he didn't see Boy. "Where is he?" he whispered.

He looked off to the most distant scene, the snow field and the mountains. *Maybe, if I run into those mountains, no one would find me. I can't do this job. I don't know how. I don't want it. I need to get out of here.* His heart pounded loudly. He stopped looking around for Boy and dashed toward the snow field. He galloped full-speed, afraid that Boy would spot him. *Fleeing is definitely the best idea—disappear and never be seen again.*

As he approached the snow, the many dogs playing in it stopped to watch him with perked ears, their faces lovely with joy. They seemed to be wondering, *Why is this frightened-looking Aussie racing toward us?*

Guilt grabbed at Ivan's heart. With a clear vision of Jolly, Carl, Beauregard, Stealth, and Murphy waking to find him gone, he stopped. He was belly-deep in snow. All the snow dogs watched him. He felt transparent, as though they read his mind and knew he was doing a bad thing. He wanted to crawl inside himself. Their innocent expressions were more than he could bear. He felt more shame than he could ever remember. *How can I abandon the others? How can I let Boy down? How can I be given a job and not try to do it? Ohhh. I'm a terrible dog. I'm really very, very bad.*

He hung his head and turned around, hoping the

snow dogs couldn't read what was going on inside him. He tucked his hindquarters under and pushed back through the snow. Once more on dry land, he trotted fast toward the living room. He kept his head down and stared only at the ground in front of his nose. Without warning, he ran into something.

"Oof!" he said as he fell onto his shoulder. He looked up to see Boy standing above him. Fear clutched him. He remained lying on his side, put one paw over his face, and clenched his eyes shut.

He waited for Boy to say something, but the Collie didn't say a word. Ivan hoped he had walked away, but he could feel his kingly presence. He waited a while longer with his eyes shut tightly. Still, nothing. Finally, he squinted one eye open and peered around his raised paw. He saw Boy looking down upon him. Ivan expected to see an angry expression, but instead, Boy's face was soft with understanding. Ivan took his paw down.

"It's not easy, is it?" Boy asked.

"How did you know?"

Boy smiled. "I know almost everything."

Ivan pushed himself up onto his elbows. He looked into Boy's deep, dark eyes. Those eyes had the greatest knowledge and the deepest love Ivan had ever seen. Big feelings welled up in his heart as he became choked up. To be in the presence of so much love overwhelmed him. Gradually, he regained composure. "Wh . . . why . . . why was I chosen to do this? I don't know what I'm doing. I'm afraid I'm going to do something wrong."

"This is part of the learning process. In order to reach the next level, you must work through this. When it's all

25

over, you will no longer have these guilt feelings. Trust me."

Ivan stood up, shook himself lightly, and pondered these ideas. "I don't know that I want to reach the next level." But this felt all wrong, and he wished he hadn't said it. "No, no, I'm sorry. That's not true. You say I'm ready, but I don't feel ready."

"Of course you don't feel ready. If you did, there would be no learning."

Ivan heard the words, and they rang true, but his brain couldn't quite grasp their meaning.

Boy continued, "When the guilt subsides, you will feel confident. You will like yourself more. It will happen. But not if you leave."

Ivan cringed and looked away.

"It is with great appreciation for who you are that you were chosen for this job. Try to believe in yourself."

Ivan heard his pulse pound rapidly in his head. He took a deep breath and tried to slow it down. "Try to believe in yourself" rang over and over in his ears. He took another deep breath and felt a little better. *Okay, I will try to believe in myself. If Boy chose me, that says something. But . . . , I ran away. I was so bad to do that. Yet, he doesn't seem surprised. He doesn't sound angry at all. It's as though he expected it. And I do feel a little better now.*

Ivan turned to thank Boy, but Boy was gone. "What?" said Ivan out loud. "Boy? Where are you?" Ivan spun his head around this way and that, searching for the Collie, but he had truly vanished. *Gosh, I wonder why he did that.*

He sat down and replayed all that Boy had said. He expected to feel cold, but instead he felt warmed. Something unexplainable had happened, but he wasn't sure what. He felt different, smarter. *How strange. How very strange.* He sat only a moment longer and gazed about the now-familiar surroundings. Propelled from something deep within, he trotted back toward the living room.

Boy's words played repeatedly in rhythm with Ivan's footsteps. "Try to believe in yourself, try to believe in yourself, try to believe in yourself . . . ." After a while he thought, *Boy didn't say "do believe in yourself." He just said "try." I think I can try.*

As Ivan stepped into the cozy living room, his head no longer spun. He no longer felt panicky. *I know that I don't have this day clearly planned, but I just have a feeling it will work out okay.* "*Try* to believe in yourself. *Try* to believe in yourself," he muttered over and over.

Ivan's entrance was an unspoken cue for the others to awaken. Murphy, still in a ball, fluttered his eyes open. He opened his mouth and yawned, licked his chops, blinked his eyes a few times, and looked around the room. Stealth was up on all fours in an instant. He tried to be alert, but sleepiness clung to him. Beauregard, still on his back, simply opened his eyes and looked around. He brought his limp tongue back into his mouth, swallowed, rolled onto his belly, and propped himself up on his elbows. Carl made a few smuffing noises and sat up, already alert. Jolly's tail awakened before the rest of her, thumping happily on the floor. Her legs awakened next and brought themselves under her body. Finally, her head lifted, and she gazed at the others sleepily.

"Good morning, everyone," said Ivan. He sounded, to himself, quite confident. He waited until they'd all looked about to get re-oriented. When they were fully awake, Ivan said, "Let's go outside for some fresh air." They perked their ears, stretched, shook, and shuffled outside. Each one jogged a respectable distance into the woods and fields, cantered a bit or rolled in the grass, and trotted back. Since they no longer needed to attend to bodily functions, they came in willingly. They didn't need to look for food or water and entered the living room ready to attend to the day's business.

Ivan took his spot in front of the fireplace, and the others gathered before him. He felt relaxed as he cleared his throat and began, "Today . . . ," but Jolly interrupted him.

"Can we go back to Earth again? I really want to."

Refusing to be annoyed by her interruption, Ivan said, "I think that's a good idea. But this time, let's do it with a purpose."

"Like what?" Carl asked.

"Well . . . , you know we need to better understand our past lives so that we can plan our next one, right? So how about focusing on that question—what did we learn in this last life? Why did we choose these particular people? And what did we learn about ourselves?"

While Carl, Murphy, and Stealth nodded, Beauregard and Jolly looked perplexed.

Rather than explain further, Ivan said, "Just go back, and while you're there, see if you can learn something about yourselves. Remember how?"

Jolly offered, "Close our eyes and pretend we're there?"

Ivan nodded. "That should do it."

Carl jumped into the leather chair and leaned against the back with a dreamy look. Beauregard, Jolly, and Murphy found their own comfortable places in the living room and did the same thing. Stealth, however, just stood and stared at Ivan. "Not sure you want to go back?" Ivan asked.

"I likes it here better," Stealth said.

"Was there anything good about being on Earth?" asked Ivan. Stealth looked to one side, thinking. He didn't answer. "Or," said Ivan, "maybe you need to re-experience what was unpleasant in order to understand it."

"Ah," said Stealth as though that idea rang a bell. Ivan watched the tough-looking dog clench his jaw and concentrate on what appeared to be something painful. He almost told Stealth to stop but sensed he shouldn't interfere. Stealth had to battle with himself to make the transition happen. His strong jaw was tight, his whole body was tense, and a low growl rumbled in his throat. Finally, after trying and trying, Stealth's body relaxed and went into a dream state like the others.

"And now my dear Sarah," Ivan sighed. He lay down, put his chin on his paws, and remembered how close he'd felt to her yesterday. In a mere moment, he was again at her side, this time on her bed as she slept. It was mid-morning, long past her normal waking hour. Her leg with the cast was outside the covers. He saw that people had written words on it, mostly messages of "get well soon." Someone, however, had drawn a dog paw print in heavy blue ink. Next to it were the words, "In loving memory of Ivan. His love will always be with you."

This struck Ivan like a chime. "My gosh!" he whispered out loud. *Someone knows. Wow.* Whoever had written this had signed it, but Ivan couldn't read the writing. He thought about all of Sarah's friends. There was one, a fellow named Don, who seemed to know all about heaven and spirits and life after death. Maybe it was he. Ivan scrutinized the signature again, trying to decide if the first letter was a D. He couldn't tell. Sarah stirred and turned onto her other side, dragging the heavy cast across the covers. Ivan slid off the bed and walked around so he could look at her face. He expected her to look peaceful in her sleep, but she didn't. Her eyebrows were furrowed, her lips stuck out like a duck's bill, her skin looked too red, and her breathing was rapid and uneven.

Without thinking, Ivan leaped back onto the bed and curled up against her belly. She put her arm over him, and he scooted as close as he could. He pressed his face against her shoulder and saw her brows go smooth, her lips relax into a slight smile, and her breathing slow. *Now this is heaven*, he thought and lay there for what felt like hours.

When he heard a knocking on Sarah's front door, he leaped off the bed, raced to the entryway, and barked fiercely. He felt a divine joy in protecting her and barked with all his might. When the door opened, its mass passed right through him. Ivan was amazed, because he felt nothing. A man carrying some plastic grocery bags and a bouquet of flowers stepped in and walked right through Ivan. Ivan growled and grabbed his ankle, but the man didn't notice. He set the bags down on the dining table and carried the bouquet into Sarah's bedroom. Ivan barked, growled, and tore at the man's pant leg, but the man still didn't notice. Angry, Ivan leaped up and grabbed the man's forearm. He dug his teeth in as hard as he could, but again, nothing happened.

The man stood in the doorway and looked at Sarah, who smiled sleepily. "Hi, Donald," she said.

"I brought these for you," Don said.

Sarah smiled and pulled herself up to lean back against her pillows. Ivan took a second look at the man—at his face this time—and saw that it was, in fact, Sarah's friend. For the first time, Ivan was grateful he was dead. He wanted to crawl under the bed and not come out. *How could I have attacked such a nice person?* He cringed as he imagined the damage he would have caused if he'd been a live dog. He emitted a whine to see if Sarah and Don could hear him— one last test to make sure, but they paid no attention.

Feeling freer, he leaped onto the bed and snuggled next to Sarah. Automatically, she laid her hand across his back and stroked him. As he soaked up the feeling of her touch, Don asked, "What are you doing?"

Sarah pulled her hand back. "Oh my gosh! I thought Ivan was here. I could feel him. Oh my goodness!"

Don smiled. "Maybe he is here. You miss him a lot, don't you?"

Sarah burst into tears. "Oh, I do—so much that I feel like he's here sometimes." She sobbed hard. Don sat down next to her, hugged her, and stroked her head.

Ivan licked Sarah's tears and leaned against her shoulder. *I made her cry. It's my fault. Oh, my dear Sarah, I'm so sorry.*

"God!" Sarah cried out. "I swear I can feel him some-times. Like right now. It feels like he's sitting here. It even felt like he was licking my face. My poor boy. Such a won-derful dog."

"You have to wonder about those doggie spirits," Don said. "I think they have their own way of getting around. Maybe he *is* here."

Sarah laughed as she wiped the remaining tears away.

"Do you think so? Hey, Ivan! Are you here?" Then she giggled nervously. "Yeah, and the looney wagon's gonna arrive any minute, right?"

Don cocked his head to one side. "Maybe. Maybe not." Sarah smiled at him and lay back against her pillows. Don said, "Well, hey, what do you say we do something fun. I rented a movie. Your favorite."

"*You've Got Mail?*"

"Yep."

"Oh, good. I could use something light-hearted. Will you set it up, and I'll hobble out there in a few minutes?"

"Sounds good to me," said Don and walked out of the bedroom, closing the door behind him.

Ivan decided to stay and help Sarah. He jumped off the bed, stepped over by the window out of her way, and watched as she lifted her bulky leg with the cast. She swung it down so her heel touched the floor. She groaned. She wore a sleeveless nightgown, and Ivan saw, for the first time, the severe red marks on her arms. He gasped with horror at a raw-looking set of cuts on her cheek and neck. The sutures looked painful. *Oh, my beautiful Sarah. Her pretty face has been scarred.* Without thinking, he leaped back onto the bed and sniffed them, then gave them a few gentle licks. Sarah absent-mindedly touched the places that he'd tickled.

"Oh, you Ivan boy. Did you just kiss me?" She giggled nervously as she limped into the bathroom. Ivan lay down and waited.

After awhile, Sarah came out fully dressed and made her way into the living room. Ivan followed. Don had the DVD in the player, and he had set out some snacks. Sarah sat on the sofa, Don pushed the "on" button, the film began, and Ivan crawled up and snuggled next to Sarah. Entirely content, he drifted off to sleep.

When he awoke, he found himself back in the living room with Jolly, Murphy, Beauregard, Stealth, and Carl. He glanced around quickly, looking for Sarah, then remembered that had just been a visit. Regret tugged inside his belly as he focused on the present situation. He struggled to remember all that he'd said to his dogs before they'd gone back to Earth. He had given them assignments, things to ponder about their past lives. *Now what were all the things I asked them to do? Gosh, my mind feels like mush after being with Sarah.*

The others lightly dozed as they waited for Ivan's return. Ivan felt a little sheepish that he'd stayed away the longest. He softly cleared his throat, and they awakened. Without speaking, they gathered in front of him. In his best professorial manner, he said, "Now let's review the things I asked you to do while you were back on Earth. Can someone name them?"

Carl spoke quickly, "What did we learn in this past life?"

Jolly said, "Why did we choose our people?"

Stealth, in a monotone voice and with his head hanging, said, "We was supposed to see if we learned anyting 'bout ourselves."

Ivan wanted to respond to just Stealth, to take him aside and talk about his pain, and when he glanced at the others and saw they all wore sad expressions, he said, "Oh, Stealth. You sound unhappy. Did you learn something about yourself that upset you?"

Stealth looked at the floor and mumbled, "Mmmph, yeah, I guesses so."

Carl said, "We all have a dark side, Stealth. No one is all good."

Stealth glanced at Carl. "Yeah, I guess I'd forgotten dat. I don't wanna have a dark side." He paused a long time as sorrow flooded his face. "But I does. Or, I did." He paused again. "Least it's over. I don't gotta be dat dog no more."

Beauregard, with great compassion, said "You're right, Stealth. It's over. You can breathe easy now, Buddy."

Stealth perked up at being called "Buddy." He lifted his head and took a breath. "You's right, dandy one. It is all over. And I tanks my lucky stars. It's over."

Jolly politely, tentatively, asked in a small voice, "Geez, Stealth, what did you do that was so bad? We love you for who you are now, not what you were on Earth."

Ivan was impressed. He wouldn't have guessed that Jolly could be so clear. Jolly surprised him even more when she stepped over to Stealth and began to lick the side of his face. She even licked the inside of his ear, purposefully and with tenderness. Stealth closed his eyes and leaned towards her.

With a patience Ivan knew he himself didn't have, Jolly licked and licked. And Stealth soaked it up like a thirsty sponge. Stealth leaned into Jolly so much, Ivan thought Stealth might tip over. Ivan looked at the other dogs. Each one listed to one side as if he, too, were being licked by Jolly. Ivan even found himself leaning to one side, then grinned at the sight of them all.

Eventually, Stealth opened his eyes and straightened himself. Softly, he said, "Tanks, Jolly, Ma'am. Dat felt mighty good." Jolly pulled back, gave him one last lick and returned to her spot. Murphy looked longingly at Jolly as though he were about to cry.

Rather than continue to focus on Stealth, Ivan sensed he should direct their attention back to the first question. He knew that Jolly's loving gesture had done wonders for Stealth. "Well," he said. "I think we're ready to examine that first question: What did we each learn in this past life?"

Some looked at the floor, some gazed up at the ceiling, but they all thought deeply. Carl spoke first. "There was so much. I don't think I can just, off the top of my head, name all the things."

"Me neither," said Jolly. "I learned a lot."

"Yeah, me too," said Murphy. "Taking care of a deaf person in a wheel chair made me learn tons of stuff."

Beauregard and Stealth nodded. Ivan agreed. "You're right. The question is too big. How about if we each come up with the *three* most important things."

"May I go first?" Jolly asked and wiggled her slow, wavy wiggle.

"Is that okay with everyone?" Ivan asked. The boys all nodded. "Sure, Jolly, go ahead."

"Well," she said, still wiggling, "My first one—um— the thing I learned about the most—is selflessness. Everybody know what that means?" She giggled. "It's kind of a big word, but I like it." She giggled again. "The lady of my house—the mom—Julie—she used to talk about selflessness a lot. She read lots of books on love and peace and God and psychology. She said that if all humans were like me—hee hee—the world would be a better place. She often told the children that I cared more about them than I did myself, and this was a noble thing. I guess she forgot about the time I stole the Christmas cookies. I took some other food when they weren't looking, too, but they never figured that out. Oops! Guess maybe I wasn't as selfless as Julie thought." Jolly giggled some more and then got serious.

"But every time I heard her tell one of the kids about this, I tried harder. And I think I stopped sneaking food when I was maybe seven years old or so." She giggled again and looked to the side. She rolled her eyes, giggled a little more, and went on. "By then, I believe I truly was selfless. I never complained when the younger kids hit me with a spoon or rode on my back or pulled my tail. Twice, my tail got slammed in the car door. That hurt! A lot! But they opened the door fast when I yelped, and they put ice on it and took me to the vet. But I never held a grudge. The first time it was Joseph, and the second time it was Jennifer. I was pretty mad at both of them, because that hurt SOOOO much. But I was surprised at how easy it was to forgive them. Both of them felt very badly about it. Joseph even cried. That's how much he loved me.

"I think I just listened to Julie so much that it finally sank in. I believe that during the last three years of my life I was truly selfless. I would have given my life for any of them. I never tried to grab their food—even when Joseph was two and held out pieces of cheese to me. He needed his food. I didn't. I put all their needs before my own. And you know . . . it felt really, really good to do that." She nodded to let everyone know she was done.

"Wow," said Beauregard. "That's beautiful." The others sat with mouths slightly open and their eyes large. They nodded their heads.

Murphy said, in a gentle, earnest voice, "I led a similar kind of life. I had to be selfless in order to take care of Helga. But, I don't think I had to learn it. I think I already knew it when I became her dog. It was sort of built in already. Know what I mean?" He looked at the others with a hopeful expression.

They all turned their heads to him. Beauregard hesitated. Carl thought about this, and Stealth looked at the floor. Jolly didn't know what to say. Ivan said, in a positive, helpful manner, "I agree. I think I gave selflessly to Sarah, but it wasn't something I had to learn. I was just sort of born that way, too."

Jolly puffed up. "So, are you guys saying you're better than I am? You already *knew* selflessness, and I had to *learn* it?" Jolly clenched her jaw, turned, and marched out of the room. Ivan's and Murphy's faces fell. Stealth glared at them and growled.

"Whoa!" said Ivan. "Wait a minute. Jolly! Wait! Come back!"

Stealth spun on one heel and trotted out the door after her. Murphy and Ivan looked at one another in disbelief. "I didn't mean to insult her," said Murphy.

"Me neither," said Ivan. "I don't know whether to chase after her or not."

"I'll go," said Carl.

"Me too," said Beauregard, and they trotted out.

Ivan's and Murphy's jaws hung open. Ivan said, "I feel terrible. Now they all seem mad at me."

"Me too," said Murphy. "I just thought I'd share how I'd been selfless, too. I didn't mean that I was superior because I already knew it. There must be things she learned that I didn't. Don't you think so, Ivan?"

Ivan felt no superiority to any of them and certainly not to Murphy, yet Murphy seemed to think Ivan should have all the answers. Ivan felt the shroud of despair return. He felt just as worthless as in the beginning. *How could this have happened? I thought I was getting the hang of this leadership thing, but I obviously haven't. I should have seen this coming. I should have been more sensitive to what Jolly was saying. I didn't think of her at all. I only thought about what I wanted to say, what I wanted the others to know about me. Ohhhh. I'm worthless. I can't do this job. I'm not good enough. Why, oh why, did Boy choose me? Maybe I can find him and tell him to choose someone else. I'm stupid. I'm insensitive.* He remembered, then, his mantra, the one he'd repeated to himself over and over. "Try to believe in yourself." *Oh yeah, that. Well that sure didn't work.* He started to trot out of the room.

Murphy said, "Wait, Ivan. Don't leave me here. Where are you going?"

"I'm going to find Boy and tell him to give this job to someone else."

Murphy followed Ivan outside. "What if he won't let you quit?"

"Well . . . I'll quit anyway."

"Where would you go?"

"Go?" Ivan stopped in his tracks. "I don't know. Maybe up into those mountains."

"And do what?"

"Do?"

"Yes. What would you do up there all by yourself?"

"I don't know. Maybe there are other dogs I could hang out with. Or maybe I should just be a hermit. I'm not very good with other dogs anyway. That should be pretty obvious to you, Murphy." Murphy's ears dropped, and Ivan took a quick breath, because, even to himself, he'd sounded condescending. *Oh! I'm such a curmudgeon.*

Ivan surveyed the grounds. The retrievers were still retrieving, the herding dogs were still guarding flocks of sheep, the terriers were happily digging holes, and the coursing dogs were galloping like the wind. Ivan saw Jolly, Stealth, Beauregard, and Carl standing together talking. They glanced at him and Murphy, then resumed talking. Ivan looked over near the tunnel entrance and saw Boy speaking to a few new dogs. When Boy was finished, as if he knew Ivan was waiting for him, he headed their way.

Ivan hung his head, and his ears fell flat against his skull, but he met Boy's warm, wise eyes. Boy came nearly nose-to-nose with Ivan. He said nothing but waited for Ivan to speak. Ivan, propelled by his emotions, said, "Boy, I cannot do this job the way it should be done. I'm a failure. I'm not smart enough or sensitive enough. I think Murphy would be much better."

Murphy looked up at Ivan in shock and said, "Oh no. Carl. Carl would be much better. He's so educated." He edged closer to Ivan and gazed with awe at Boy. Ivan expected Boy to ask Murphy's opinion. Instead, Boy said, "Okay. I'll tell Carl he's in charge. Ivan, you must go up into the mountains. Alone. While there, you will think about yourself. You will not be able to go back to Earth to visit Sarah. When you believe that you have truly come to know yourself, you may return. At that time, you may visit Sarah again and resume your leadership of the group. Once every twenty-one days, Murphy can bring you news of the group's

39

progress, but you may not direct the group in any way, and Murphy may bring any information about you back to the group. Murphy, go with Ivan now to the edge of the mountains. Find a spot that you will both recognize, and twenty-one days from now, you must travel to your meeting spot and tell Ivan what has transpired under Carl's guidance."

"But that means Murphy has to travel through deep snow," said Ivan. Murphy began to shiver and huddled closer to Ivan.

"No one is allowed into the mountain realm without a messenger. Murphy has chosen to be your messenger."

Murphy looked surprised. "I have?" He shivered harder.

"Of all the dogs in the group, Murphy is the only one who shouldn't have to travel through snow," Ivan insisted.

"Unconsciously, he chose this path."

"Wha-?" Ivan started to say. *This makes no sense. Why punish Murphy for my inadequacies?*

"The other option is for you to remain with your group. Either way, you will learn the necessary lessons."

Ivan searched his mind for any rationale that would support Murphy's having to trudge through icy-cold snow. Anguish ripped through him. *What an unfair choice!* He looked down onto the top of Murphy's small, round skull. The white and brown fur made an equilateral pattern. On either side of his skull, long, silky, black, white, and brown wisps of hair flowed down each ear, ears that hugged the little dog's shivering head. Ivan felt his heart swell with compassion as Murphy's trembling body pressed against his own. Yet, like a small, inner voice, something convinced Ivan that Murphy did, in fact, need to trudge through the snow, that this would somehow benefit him. He felt one last surge of guilt pass through his chest before he spoke.

"Okay. I'll go to the mountains." Murphy threw his head back. Tears sprang into his eyes, and his mouth fell open. He pushed away from Ivan, pain emanating from his face. Ivan turned to Boy. "Shall I leave now?"

"Yes," said Boy. Ivan turned away and began to walk. "One last thing, Ivan."

Ivan stopped and turned to look at the Collie. "Yes?"

"Be true to your heart."

Ivan nodded, hung his head, and walked away. He walked slowly enough that Murphy could keep up. Carl, Jolly, Stealth, and Beauregard, a short distance away, watched Ivan and Murphy but didn't try to call to them or follow them. Ivan felt nauseous. He glanced back at Murphy just once before they reached the snow field, then stopped and said, "I never dreamed Heaven would be like this, did you?"

"Certainly not. I expected I would be warm. Forever." Ivan heard a definite edge in Murphy's voice.

"I bet you did. I would have thought so, too." He paused. "I thought I'd be able to run and play, maybe herd some sheep, play with angels. You know, kick back and enjoy the love and beauty."

"It was beautiful at first."

"Yes, it was. What happened? I never dreamed I'd have to work once I got here."

"Me neither. I thought I'd see Helga again and just be able to sleep in her lap and do all the things we'd been doing together when we were alive."

"I know." Ivan gazed out over the snow field. A variety of large, fluffy, working-type dogs played together and seemed to be having a wonderful time. "How come they get to play, and we don't?"

Murphy stepped up beside Ivan and watched the Saint Bernards, Newfoundlands, Great Pyrenees, the Eskimo Dogs, the Samoyeds, and others as they frolicked in the deep snow. "Maybe they're not real. Maybe it's all a trick," he said.

"Really? You think that?" Ivan asked.

"I don't know. I just don't get it," said Murphy.

"They look real to me."

"Yes, I guess they do to me, too."

They stood and watched the snow dogs play for awhile. Ivan looked toward the mountains. He saw no path through the snow, just acres and acres of deep, unblemished whiteness. He said, "I guess we should continue. I don't know how you're going to get through this, though."

Murphy studied the edge of the snow field. Ivan waded into it until it reached his shoulders. He turned back to see Murphy shivering on the grass. His face was filled with terror. "I don't think I can," said Murphy.

"I don't think you can, either, even if I go first." Ivan felt anger well up in his chest, anger at Boy. *What kind of dirty trick is this? How can this be Heaven?* "Maybe this is really Hell," he said.

"No, I know it's not. My Helga wouldn't be here if it were Hell."

"You're probably right," said Ivan. He sat down. "So now what?" He thought for a moment. "Maybe we have to go back. Maybe this is Boy's way of getting me to face my problems and continue to lead the group."

Murphy's face brightened. "Oh yes, that must be it.

Let's go back." He started to turn when a Saint Bernard and a Newfoundland left their play group and plowed through the snow in Ivan and Murphy's direction. They came right towards them with happy faces, laughing.

"Hey ho!" they said in unison. "Where are you going?"

"I guess they're real, huh?" whispered Ivan.

"Need some help?" they asked.

Ivan and Murphy nodded slowly.

"I'm Reva," said the Saint Bernard.

"And I'm Sebastian," said the Newfoundland.

"We'll help you through the snow. Just follow us!" They laughed heartily and made a clear path with their large feet. Ivan could barely see over the top of the surface, and Murphy didn't try. He hurried along behind Ivan and made sure he stepped into Ivan's paw prints, which were inside the paw prints of Reva and Sebastian.

After several minutes, Ivan called back over his shoulder, "Are you warm enough, Murphy?"

"Actually, I'm panting I'm so warm. Those big dogs walk awfully fast. And so do you!"

Ivan felt happier now and called back, "At least you're not cold!" Murphy didn't comment.

Eventually, they reached the base of the first mountain. The snow ended, and the mountainside rose adjacent to them. It was composed of jagged rocks, tall pine trees, and lush greenery. Ivan spotted a path leading up to the right and knew he would take that path. He glanced around for a place to meet Murphy in twenty-one days.

"That's a good spot there," Reva and Sebastian said in unison. They pointed their snouts toward a perfect waterfall with a sunny, grassy clearing at its edge.

"Oh," said Ivan. "That does look nice. And it's so close to the path here. What do you think, Murphy?"

"Looks nice," Murphy said. "And warm." He stepped around the big dogs and sat in the center of the grassy area where the sun shone brightly on him. He closed his eyes and lifted his face.

"We'll wait over here. You guys say good-bye," said Sebastian. "When you're done, we'll take Murphy back."

Ivan quickly stepped over and sat down facing his friend. "Well, I guess I'll see you in three weeks. Reva and Sebastian will lead you back through the snow again. They're awfully nice."

"Very, very nice," agreed Murphy.

"I don't know what to say," said Ivan. "I'm a little scared. But I think this is the right thing. Tell the others to not be too mad at me. I think they'll understand, don't you?"

"I don't know," said Murphy. "We hurt Jolly's feelings pretty badly. And the others seemed to take her side. I feel like such a fool."

"No worse a fool than I am, and I was supposed to be the wise leader. Oh!" he said and stamped one foot on the ground. "I'm just so stupid sometimes." He looked at the path that led up the mountainside. "This is the right place for me."

Murphy looked up the path, too, sighed sadly, and said, "I'm gonna miss you, Ivan. You take good care of yourself. Don't talk to strangers, as my Helga used to say."

Ivan chuckled. "I hope there *are* some strangers here, or this could be an awfully lonely few weeks."

They looked at each other for a long moment. Ivan

lifted his front paw and brushed Murphy's shoulder. "Tell Carl thanks for me, okay?"

"Sure. Good-bye, Ivan. Good luck." Murphy turned and walked toward Reva and Sebastian, who wagged their tails happily and started back down the snow path. Ivan watched Murphy's small legs skip along, making sure he didn't step in any untrodden snow. Ivan felt his heart warm for his cold, little friend and watched them disappear around a bend in the path.

Chapter Three

Ivan gazed up the mountain trail. It beckoned him with friendly greenness. The path itself was free of rocks and plants—a smooth surface made of soft, packed soil. He couldn't see where it went, because it curved out of sight. Gingerly, he stepped onto it and sniffed the ground. There were no familiar odors, just an aroma that was inviting. His heart quickened. He felt as though an adventure lay ahead. The soil under his paws felt firm yet cushiony, moist yet dry, and somehow filled with a new kind of energy that caused a spring in his step. He felt strong. He took a deep breath of brisk air and pushed into a trot.

He jogged through pine forest so dense that he couldn't see very far in any direction. The ferns became thicker, the air became more humid, and yellow, lavender, and fuchsia wildflowers became abundant. He stopped once to take in the scenery. "This is exquisite," he breathed. The path appeared to gradually climb as it turned this way and that around the mountain. Ivan hoped he would come to an overlook so he could see how far he had come. He trotted for a few hours, yet nothing changed. The incline continued at about the same degree, the wildflowers remained plentiful as did the trees and ferns, and the path remained soft. Before long, doubts began to enter his mind. *I wonder where I'm headed. Is it possible that this path never changes, never goes anywhere, and no one else is on it? No, I must remember this is Heaven. If there are mountains, there must be a purpose to them. And why would Boy send me here if there were nothing? I can't imagine what I could possibly learn with only this.* He sat down.

Funny to never experience thirst or hunger. He looked down at his paws. They looked the same as when he was alive. He felt as though he were a physical being. *Yet, I'm not.* He recalled how Sarah's front door and Don had passed right through him as though he were air. He patted one paw with the other. It felt solid. *Weird.*

He gazed about and thought, *Nothing here but me and the trees.* He peered through them, trying to see sky, different kinds of trees, any hint of diversity. Always, when he'd hiked in the mountains of Colorado with Sarah, they had come to openings where the trails hung on the outer edges of the mountains, where no trees obstructed breath-taking vistas of deep valleys and distant mountain ranges. But this path seemed to always be in the interior of the mountain-side, far from the edges.

I wonder where I am in relation to our living room. My sense of direction is all turned around. I wonder what's on the other side of these mountains. Cat Heaven? Horse Heaven? Gerbil Heaven? He imagined that these mountains sat in the middle of all the different kinds of heavens, that it was a hub around which all the other animal spirits had their separate areas. *But who knows? Maybe this is just for dogs. Maybe it's only an extension of Dog Heaven.* Now, suddenly, questions of all sorts danced in his mind. *How long did Sarah spend in Human Heaven before she went back? Why did she get to go back and I didn't? How will I know when twenty-one days have passed to meet Murphy? How much far-ther should I go today? Is there anyone else up here, or will I spend these twenty-one days all alone? Oh, I hope there are others. I don't like being all alone. I'm a social being. I like companionship. I like conversation.*

He lay down. *Am I supposed to just wander around these woods asking myself questions? I'll go crazy. Maybe I could pray. People pray. People believe in a god or creator of some kind, a source of life. But I'm not alive. I'm just a spirit. And there are many other spirits. So, there must be something that creates life. Why do people pray? They ask for things. Sometimes they get what they ask for. Sometimes they don't. Why not? Why sometimes and not others?*

He looked around at the forest. "I wish there were someone to talk to," he said out loud, softly. "Is there anyone out there? Hellooooo?"

He heard a small rustle in the ferns behind him. He turned quickly to see a small, grey snout and two beady eyes poke out between some fronds. He gasped, then lowered his head to see better. He sniffed. It was a strange odor, one he couldn't identify. It wasn't a cat or a mouse or a rat, not a skunk, a rabbit, nor a squirrel. He looked closer. It had a pleasing face with medium-sized, dark ears set on its head like those of a human. Its small black eyes were surrounded by rings of black fur, and the snout was long and narrow. Ivan poked his face closer to it. It darted back behind the ferns.

Ivan sniffed harder. "Hello?" he whispered. "Are you still there?"

The face poked out again and smiled. "Yes, I'm here. Are you here?"

Ivan chuckled. *Silly question.* "What are you?" he asked.

"I'm me. What are you? Are you a dog?"

"Of course I'm a dog. What did you think I was?"

"Mmm. Don't know. A snippety wicket?"

"A what?"

"Oh, never mind."

"What are you doing here?" Ivan asked. "Do you live here?"

"I belong in a desert."

Oh great. This isn't the kind of conversation I had in mind. This critter, whatever it is, is rather strange. "If you belong in a desert, why are you in these mountains?" The animal ducked back behind the ferns again. "No, wait!" said Ivan. "Don't go away. Come back, please."

The little animal poked its head out again and said, "Please? Did you say 'please'? What does that mean?"

"Where are you from?" Ivan asked. "Are you a spirit? Where on Earth did you live?"

"I'm from Africa—the Kalahari Desert. South Africa to be exact."

"Why are you in the mountains?"

"Been here a long time. It's my job now."

"To do what?"

"Did you say you're a dog?" the animal asked again.

"Yes. Yes! I'm a dog. What are you?"

"Meerkat."

"What?"

"Meerkat. I'm a meerkat. *Suricata suricatta.* Rather, I used to be a meerkat. Like you used to be a dog."

Meerkat? Meerkat. Must be some kind of cat. He liked the sound of it. *But what were those other words? Maybe they were African words.* "So how are you different from a real cat?"

"Don't ask. Don't ask."

"But, I'd like to know."

"There are many things you'd like to know."

"How do you know that? Like what?"

"Bumble bee's in a shooting trap. Screeeeeeeeeech!!!"

Ivan's ears rang with the piercing sound. He turned his head away.

"Screeeeeeeeech!!!"

"Geez!" said Ivan. "Do you have to make that noise?" When he turned back, the meerkat was gone. Ivan started to call out for him but thought, *Maybe I should get away while I can.* He peered at the ferns, but the meerkat didn't come out. Ivan decided not to call out to him. *I think I best be on my way*, he thought and continued up the path.

What did the meerkat say about bumble bees and shooting something? Cap? Trap? He wasn't sure he'd heard him right. It made no sense. He tried to forget the little critter and see what he could find ahead. He shuddered a little as he thought about the strange conversation.

He trotted along for a while. He felt the path continue to climb, but the scenery still did not change. He did notice that the light in the sky was becoming dimmer, though he couldn't actually see the sun through the trees. *How will I know when twenty-one days are up?* he asked himself a second time. He looked around for some place to make a mark in the soil or maybe chew a tree limb. If he did that every day, then after twenty, he would head back down to meet Murphy at the waterfall.

He searched the area for some unique spot, a special tree or rock or patch of flowers, but everything looked the same. *How would I ever find this place again?* His heart beat a little faster. *Maybe I better go all the way back down now.*

Maybe I should just spend every night at the waterfall. I'll find a way to make marks down there, then I'll know what day it is. He turned abruptly and cantered down the trail. It was much easier going down. After a short time, he sniffed the air, trying to locate the meerkat again, but he didn't detect its scent. He cantered and cantered until it was almost totally dark. He could hear the waterfall and breathed a deep sigh when he smelled its fresh mist. He sniffed the ground until he picked up Murphy's scent. He turned in a couple circles and lay down right on the spot Murphy had sat upon. He fell sound asleep and didn't awaken until he heard birds singing in the morning.

He sat bolt upright and tried to get his bearings. He had slept so deeply for such a long time, he couldn't remember where he was or why he was in this beautiful place with the waterfall and mountain to his left and the huge snow field to his right. He couldn't figure out whether he was dead or alive. He shook his whole body hard, then stepped over to the pool of water. He dipped his chin in and lapped at it. Its cold, sweet flavor filled his mouth. It was as satisfying as the chilled vanilla pudding Sarah used to give him on occasion. It was her favorite snack, and she made it for herself often. She always let him lick the bowl and once in awhile let him have a small dishful of his own.

Oh, Sarah. Why am I here all by myself without you? This isn't fair. I'd give anything to be back in your life. He sighed and lay down again. He gazed at the snow field and thought about poor little Murphy having to travel through it, although that hadn't turned out so badly with Reva and Sebastian's help. He scanned the horizon of the snow field but saw no dogs at all. He glanced at the path going up the mountain, and it beckoned him again. He thought of the strange meerkat and wondered if he would encounter him again today. Then he remembered why he'd come back down. He had to figure out a way to count the twenty-one days until Murphy returned. *Well*, he thought with a smile, *only twenty now. One's gone already.* He had an idea.

He stepped off the grass to the side of the path, onto an area of coarse gravel. He picked up a few stones in his mouth and carried them back to the edge of the water. Then he went back and gathered more until he had a pile of twenty-one. He counted them again to make sure, picked up one in his teeth, and tossed it into the pool of water. *Ha ha! Am I brilliant or what? Every day I'll toss another rock into the pool. When they're all gone, it will be the day Murphy arrives.* He felt energized. *Now, I'll go back up this mountain and find out why Boy sent me here. It must be something good.* With his head held high, he stepped onto the path and trotted forward.

It looked the same as yesterday, but today he made better time, because he didn't slow down to look around. When he sensed he was near the place where the meerkat had been, he slowed to a fast walk, dropped his nose to the ground, and sniffed, zigzagging from one side of the path to the other. One whiff brought him to a dead stop. He had it. He smelled the meerkat. He started to call out but decided he shouldn't. *I'm not sure I like him, although he seems to be the only other animal up here. Maybe he knows about others. I should see what I can find out from him, and then I'll be on my way.*

"Meerkat? Are you here?" Ivan peered into the ferns, expecting to see the pointed grey snout emerge. He perked his ears for any sounds of movement. The foliage remained still, yet Ivan was sure he could smell the critter. He poked his nose low into a thick growth of ferns. He could smell the meerkat very clearly, so he followed the scent. He pushed through the ferns with his chest until the scent was extremely strong. He touched something soft and pulled back.

There lay the meerkat. At first Ivan thought he was dead, but upon looking harder, he could see him breathing. "Meerkat," he whispered. "Wake up. It's morning."

The meerkat fluttered his eyes open and turned his head to look at Ivan. "Let me sleep," he said and rolled over onto his side.

"Just one question," said Ivan. "Is there anyone else up here?"

"Yeah, sure," the meerkat muttered. "Lots. One like you. Blue merle. A snippety wicket."

"What's a snippety wicket?" Ivan asked, but the meerkat was sound asleep again and didn't answer.

Just as well. I don't want a lengthy conversation with him anyway. He continued trotting up the mountain. *What's a snippety wicket? And what was that about a blue merle? I've seen many blue merle Aussies at competitions with Sarah. I like the mottled blue-grey coats of those dogs. They're more interesting than the solid black parts of my own coat. And the meerkat said there are "lots" of other animals up here. Well, I'd sure like to see some.*

He went way past where he'd stopped yesterday. He could tell, because the trees were farther apart, and the foliage was less dense. He sensed he was quite high on the mountain and that the scenery would change soon. He turned right around a bend and came to a clearing, which struck him like a blast of cool air on a hot day. He stepped to the edge of the path and saw a vast panorama of green mountains spotted with blue tarns as vivid as turquoise stones. "Oh!" he breathed. "How lovely." He could not see the snow field or any sign of canine heaven. He figured they were well behind him now.

Wow. Where shall I go? He gazed down on the dozens of mountains, looking for anything that might draw him to it.

A voice behind him said, "Hard to know where to go, isn't it?"

Ivan swung around and was face-to-face with another Australian Shepherd, but this one had one blue eye, one brown eye, and was a blue merle with a wide, white blaze down one side of his face. Ivan didn't know whether to be elated or frightened. He was happy to see another dog, but this one gave him a bad feeling.

"Hi," said Ivan. He couldn't think of anything else.

"Anubis sent you up here, didn't he?"

"Yes," said Ivan. "How do you know that?"

"He probably asked you to take charge of a group of dogs and be their leader, right?"

"Why, yes," said Ivan.

"And then he probably expected you to do things you didn't know how to do, right?"

"Wow. Yes!" Ivan was beginning to change his mind about this dog.

"And the other dogs in your group also expected you to be something you weren't?"

"Oh my gosh, yes."

"And the pressure got so great, you just couldn't handle it."

"Yes."

"Then the others turned against you, and you wanted to quit—just get out of there?"

Ivan nodded his head.

"Happens a lot," said the blue merle.

"And they come up here to find themselves?" Ivan asked.

"You got it."

"What happens then?"

"Most decide to stay up here where life—or rather, death—is much better."

"Really? It's better here? Why? How?"

"You're quite inquisitive."

"I want to know what I'm supposed to do here."

"Of course." The blue merle turned and began to stroll away, assuming Ivan would follow.

Ivan hesitated. He felt ambivalent about following and almost stayed behind, but there was so much he needed to know, so he trotted and caught up quickly. "What's your name?" he asked.

"Garmr."

"Gar Mur?"

"Garmr. One syllable."

Ivan whispered the name over and over to himself, trying to say it without two syllables. *Weird. This whole place is weird.* "What kind of name is that? Who named you?"

"It's an ancient name. Very ancient."

"Oh," said Ivan. With a crooked feeling in his stomach, he followed Garmr, then asked, "Have you met the meerkat who lives down the path?"

"Which one? There are many."

"Really? Oh, I don't know. I didn't get his name. He talked in riddles."

"They all do."

"You said most dogs decide to stay up here. Where are they? What do they do here?"

Garmr nodded down below. "Mostly they live down there." He motioned his head toward the numerous mountains Ivan had seen from the clearing. "They spend a lot of time visiting their people, the ones who are still alive on Earth."

Ivan's heart fluttered as he thought of Sarah. "Oh, I would love to do that. My Sarah is still there. We were in a terrible car accident. She's all cut and broken, but she'll be okay. I love visiting her. She still needs me, and I want to be with her as much as possible."

Garmr smiled. "If you decide to stay up here, you can visit her as often as you wish. Forever."

"Oh, that would be wonderful," Ivan exclaimed. He looked at Garmr. Garmr's ears fell, his face softened, and the blue eye and the brown eye blended in an expression of generosity that Ivan had not seen in Boy's eyes. Yet . . . something about Garmr made Ivan uneasy. "I'd like to meet some of the other dogs," he said.

"In time. I'll take you down there. But first, let's get better acquainted—the two of us. Tell me some more about your Sarah."

"Ohhh," murmured Ivan as he drifted into a reverie. "My Sarah is beautiful. She's kind and fun. She's generous and smart. I love her very much. And I miss her terribly."

"Tell me about some of the things you used to do together."

Ivan talked for hours about the dog shows, the herding competitions, the agility trials, the hikes in the mountains, and all the quiet, loving times in between. Garmr was an excellent listener, and Ivan talked until it was nearly dark. The darkening sky caught him by surprise, and he realized he must gallop back down to the waterfall to throw a stone into the pond. He told Garmr he had to leave.

"Come back in the morning," said Garmr, "and I'll show you around."

Ivan said, "Okay," dug his heels into the soil, and peeled away as fast as he could. It was totally dark when he arrived, but the sound of the waterfall guided him. He found his pile of stones, tossed one into the pool, and lay down on Murphy's spot.

Chapter Four

Ivan expected to drift off to sleep immediately. It had been such a full day. Yet, he couldn't find a comfortable position as images of Garmr flashed repeatedly inside his closed eyelids. The images were mostly of Garmr's face as he'd listened to Ivan's stories of Sarah. Most of the time, Ivan had been so involved in describing his life with Sarah, picturing in his mind how she'd done this and that, the cheerful, encouraging tone of her voice, and the way she'd jumped for joy when he'd done something correctly, that he didn't study Garmr. Yet, indelible impressions of Garmr's countenance were burned into Ivan's memory. The way Garmr tilted his head just right or squinted whenever Ivan told of something emotional were too appropriate. The expressions looked genuine, yet something didn't ring true.

Maybe it's just because his eyes are two different colors, thought Ivan. He'd seen plenty of Aussies with one brown and one blue eye, yet he'd never become acquainted with any of them. There had been quick glances, little whines, sometimes an occasional soft growl at a dog show or competition, yet he'd never really formed an opinion of their characters. To him they were just like the Aussies whose eyes were both brown or both blue. *No, it's not his eyes,* he concluded. *Maybe it's just my imagination. Maybe, because I've come to not trust Boy, I'm leery of anyone like Boy. I mean, Garmr must also be a higher-level dog spirit or he wouldn't know so much. He did say he's ancient, or at least his name is ancient. Maybe he's the guardian of the mountains, the one that helps dogs like me figure out how to do their job back in Anubis's realm. That must be it. I must not question his intentions. He wouldn't have listened to me for so long and cared so much if he were a bad dog. Boy wouldn't have sent me to be with a bad dog.*

That settles it, he thought, and rolled over onto his side, ready to fall asleep. A few moments later, he tried lying on his other side. He tried lying on his belly. He even rolled onto his back and gazed up at the stars. He tried counting the stars. Nothing worked. He got up and walked to the waterfall pool, lapped at the sweet water, then lapped some more, not because he was thirsty but because it tasted so good.

He could barely see his pile of stones in the darkness, but he knew there were nineteen left, nineteen days before Murphy would meet him here and tell him how things were going back in the living room. *Gosh, I hope the others didn't stay angry at Murphy. I hope Jolly realized he was only trying to be helpful. I wish I were there to hear what they're saying. Ohhh, geez, I miss them. It's odd that Garmr doesn't make me feel like I have a friend. I wish Carl were here, and Murphy and Jolly, Beauregard and Stealth. Oh, poor Stealth. I hope he becomes able to talk about some of his experiences. Poor guy must have had a very unpleasant life.*

Ivan looked up at the night sky. A faint glow from the stars allowed him to see an outline of the mountain next to him and the snow field's glowing, hushed-blue whiteness. He wished he had a campfire like the ones Sarah used to make, a friendly-feeling, crackling, orange fire. He sighed heavily. *I wish there was someone to talk to.*

He'd barely wished the wish when he heard scritching

noises on the stones near the path. He sniffed the air and was sure he detected the meerkat. He peered hard into the darkness and saw a small, wobbling figure amble toward him. It was the meerkat! *How about that. All I have to do is wish for him, and he appears.*

"Hello, meerkat!" Ivan said.

"Greetings, greetings. What the heck you callin' me this time of night for? Can't you let a fellow sleep?"

"But, I didn't call you," said Ivan. "I only thought about it."

"That's all you gotta do is think it—around here anyway."

"How can that be? How did you hear me?"

"Oh, it's why we're here—to honor your wishes. They went and assigned me to you. Wish they'd left me alone. But, it was my turn, I reckon. You are the dog I met yesterday, right?"

"Yes, I am he. Who's 'they?'" Ivan asked.

"What kinda sentence was that! What are you talking about—'he,' 'they?'"

"Ohhhhh!" said Ivan. "You're so hard to communicate with."

"Look who's talking! Barely a smidgen of what you say makes sense to me. Let's go to sleep." The meerkat started to walk away.

"Where are you going?" Ivan demanded.

"I'm going to curl up over here by the fire."

"Fire? What fire?"

"I could've sworn I heard you wish for a camp fire. Dang it. You're impossible. Now go to sleep, stupid dog."

"What?" asked Ivan. But when he turned around to

follow the meerkat, there was a lovely campfire, exactly like the one he had just imagined, and the meerkat was curled into a ball, sound asleep next to it. The orange light flicked and crackled and made a dancing pattern on the meerkat's coat. His sleeping face was peaceful.

Ivan stood with his mouth open. He couldn't believe this. Was it true that all he had to do was wish for something, and the meerkat would make it happen? *I better be careful what I wish for.*

Ivan stepped close to the meerkat and looked at the little face with its pointed snout, the eyes that appeared larger than they were because of the dark rings around them, and the human-like ears on the sides of his head. *What a cute fellow. I guess he'll be my friend, my only friend, for now.* With a warmth in his belly, Ivan lay down by the fire, not far from the meerkat, and drifted into sleep.

When he awoke, all signs of the campfire were gone as was the meerkat.

"Meerkat!" Ivan called, but the meerkat didn't appear. Ivan searched around the waterfall and pool, around the trailhead, and scanned the snow field but did not see the meerkat. He stomped one foot. *Darn. I should have asked him his name. He'd probably like to be called something other than "Meerkat." Well, next time.*

He stretched, looked up at the mountain, heard the birds singing, listened to the splashing of the waterfall, and decided things were pretty good. Then he remembered his appointment today with Garmr, and his stomach tightened. He drank a couple mouthfuls of water from the pool, and thought, *I better get going. I better start walking up the path.* He didn't trot this time and felt guilty about dragging his feet. *Garmr's probably waiting, wondering when I'll arrive.*

I suppose I could just not go up there. He considered this option but felt compelled to go anyway. He wondered if this was how Sarah felt whenever she had a dentist appointment. She didn't want to go but knew that it was best that she did. And, as Ivan recalled, it was never as bad as she anticipated. *This is probably just like that—this is good for me even though there's something unpleasant about it.* Still, he couldn't conceptualize just what it was that was unpleasant about Garmr. *He says all the right things, does all the right things, looks fine, but there's some little something I can't pinpoint. Oh well. Maybe that doubt will be gone today.* He raised his chin and pushed himself from a walk into a medium jog.

As he rounded a certain bend in the path, he thought he recognized it as the spot where the meerkat had been. He sniffed the air, but the scent was too faint for the meerkat to be present, so he kept going. After awhile, he reached the clearing. The summit was only a short distance further. As he strode across the grassy mountain top, he looked all around but didn't see Garmr. Then, Garmr appeared out of nowhere. Ivan did not see him walk towards him from someplace else. He just—poof—appeared.

"How did you do that?" Ivan asked.

"Good morning," said Garmr. He waited awhile, then said, "You mean, how did I just appear out of nowhere?"

"Yes. I didn't see you coming."

"We ancient ones have a way of doing that. Don't worry about it. You yourself are actually capable of the same thing. You just haven't figured it out yet."

The uneasiness returned to Ivan's core. *I just don't trust* him. *Plain and simple.* He took a deep breath and faced the other Aussie. He was about to tell him that he was going for a walk or maybe head down into the valleys. He just wanted to go exploring today, but he kept these thoughts to himself.

Garmr said, "Oh, but you can't go down there without an escort. That is forbidden."

Ivan jumped. He knew he hadn't spoken those words out loud. "You read my mind," he said. He gasped when he realized he had also thought to himself that he didn't trust Garmr. *Oh my gosh. I have to be careful what I think around him.*

"It doesn't all come through to me," Garmr assured him. "—primarily the wishes and desires, although I did pick up something about your not trusting me. That's understandable. This is a strange, new place, there's the odd little meerkat, whom you should be careful of, by the way, and you don't know what you're supposed to be doing here. Of course you're on guard. You should be. But, do try to trust me. I have only your best interests at heart." Garmr's head tilted to one side with a sweet expression.

Ivan froze. He was afraid to think, afraid to move, afraid to wish for anything.

"Come," said Garmr. "Let me show you some of the activities the other dogs enjoy here. Follow me." He walked away, and Ivan followed, rigid with apprehension.

He followed Garmr down a long path that looked very similar to the one he'd taken to the top of this mountain—countless spruce trees, ferns, and wildflowers. They walked for hours down and down and down. Ivan was in a sort of trance. He was afraid to think anything specific for fear Garmr would read his mind, so he let his brain go limp and concentrated on Garmr's white hocks jogging at a leisurely pace in front of him.

Finally, the woods opened onto a large meadow. Here, Aussies of all colors—black tri-colored ones, red tri-colored ones, red merles, blue merles, solid reds—herded sheep. Ivan perked his ears, because he always loved the herding competitions with Sarah where he herded sheep through prescribed courses. Sarah had trained him well, and nothing excited him more. It made his blood rush through his veins like nothing else. "Oh," he said to Garmr. "I love to herd."

"Most Aussies do. If you stay here, you'll get to do this all day every day."

"Really? Wow," he said, forgetting to not think. "That would be terrific. I love it more than anything."

"I know," said Garmr.

"Of course, I love Sarah even more, but that's different. She's a person."

"Yes," said Garmr knowingly.

Ivan watched as a red merle and a black tri-colored dog like himself rushed several sheep this way and that, funneling them into a small pen. When the sheep were all enclosed, the dogs shut the gate, then re-opened it, let the sheep back out, scattered them throughout the meadow, then began herding them back toward the pen again. Ivan itched to join them, but Garmr had walked on, so Ivan followed until they came to another section of meadow where some Pembroke Welsh Corgis herded cattle in a similar fashion. The short-statured corgis' faces were gleeful whenever a cow's kick missed them, as though they understood and enjoyed the reason for their having been bred to be so low to the ground.

Garmr led the way into a small woods where various types of retrievers swam towards ducks sitting in a large lake. Some of the ducks flew away, circled the lake, and alighted on the water again while other ducks allowed themselves to be caught and carried in the mouths of the retrievers back to shore. Once the dogs set the ducks down on the ground, the ducks would fly away, seeming to enjoy the game, circle the lake, and land on the water, only to be retrieved again.

They walked further into the woods and came upon a group of English Foxhounds charging through the trees after a sly red fox who ran through streams, across fallen tree trunks, and through thick hedges. Shortly after, a herd of deer bounded across their path followed by several Scottish Deerhounds. A small clearing was filled with Cairn Terriers digging for rodents.

"See," said Garmr. "In this land, every dog is fulfilled by doing what he or she was bred to do. They find it very gratifying, as you can well imagine."

"Oh, I know I would love to herd sheep all day. Do those dogs ever get to visit their people?"

"Oh my, yes," said Garmr. "But let me show you that tomorrow. As you might have noticed, the sky is beginning to dim, and I think you have a stone to toss, don't you?" he chuckled warmly.

Ivan looked up at the sky in surprise. Garmr was correct. The light was waning, so Ivan turned to go back the way they had come. "Wait," said Garmr. "Let me show you a short-cut." Ivan followed Garmr once more, this time to the edge of a meadow filled with wildflowers but no dogs. The wildflowers were a magnificent mixture of every color of the rainbow. Garmr motioned with a toss of his head. "If you walk across this meadow, you'll find a path on the other side that will lead you to the top of the mountain. There you'll find your trail to the bottom."

"Oh," said Ivan, somewhat disappointed. He wasn't in the mood to be alone, perhaps because, even in Garmr's company, he felt strangely alienated. The meadow was vast, and although it was beautiful, Ivan didn't much feel like trudging through it by himself.

"Good-bye, Ivan. See you tomorrow. Have a good night's rest," said Garmr, who turned away from Ivan, then vanished with the same sort of poof he'd appeared that morning.

Ivan stood still. He wanted to sort through this day, but his mind was numb. He realized that he'd forgotten to not think. He'd been so caught up in all that Garmr had shown him, he had let his guard down. He tried to remember if any of his thoughts had been private. Now his mind felt like cotton balls. He shook himself hard. That helped a little. He sat down and pawed at his head. He rubbed his eyes on his wrist. This helped some, but mostly his mind felt vacant, so he shook again, trying to rev up his thought circuits. *Geez, this is weird.* He backed away from the flower field and looked into the woods. *Maybe if I jump into the retrievers' lake, the cool water will wake me up.* He could see a distinctly-worn path that he and Garmr must have walked on. *Funny that I didn't notice this path. I was just following Garmr. Maybe it was here the whole time.*

He felt better taking charge of his own direction and

broke into a canter. He passed through the area where the hounds had chased the fox, and he arrived at the lake where retrievers and ducks were ending their day. Ivan didn't want to disturb them, so he found a little round bay off to one side. Despite his general dislike for swimming, he knew he needed this and slipped into the water. It was much colder than he expected. A zing traveled across his entire skin surface as he ducked his head under the water several times. He was delighted to feel his brain awaken, so he ducked under the water over and over and then leaped out. "Whoo!" he shouted quietly and shook as hard as he could to get the water out of his coat, then shook some more.

"Oh, that's better," he whispered. "Now I should hustle." He cantered back to the flower field and right into it. The foliage was so thick, he had to hop, but he was determined to get through it quickly. About a third of the way through, however, he noticed that he had trouble thinking again. Intuitively, he realized the flowers themselves had a numbing effect on his mind, and he galloped back out the way he'd entered. He stood a short distance from the field and shook himself, but his brain felt like cotton balls once again. "Well darn it," he whispered. He stepped further away. He trotted away from it, back down the path to the lake. *This time I'm going to stay away from those flowers.* When he arrived at the lake, he jumped right in and stayed under the water as long as he could. He popped up and gasped for air. Once again, he felt his brain recharge, so he shook off all the water. He noticed the sky had turned a dark shade of grey.

"Oh no," he said aloud. "How will I get back to the waterfall? I don't know where I am. Well, yes I do. If I go back to the flower field and run around it, I should be able to find the path on the other side."

He sped back to the flower field, spotted what he thought was a trail going up a hill on the other side, and galloped to the left around the field. His heart pumped fast as he breathed hard, and his mind remained clear. He kept an eye on the spot where he'd seen the trail. When he reached the other side, he felt his heart booming inside his ribs. The trail was gone. He criss-crossed back and forth across the face of the hill, searching for it. *Maybe, because it's almost dark, I just thought I saw it. Well, this is just great. Now what? Maybe I'll just go to the top of this hill, and I'll spot it from there.* He dug his heels in, raced to the summit, and scanned the whole area, but he saw no path. Fear-laden adrenaline pumped into his heart. *I don't trust this place.*

The mountain should be right behind me here and over to the right, but I don't see it. It's nearly dark. I can't even make out the woods and lake from here. What am I going to do? I can't even sniff my way back. He sniffed hard at the air and at the ground but smelled nothing familiar. His throat constricted. He felt like an abandoned puppy. *I wish I had a friend here.*

Within a few seconds, he heard a small, familiar voice. "I'm here," said the meerkat.

"Oh!" Ivan exclaimed. "I'm so happy to see you. Can you help me get back to the waterfall?"

"Of course. See, you *are* a stupid dog. Dogs don't get lost. Follow me." The meerkat turned and trotted away. It was so dark now, Ivan could barely see his little friend, but he could smell him and was sure to keep up.

"What's your name?" Ivan asked, glad he'd remembered this time.

"I told you already—*Suricata suricatta*. It's Latin."

"It's an awfully long name. Can I call you Surri?"

"Or Catta."

"I like Surri," Ivan replied.

"All right, all right. You're the one who's lost. You can have your pick."

"Thank you, Surri. How did you find me?"

"We talked about this already."

"Has anyone ever told you you're difficult to converse with?" Ivan asked.

"Has anyone told *you* that *you're* difficult to converse with?"

"I don't have trouble with other dogs."

"I'm not a dog."

Ivan didn't want to push it. He was grateful to have Surri rescue him, and even if communication was difficult, it was worth it. "How do you know how to get back?" Ivan asked.

"I just do."

Ivan couldn't think of any more questions, though he found the silence awkward. "Thank you," he added and kept his nose to the ground so as not to lose Surri's scent.

"You're welcome," said Surri. Ivan noticed that Surri seemed to have nothing to say unless Ivan asked him a question. Head to tail, they proceeded down hills, up hills, around bends, and then down a long descent. Ivan was sure this was their original mountain. Soon he heard the whisper of the waterfall and breathed more easily. Surri escorted Ivan to the spot where he had slept the previous two nights. Ivan sniffed the ground and could still detect Murphy's aroma.

"Thank you," said Ivan. "Wait!" he added, afraid Surri would vanish. "Could I have another campfire?"

"You bet," said Surri. A campfire appeared. It was just the right size, not too small, not too large.

"Thank you," said Ivan.

"You're welcome," said Surri as he vanished.

"Wouldn't you like some casual conversation?" Ivan called, but there was no response.

Grrrr, Ivan thought. *Surri is so frustrating.* He focused instead on the fire, staring into the orange flames as they licked at the burning branches of wood. Deep in the center, red embers turned to white, and at the very tips of the outer flames, licks of blue played in the darkness. He stared into them and tried to relax, but he couldn't as he began to think about his day. Unpleasant sensations arose in his belly—fear of Garmr's realm and mistrust of Garmr, yet a strange attraction to him. The ambivalence was too uncomfortable to dwell upon, so he allowed the fire to mesmerize him and soon fell asleep.

When he awakened, he noticed his pile of stones and realized he hadn't thrown one into the pool last night, so he quickly got up, snatched one in his teeth, and tossed it in. *Eighteen. That's an awful lot of days till I see Murphy. What am I going to do with all this time?* He thought about his promise to meet Garmr up there again today, but his innards sank at the idea. "I'm just not going to go," he said aloud. "I'll stay down here, wander around, maybe call Surri to come talk with me. Yes, that's it! It seems as if all I have to do is wish for something, and he grants the wish. I will wish to have a conversation with him."

Ivan closed his eyes and thought, *Surri, I wish you would come and talk with me.* He wished the wish sincerely, and when he opened his eyes, there stood the meerkat, slowly tapping his foot.

Ivan said, "So, you'll have a real conversation with me?"

"I'll have a conversation with you."

"So . . . what would you like to talk about?" Ivan asked, feeling a little silly.

"This is your wish, not mine."

"Oh! You're so difficult!"

"Mmm." Surri watched Ivan and waited.

"Okay, do you know an Australian Shepherd named Garmr?"

"Know him?"

"That's what I asked."

"I know *of* him. Can't say I've encountered him directly."

"What do you know about him?"

"He's a snippety-wicket."

"What's a snippety-wicket?"

"A snippety-wicket is a being, a dog in your case, who is important for you to know."

"What?"

"Just what I said."

"Well, what does that mean? Why is it important that I know him? I don't trust him."

"Mmm hmm."

"So, tell me more," Ivan pleaded.

"Like what?"

"Oh!" Ivan stamped his foot and walked in a small circle. "Like what I just asked you—why is it important than I know him?"

"I don't know."

"But, you just *said* it's important that I know him."

"Yes, I did say that," said Surri.

"But why?"

"I don't know."

"You just said *that*!" Ivan felt himself becoming angry. "You're talking in circles."

"You're asking questions in circles."

"Oh! You're SO difficult!"

"Mmm."

Ivan tried again, "So why is it important that I know him?"

"I don't know why. It just is. You have to find that out for yourself. For your SELF. See the difference?"

"What?"

"Oh!" Surri mimicked Ivan. "You're so difficult." He added, "It is your SELF that needs to know him."

"Oh," Ivan said, thinking. "But why?"

"How many times do I need to repeat this? I do not know. You'll find out."

"Oh," said Ivan. "So, I *should* go back up there and meet him?"

"I didn't tell you what to do. I never will."

"Why not? You live here. I don't."

"Mmm."

"Oh, geez," Ivan said and paced in a circle again. He sat down and faced Surri. "Well, I don't like him. No, that's not entirely true. There's something very appealing about him." He paused. "I don't trust him. That's more accurate. He showed me what a great place he has up there. He showed me different types of dogs doing what they love to do, what they were bred to do. He showed me Australian Shepherds like myself herding sheep. I love to herd sheep. He said that if I stay, I can do that every day. I can't think of anything better."

"I guess you wouldn't," said Surri.

"But then, when it was getting dark, he showed me a short-cut across a field of flowers. As I stood near the flowers, I began to feel weird in my head and couldn't think clearly. So, I jumped into a lake and felt better. When I ran back into the flower field, my brain got numb again, so I had to jump back into the lake again. I tried to go around the flower field, and that's when I got lost and called you."

"I'm glad you did," said Surri. "That's my job."

"I realize that," said Ivan, "but what was going on with those flowers?"

"He's a snippety-wicket."

"What? Why don't you just say what you mean? Why do I have to keep trying to guess what you mean?"

"Because you're a dog."

"Oh! Oh, oh, oh!"

Surri nodded. "It's frustrating. For me, too."

"Well then, why don't you just talk like I do?"

"Because I'm not a dog."

"Oh! Geez! Okay. Well, just forget it. But you'll still come if I call you? If I go up there and get lost again, will you come?"

"Of course," said Surri and closed his eyes. For the

first time, Ivan saw that Surri was very old. He felt strangely blessed to have him as his friend. He wanted to spend
more time with him, because he sensed that he could learn
a great deal from him. Yet, Surri was so difficult to talk
with, Ivan decided to let him go for now.

"Thank you. I suppose I should go up there. I don't really want to. But, if what you said is true, I suppose I need
to find out *why* he's a snippety-wicket."

Surri nodded again with his eyes half shut. "It is true.
Good luck, my dog."

Ivan smiled, and Surri ambled away, disappearing
into a clump of ferns. Ivan's belly warmed as he watched
the little tail disappear into the vegetation.

He stood at the trailhead and contemplated the path.
With a heavy sigh, he placed one foot in front of the other
and started to climb. About halfway up, he began replay-
ing the last two days' events in his mind. He recalled
Garmr telling him he should be wary of Surri. That's odd,
Ivan thought. Surri doesn't seem to like Garmr either. Of
the two, Ivan's gut said Surri was the more trustworthy.
Yet, he still felt drawn to Garmr and felt he was doing the
right thing. He knew his upcoming experiences may not
be pleasant, but this was what he had to do. He imagined
himself staying down here and hanging around by the
waterfall for eighteen days and knew it would not fulfill
his mission.

When he reached the apex of the mountain, he studied
the vistas below. They were all the same no matter which
way he looked. All 360 degrees consisted of smaller green
mountains and turquoise-blue tarns. Here and there a few
grey clouds shed rain, but right beside them the sun's rays

created not magnificent rainbows but mediocre ones. Ivan breathed the air deeply into his lungs, readying himself for the day.

"So you did come," said Garmr. "I wondered if you would."

Ivan, only partially startled, turned around. "Why?" he asked. "Did you think I might not, because I got stuck in the flower field? Why did you trick me like that? What would have happened had I stayed in there?"

"It was just a little test—a test to see if you have a mind worthy of inhabiting this splendor-filled place. Not all dogs have what it takes. Any dog who chooses to live here must be of the highest intelligence, have quick wits, and be able to fend for himself. Your jumping into the lake was very impressive. I'd say you've earned the privilege of herding sheep for a day. Would you like that? You can have your own field, your own herd, and your own pen."

Ivan's heart quickened. His blood rushed. His muscles fired. "Ohhh, would I," said Ivan. "Is that really possible? You'll let me?"

"Come," said Garmr and trotted away. Ivan followed him down the path they had taken yesterday. They traveled across meadows, hills, and valleys, but Ivan saw no dogs as he had the day before. Soon he smelled the aroma of sheep, and when he and Garmr emerged from a forest into a huge meadow, he saw that it was filled with grazing sheep. His heart jumped, and adrenaline surged through his body.

Garmr, with Ivan on his heels, trotted through the middle of the herd until they reached a large, fenced-in area. A wide metal gate stood open. "How many would you like?" Garmr asked. "Ten or so?"

"Sure," said Ivan.

"I'll help you. Let's round up that group over here." Garmr scooted to the far side of a group of sheep. "You take them from that side," he motioned.

Ivan understood, and the two galloped out a little beyond a group of ten sheep. Garmr chased five sheep toward the open gate. Ivan did the same with the other five. A few broke loose and tried to join the larger herd, but each time, Ivan or Garmr raced around the sheep, nipped at its heels, and guided it back. Before long, the group of ten grazed inside the fenced area. Garmr showed Ivan how to push the gate shut and, with his teeth, pull the chain across a slot in the metal to secure it.

Both dogs panted heavily, their tongues hanging out the sides of their mouths. Ivan saw fire in Garmr's eyes and knew the same kind of fire blazed in his own. There was nothing more exhilarating than herding. They glanced at each other with appreciation for what they both felt, and Ivan felt a sense of camaraderie with Garmr, maybe even trust.

"Wow," he said. "That was great."

Garmr concurred. "Yes, it was. Shall we let them all out and do it again? Maybe if we scatter them out further, more will try to join the big herd." With a gleam in his eye, he added, "But, what will keep the others from trying to do the same? Maybe one of us should keep the whole group together while the other chases the singles."

"Sounds like a good plan," said Ivan.

"Which job would you like?" Garmr asked. "Take your pick."

Ivan chose to round up the singles. Together, they unlatched the gate and pulled it open. Ivan circled around to the right, and Garmr circled to the left. When they reached the far side, they drove the sheep back out the gate and scattered them far and wide. When the sheep were far enough out, Garmr asked Ivan if he was ready, and Ivan called, "I sure am!"

It took longer this time, and both dogs had to run farther, harder, and with more quick turns, but eventually they drove all the sheep into the fenced area. When they caught their breath, Garmr suggested Ivan plan the next game. Ivan did, and together they herded the sheep back out, then back in. The next time, Garmr created a game. Then Ivan. Suddenly, the day was gone. The sun was low in the sky, and Garmr suggested Ivan head back to his waterfall. This time, Garmr led Ivan directly to the return path, and Ivan trotted back to the waterfall by himself.

The exhaustion he felt was gratifying. He couldn't have wished for a better day than this. He didn't need a campfire. He looked up at the stars, listened to tree frogs chirping, and bathed in the lovely sound of water cascading into the pool. At this moment, he didn't need Surri. He didn't care about Murphy, Stealth, Jolly, Beauregard, and Carl. Even Sarah was but a distant memory. *If every day could be like this one, I would be happy.*

Just as he was about to fall asleep, he remembered his pile of stones. He shrugged and thought, *Oh forget it. I'm not going back there anyway. Why would I want to manage a group of arguing dogs? That Jolly's so selfish and temperamental. Beauregard is so gorgeous and too good for anyone else. Carl is stuffy with his over-educated ways. Murphy has sunshine all around him; you'd think he'd have warmed up by now. And Stealth. I'm tired of trying to find out his story. If he wants to keep it to himself, let him. As for finding one's purpose, I know the answer—do what you were bred to do. Simple as that. I have found Heaven at last.* With a smile on his face, Ivan fell fast asleep.

Chapter Five

He awoke the next morning to the same birds, the same sunshine, the familiar waterfall, and the same trees and flowers but a whole different outlook about this excursion. Instead of feeling tentative, instead of wishing Surri were better company, instead of wishing Murphy were here, he awoke knowing what he wanted. He could hardly wait to dash up the mountain to find Garmr and spend another day herding. He recalled a dream he'd had about a new game Garmr would love.

He galloped full-speed up the path, and when he reached the top, he looked this way and that, expecting Garmr to appear. But, Garmr didn't appear. *Maybe he expects me to meet him down by the sheep. I'll wait a little longer, then head down there by myself.* While he waited, he peered down into the mountains, trying to spot the sheep meadow and pens. He looked for groups of dogs, but he couldn't see anything but the hills, valleys, and mountain lakes. He sighed and sat down. Garmr probably has other dogs to attend to, not just me. I wonder where they are. He looked around. *You'd think there would at least be other Aussies here with me. I wonder if he shows other breeds around as well, though I can't imagine him retrieving ducks or digging for rodents.*

He paced back and forth across the mountain top, trying to be patient. He could already feel the charged-up energy in his muscles. He played out the new game he'd dreamed of. He imagined the herd of sheep, and he imagined Garmr there with him. He practiced dashing this way and that, cutting sharply in each direction to block a crafty sheep. When, in his imagination, he and Garmr had successfully penned up the herd, he sighed again and sat down. Then, without thinking, he headed down the path toward the sheep meadow.

Maybe he told me to meet him down there. When he tried to recall Garmr's exact words, he couldn't. *Besides,* he reassured himself, *with his powers, he can find me anywhere. And it's not like this is my first time. I do know my way.* He trotted merrily along, anticipating each curve, each switchback, and each straightaway until he reached the bottom where an open area stretched before him. He cantered across it with confidence and continued along the path. He passed by the lake, but no retrievers were there. When he passed through the woods, no hounds came charging through. When he passed by more meadows, no terriers were digging. He never saw the flower field, and when he arrived at the meadow where the sheep had been, the fence and pen were gone.

"Okay, Garmr," he said aloud. "This is another test, right?" With a chuckle in his throat, he looked around, but Garmr did not materialize. "Let me see if I can figure out what you're testing me for this time," he called out in a friendly tone. He sat down and thought, *Well, he didn't greet me at the top, so he's probably testing my ability to navigate my way here, and I think I passed that test.* He paused. *Except, why aren't the sheep here? Ahhh! Maybe he's hidden them to see if I can find them on my own.* Ivan cantered in a huge circle all around the meadow, through the woods all around it, and sniffed the air for sheep, sniffed the ground for sheep, and listened for their bleating, but he found no sheep.

He sat down and thought some more, trying very hard to remember what Garmr had said. *I don't think he said anything. I just assumed we'd meet at the top. Uh oh,* he thought as his heart stopped for a second. *I think I may have made a big mistake. I recall him saying that no one is to come down here without an escort, that it's not allowed. That was the first day. Uh oh. What have I done?* He stood up quickly. *Maybe that was the test—to see if I could contain my desire to herd and obey his original command. Uh oh. I should have stayed at the top. Oh boy, I better get back up there. I hope he hasn't already seen what I've done.* Ivan noticed a definite tremble in his legs as he galloped back. When he reached the top of the mountain, he sat and waited. He tried to send thought waves to Garmr. "Garmr, this is Ivan. I'm here on the mountain top waiting for you. I'm ready to go herd. I have a new game for you."

When Garmr still didn't appear, Ivan thought, *He must be very busy today. Maybe he has more new arrivals. But where are they? Gosh, I'm so full of energy. I'm so ready to try out that new game. But, I must be patient. I'm sure he has a good reason for not being here.*

Ivan lay down with his head on his paws. He tried to sleep. The sun and the air were a nice temperature, but he wasn't sleepy. Instead, he wondered if Garmr had simply forgotten him. *Maybe I wasn't good enough yesterday. Maybe an Aussie has to be a spectacular herder to be able to live here. I thought I was good, but I could have been quicker with a few of those sheep, and there was that one that got past me. Maybe he just doesn't like me. Maybe he's spending time with dogs who are better than I am. That must be it.*

"You had it right before," said Garmr from behind Ivan. Ivan leaped up and whirled around. "It was a test, a test to see if you would ignore what I said to you the first day, that no one is allowed down there without an escort. You disobeyed, Ivan. And I must take that into consideration. I don't know that I could trust you to reside here. Rules are rules for a reason."

"Oh, Garmr, I'm sorry. I just forgot."

"That's not a good excuse, Ivan. How can one forget a rule so easily, the only rule I gave you?"

"I—I don't know. I was excited. I thought of a new game with the sheep—for you and me."

Garmr looked at Ivan hard. Ivan thought Garmr's eyes turned different colors, but he wasn't sure with the sun shining right into his face. Garmr appeared larger today, and his stern demeanor was chilling as he said, "I think you should go now."

"Go? But where? I thought I was supposed to spend time with you."

"Who said that?" Garmr's voice boomed.

"Oh, gosh," said Ivan, cowering. "I don't remember. Maybe no one. I'm sorry. I'm very sorry. I'm not sure why I said that."

"Ha! Why should I believe you? You lie."

"Oh, no, no. I don't lie. Or I don't mean to. I just did what I thought you wanted."

"How dare you try to read my mind."

Ivan peeked up at Garmr. *How could he have been so much fun yesterday and so mean today?*

"Mean!" Garmr boomed again. "I am not mean. I did nothing wrong. You are the one who did something wrong. Do you understand?"

"Y-y-yes," said Ivan. He cowered again. He tried not to think, because he knew Garmr would read his mind. He began to tremble. He shook so hard, he couldn't believe it, and he couldn't make it stop.

"Go back down to your waterfall. Give yourself some hard thought. In three days I will give you one more chance. Meet me here then, and we'll talk." Garmr turned his back on Ivan and vanished.

Ivan lifted his head to see where Garmr had gone. He still shook—like a leaf in a wind storm. His teeth chattered. He sniffed the air. He perked his ears. He couldn't detect Garmr at all, so he made a dash for the trail. He cantered clumsily all the way down his mountain as though he had a tail tucked between his legs. When he reached his pile of stones, he hovered close to them. Still shaking, he grabbed last night's stone and tossed it into the pool. With a blank mind, he sat and stared at the trail, not even sure his soul existed.

Feeling like a hunk of lead, he collapsed on top of his pile of stones. He circled his body around them, nurturing them as if they were his life, and remained in a stupor for nearly three days. As each nightfall arrived, he tossed a stone into the pool and waited for the three days to end but had no idea what he would do when they were over. He knew he could call Surri, *But why?* he asked himself. *It would only be difficult.*

On the third day he stood up and wandered over to the pool, which was clear and calm. The ripples from the falling water usually created small rings, but this morning they didn't, leaving a mirrored surface into which he peered. He'd seen his reflection in Sarah's mirrors and knew he was a handsome dog. The black, copper, and white fur made a nearly-symmetrical pattern on his head. The white blaze that saddled his snout and extended onto his forehead was shaped just right, his brown watch eyes were perfect, and the areas of brown fur on his cheeks were evenly matched in size and shape. His neck and chest were all white against his black shoulders and upper legs. His belly and lower legs were white as well.

He stared at himself. "Who am I?" he asked the reflection. "Am I a dog who is a leader of other dogs, or am I a sheep-herding dog, a handsome, show-quality, smart, fast, energetic dog who likes to work?" As he gazed at himself, he began to fall in love with the image. He began to appreciate who he was. He recalled the excitement of working the sheep with Garmr and how nothing was more fulfilling. The thought of coddling Murphy, Jolly, and the others was sickening in comparison. And, he'd almost forgotten about Garmr's promise that he could visit Sarah every day. Maybe Garmr would show him how to do that.

He looked hard at his reflection, cocked his head, perked his ears, then bowed quickly as if he were going to lunge at a sheep. He watched himself sideways and thought he looked very good indeed. He was built to herd sheep, no doubt about it, so this is what he would do. He detected a slight movement over by the ferns and looked to see Surri watching him. Surri said nothing and made no gesture, so Ivan decided he wouldn't either. The two stared at each other until Ivan's belly tightened, so he looked away. He started for the path, but something made him go back, and, just for a laugh, he counted the stones remaining. Fourteen. *So, who cares?* He turned on his heels, and loped briskly up the trail to meet Garmr.

At the top, Garmr sat waiting. "Good morning, my son!" he shouted warmly. "I'm so glad you came." Without waiting for a response, he turned and headed for the path down the other side. He called over his shoulder, "So, are you ready to show me that new game?"

"Oh, yes, I am," Ivan replied and cantered to catch up. In a surprising flash, they were in the sheep meadow without having to traverse all the hills, valleys, woods, and meadows to get there. "Wow," said Ivan. "That's cool." He wondered how he could travel so fast without feeling it.

"Okay, young man, show me your game," said Garmr, jovial and ready to play. No sign of the harsh, demeaning personality remained, and Ivan wondered how Garmr could be so angry one day and so pleasant three days later.

Ivan explained his game, and the two practiced it over and over all day, Garmr suggesting variations and Ivan agreeing wholeheartedly. They herded sheep, and Ivan felt grand. *Maybe this is why Boy sent me here—to obtain the fulfillment he knows I deserve.*

When nightfall came, Garmr showed Ivan into a small, wooden shed filled with clean straw. It was rich with the aroma of sheep. "You may sleep here tonight—unless you'd prefer to go back to your waterfall. This way, we can get an earlier start tomorrow."

"Oh, this looks very comfortable," said Ivan. He felt gratified after a hard day's work with the promise of another like it tomorrow. He sighed and stretched. "Thank you, Garmr. This is the greatest."

"Yes, it is," said Garmr. "See you in the morning," and he disappeared.

Ivan stood in a corner of the shed and circled around until he made a nice nest in the straw. He lay down and spoke to himself, "All that hard work, and I'm not hungry or thirsty. Pretty amazing." The next morning, Garmr stood in the middle of the shed, waiting for Ivan to awaken. Together, they herded sheep all day, taking turns making up maneuvers. Ivan did not become bored. He loved every minute of it. And Garmr came the next day and the next until a week had passed. Before retiring for the night, Garmr walked with Ivan into the shed.

"Tell me, Ivan," said Garmr. "Would you like to continue this way of life?"

"Oh yes," said Ivan. "I never tire of it. I never will. This is what I want to do."

"Well, I think you have shown your worthiness. You shall have your wish." Garmr beamed with joy. "Are ready to commit to this way of life?"

"I just have one question, though," said Ivan. He now felt assured that Garmr truly liked him. "When we first met, you said I could visit Sarah every day. I haven't visited her once since I've been here, and I'd like to do that. Can you show me how? Is it the same procedure as in the realm of Anubis?"

Ivan was shocked to see Garmr grow larger. Garmr's whole body vibrated, and his bluish coat began to turn red. Ivan gasped and stepped back. He blinked his eyes to see if this were real. Garmr saw Ivan's expression and immediately shrank back to normal and said calmly, "Ivan, we don't speak of Anubis here. You must never mention his name again. Do you promise?"

"Oh, s-sure. Of c-course," Ivan stammered. He started to ask why but knew that would be a mistake.

"Sit," said Garmr, and Ivan sat. Garmr sat down next to him. "Do this." Garmr lifted his left paw, pads down, and held it in the air in front of his face. "Make circles, counter-clockwise, and say her name three times."

Ivan did as Garmr directed, saying, "Sarah, Sarah, Sarah." Slowly, an image of Sarah sitting at her computer materialized. She happily hummed along to a song on her radio as she worked on her teaching materials. Her one leg was still in a cast, but the cuts and bruises were less noticeable.

"She looks happy," said Ivan.

Garmr gazed with interest at Sarah and said, "Yes, she does, Ivan. She seems to be feeling better these days."

"Can she hear us talking?" Ivan asked.

"No, she can't."

Ivan stepped into the image and sat next to Sarah. He leaned against her hip. This time, Sarah didn't seem to notice him and continued typing and humming. Ivan leaned his body into hers, but she showed no signs of feeling him.

"They don't always feel your presence," said Garmr with kindness. "Don't be disappointed. She's doing well, and you should be happy for her."

Ivan did feel happy for her. She had better color in her face, and her voice, as she hummed, had more of its old energy. He did feel an ache in his belly, though, that she hadn't responded to his touch. *But Garmr is right. I am just a spirit, and people aren't supposed to feel spirits.* Her image dissolved too quickly, and Ivan stepped back. He turned to Garmr to see what he'd done wrong. "What did I do?"

"Oh, I'm sorry," Garmr said. "Did you want to spend more time with her? You can bring her back. Just make the circles again."

"That's okay," said Ivan. "I can check in on her again tomorrow. Thanks for showing me how to do it."

"That's what I'm here for," Garmr said warmly. "To close the image, just step back from it. Tomorrow then, we'll perform the initiation, and you can spend eternity here with me. You can herd sheep, you can visit Sarah. Life is truly grand. I'm so glad you've followed your heart."

"Thank you," said Ivan as Garmr vanished.

Ivan tried to get comfortable in his corner of the shed. He nestled into the fluffy straw and relished the pleasant exhaustion after another day of herding. He expected to drift off to sleep, but he couldn't. He thought about Sarah. He missed her so much. *Well, gosh. I'll just visit her again.* He sat upright, lifted his left paw the way Garmr had shown him, made three circles, said, "Sarah, Sarah, Sarah," and her image materialized. She still sat at her computer, typing and humming with a song on the radio. Ivan beamed love at her, but she didn't seem to notice. He stepped over to her and set his chin on her knee. She didn't feel him this time, either, so he sat back and watched. He glanced at the computer screen to see what she was working on. It looked like lecture notes for a presentation on Tolstoy. *She must be getting ready to go back to work. I wonder how long she'll have the cast on. She seems to be deep in thought and isn't doing anything but typing and humming, so I'll just check on her in the morning.* He stepped back from her image, and the scene closed.

He curled up in his corner again. He could hear a few sheep bleating outside, and a half moon brought some light through the small windows. He noticed that the shed always smelled of sheep, yet sheep never seemed to come in here. It was always clean and neat, just the way he left it every day. *I guess this is just how it is in Heaven.*

He sat up again. *Maybe I can't sleep because I'm excited about the initiation. I wonder what it involves. I hope there won't be any more tests. I think I've passed enough of those.* He gazed around the shed. It was extremely quiet. *Funny how I've never noticed this before. Maybe I've just been too tired. I've always gone right to sleep.* He got up and sniffed every corner of the shed. He looked out every window. He felt alone. *I kind of wish Murphy were here. Or Carl. Even Beauregard would be company. Jolly and Stealth are too much trouble, but I wonder how they're doing.* He imagined Carl leading the group in discussion and knew they were in good hands.

It sure is quiet in here. Morning is a long way off. I wonder if I'll ever get to sleep. He walked to the doorway and looked out into the meadow to see the sheep sleeping, though a few continued to graze by the light of the moon. Their white bodies cast little lumps of shimmery-white glow. *What a lovely sight. What a wonderful existence. Sheep all day, sleep all night. I can check on Sarah whenever I want.* He felt content, went back into the shed, and lay down in the corner.

He just wasn't sleepy. He looked about the shed some more and felt very, very lonely. "Surri!" he whispered.

"Would you come talk to me?" Instantly, Surri appeared. He rubbed his eyes as if he'd just been awakened.

"Gotta call me at night, don't you? Can't let a fellow sleep, eh?"

"Sorry."

"It's okay. Like I said, if you need me, you should call. It's why I'm here."

"Why?" asked Ivan

"Huh?

"Why are you here for me?"

"Why? Why ask why?" Surri asked, holding out his palms.

"Ohhhh, no," said Ivan. "Can't we just have a normal conversation?"

"I'll try," said Surri. "I think I'm getting better at understanding you."

"Oh," said Ivan, brightening. "I'm happy to hear that."

"Mmm." Then Surri sat silent, waiting.

"So?" asked Ivan.

"So what?"

"Grrrr. Are you going to answer my question?" Ivan asked.

"You mean 'So what?' I don't understand that one."

"No, no no. The other one—why are you here for me?"

"Oh, that one. It just is."

"What? What just is? What are you talking about?"

"See," said Surri. "You don't understand me either. We do have a problem, don't we?"

"I'd say so."

"Well, what can we do about it?" Surri asked.

"I thought you were the one with all the answers," said Ivan.

"Well, you have a point there. It's just that you ask me questions I haven't answered before. You're a challenge. A bright one. You keep me on my toes." Surri looked at Ivan as if Ivan were supposed to respond.

"What?" Ivan asked. "Why are you looking at me like that?"

"I thought you had something to say," said Surri.

"I thought YOU had something to say. I did ask you a question that you still haven't answered."

"Which one was that?" Surri asked innocently.

"Well, I asked two that I'd like answers to. The first one is Why are you here for me? The second one is What can we do about our communication problem? Actually, you asked that one, but I think you have the answer, not I."

"Okay," said Surri. "Let's just go slowly. That might help."

Ivan nodded his head hard. "Yes, let's go slowly. First question: Why are you here for me?"

"Because that's how it is. I just am."

"Well, there must be a reason. Don't you ever wonder why you have this job?"

"I used to. And then I discovered that it's because it just is."

"Oh, I don't know if I can accept that. There must be some reason, some explanation," Ivan insisted.

"It's part of the Grand Design," said Surri. "It's because this is how things work best. If you didn't have me, what would you do?"

Ivan pondered that. He thought about encountering Surri the first time and how glad he was to find another animal in the forest. He thought about Surri rescuing him when he was lost and how appreciative he was. He thought about how Surri had made him campfires and talked with him when he was lonely, like now. He also thought about how difficult conversation was. "Then why is it so difficult for us to talk to one another?" he asked.

"Because we're different kinds of beings. I communicate more easily with my own kind, and you do too. Aren't dogs the easiest for you to talk with?"

Ivan nodded. "I suppose that makes sense." He thought a moment. "I think we got off the track. Let's go back to why you're here for me. You said it's because this is how things work best. I don't understand."

Surri sighed. "How can I explain this? Okay, let's use you and Sarah as an example. Why were you there for Sarah? What purpose did you serve?"

"Oh, that's easy. I was there so she had a companion and a protector."

"Okay, so what would she have done without you?"

Ivan thought. "She would have been lonely. No one would have protected her. She wouldn't have had as much love in her life." Ivan looked at Surri with pride. Then his face fell. "Oh no, oh no. And that's how it is for her now . . . without me."

"Let's not dwell on that—just for the moment, okay? So . . . why do you think it works this way? Why are dogs there for humans?"

"To make their lives happier . . . , brighter . . . , safer . . . , filled with love . . . , and to give them fun things to do."

"And without dogs, their lives just wouldn't be as full in many ways, right?"

"Yes," said Ivan.

"So, why is it this way? Who or what created this system?"

"I don't know," said Ivan. "That's just how it is."

"Aha! See! Exactly right. That's just how it is. No one questions it to any extent. It's good, it works, both parties are pleased with the arrangement—just like you and me. See?"

"Well, I guess so. The human-dog thing seems natural. But this is kind of strange."

"That's just because you're now on the receiving end. On Earth you were always the giver. Now you're the receiver. See?"

"It's still rather strange, but yes, I do see. Hmm. Interesting. Okay, then. I accept you. Thank you for being here. I do appreciate your being here. It got so lonely in this shed tonight. I don't know why."

"You don't? Don't you have a big day ahead of you tomorrow?"

"You mean the initiation? How did you know about that?"

"I've been around here a long time."

"Yes," said Ivan. "You've said that before." He thought again. He didn't want to talk to Surri about the initiation. He sensed that the topic would be difficult, so he changed it. "This is going better, isn't it?"

"What?"

"Our communication. I think slowing down did help."

"I agree," said Surri. He remained silent, waiting for Ivan to continue.

Ivan's thoughts went back to Sarah. "Sarah needs another dog, doesn't she?"

"It appears that way. How do you feel about that?"

"I think she should get another one. I don't think any other dog will entirely fill my shoes, but she needs one nonetheless."

"You're probably right," said Surri.

I wish Surri would initiate more conversation. He always leaves it to me. I don't know what to talk about. But I'm glad he's here. "So, how do you like my sheep out there?"

"Sheep are sheep. I didn't pay much attention to them. How do you like them?"

"Oh boy. I love them. I mean, I love herding them. I can't say I love them for themselves. They're just sheep."

"My thinking exactly."

Oh geez. Another lull. He looked at Surri, who waited patiently. Ivan had no intention of talking to him about the initiation, but it burst out of him anyway. "What do you know about Garmr's initiation tomorrow? Have you ever seen one? Do you know what goes on?"

"Whoa. A little anxious about it? Are you worried?"

"No. Well, maybe." He paused. "I'm not sure." He paused again. "Yes, I think so. But I don't know why."

"You have good feelings and bad feelings, both at the same time," Surri suggested.

"Yes, I guess that's true. I love herding the sheep, and Garmr showed me how easy it is to visit Sarah any time I want. There's no better existence for a dog like me. Herding sheep is in my blood. Nothing satisfies me more. Well . . . , being with Sarah and protecting her is very satisfying, too, but I can't have that anymore. So . . . what could be better than to do what I was bred to do?"

"I see. Herding sheep is all there is for you anymore. You have nothing else to offer."

"I . . . I . . . I . . . don't like thinking of it that way," said Ivan earnestly.

"But, you're choosing to think of it that way. You believe your only worth is to herd sheep, because that's what feels best—because that's what you were bred to do."

"I can't be with Sarah anymore. When I visited her earlier today, I leaned against her, but she couldn't feel me. The last time I visited her, she did feel me. I guess my spirit isn't strong enough anymore."

"And because of this, you're convincing yourself there's nothing left for you to do but herd sheep. How will you feel about this, say, a year from now when you're tired of herding sheep?"

"I'll never get tired of herding sheep. Never. Impossible."

"I have an idea. What time of day is the initiation tomorrow?"

"I don't know. Probably in the morning."

"What do you think the initiation is for?" Surri asked.

"So that I'm assured I can stay here forever and herd sheep."

"What is 'forever?'"

"Forever is forever—until I don't want to do it anymore."

"Hmm." Surri looked up into the sky. "Listen. Let's get up before dawn. I want to take you over to some of the woods and fields. We'll get back in time. Garmr is not an early riser."

Ivan nodded. He was unsure but felt an uncanny faith in Surri's wisdom. He believed Surri was, in fact, here to help him, despite what Garmr had said. "Will you stay with me the rest of the night?" he asked softly.

Surri nodded his wise, old nod with his eyes half shut. Ivan liked this expression. It conveyed strength, knowledge, love, and peace, concepts Ivan never thought he would care about. It lulled him into a deep sleep.

ↄ

When Surri nudged Ivan to wake up, it was still dark out. "Let's go," Surri whispered. "We can reach several areas and return by late morning when Garmr will arrive. Surri scampered out of the shed, and Ivan trotted behind him. They passed the grazing sheep and headed into a woods. Surri guided Ivan to a spot at the edge of a lake that afforded them a wide view. The sky was beginning to lighten with a lavender glow to the east. "Any moment now, Ivan, you'll see retrievers coming out. See all those ducks on the lake? They stay there all night."

"Oh yes, Garmr showed them to me my first day. Those retrievers get to fetch birds all day. They love it, just like I love herding. This is such a wonderful place. All the different breeds get to do what they love best."

"Yes, I know," said Surri.

Ivan and the meerkat watched as the sky turned pink, gold, and then blue. Soon, a dozen or more retrievers of all kinds appeared on the banks of the lake. One by one they jumped in and swam toward the birds. They retrieved them, set them on the shore, and the birds flew up into the sky but came back to land on the water where they were retrieved again and again.

"Come," said Surri. "Let's go talk to one of those dogs."

"Really? Why?" asked Ivan.

"You'll see." Surri scuttled off around the shoreline, Ivan close behind, until they reached a wet area in the grass where the retrievers had shaken water off their coats. "Here comes one—that brown one there," said Surri. "Let's have a chat with her."

A lovely chocolate-colored Lab holding a duck pulled herself out of the lake. She set the bird down and shook a large spray of water into the air. The bird flew away, and the dog was about to turn around to jump back into the lake when Surri called out, "Excuse me, Ma'am. May we have a word with you?" He hurried over to her and said a few soft words that Ivan couldn't understand. The dog nodded her head and walked over to Ivan.

"Ivan," said Surri, "this is Bon Bon. Bon Bon, this is Ivan. Ivan here is thinking of making this place his new home. Would you please tell him how long you've been retrieving ducks out of this lake?"

She nodded and obediently said, "Sixty-four years, son."

"And would you tell him how many of those years you've been happily retrieving ducks?"

"About a third of one year I'd say."

"And why do you continue?" Surri asked.

"I can't stop," said the Lab as she turned around and sprang into the water.

Ivan sat back and looked at her as she swam away. He

looked at Surri. "What does she mean she can't stop? Of course she can stop. All she has to do is—stop. How ridiculous."

"Come," said Surri and hurried off toward the woods. Ivan followed until Surri stopped and said, "Let's wait here for a bit."

"What are we waiting for?" Ivan asked. He was beginning to wonder what would happen if Garmr showed up at the shed, and he weren't there.

"Here they come," said Surri. "I'll pull one aside."

Ivan heard a loud racket of baying Foxhounds. Soon, a silver fox galloped past them and shortly after, a pack of hounds appeared, chasing the fox. As they thundered by, Ivan held his ears against his head to dampen the sound.

"Ahoy there!" Surri called. "You, sir, would you chat with us for a quick moment?" One of the hounds pulled up next to them and stopped, panting and gasping for air. "Would you be kind enough, sir, to tell us how long you've been chasing that fox?"

The Foxhound panted so hard, he could hardly speak. "Me personally?" he asked, "or the whole pack?"

"Just you yourself."

"Let's see. I think it's been one hundred and thirteen years."

"Wait," said Ivan. "Do you still enjoy it?"

"Ha! What a joke. Would you?" and he galloped away.

"What did he mean by that?" Ivan asked. "Was he serious? If I were a Foxhound and loved to chase foxes the way I love to herd sheep, I would still enjoy it."

"Let's go," said Surri and headed for the nearby field where some Scottish Terriers were digging holes in the ground. He walked up to one and said, "Ahem, excuse me.

May we speak with you for a moment?" The terrier lifted her head out of the hole. She had soil all over her face, and she was panting. "How are you doing today?" Surri asked.

"The same as every other day," she said and went back to digging.

"Would you be so kind as to tell us how long you've been digging in this field?"

She stopped briefly to think. "Twenty-seven years," she said and dug some more.

Ivan stepped close to her. "Are you happy?"

"If I could stop now and then, I would be."

Ivan asked, "Did you have the choice to stay here or not?"

"Of course. We all did. But we didn't know until we'd been initiated that one can never go back."

Ivan sat down. Horror filled his gut. "Never?"

"Never. This is Hell, young man. Didn't anyone tell you that? Once you commit, you're here forever. And I mean forever. I wasn't as lucky as you. When I first arrived, and one of these meerkats here tried to approach me, I rejected him. Be a smart boy. Listen to your meerkat." She went back to digging.

Ivan, wide-eyed, looked at Surri. "Wow," was all he could say.

Surri hurried back toward the shed, and as Ivan trotted along behind him, he felt crushed. "I've been betrayed," said Ivan. He didn't feel like trotting. He just wanted to walk slowly and think, but Surri seemed to be in a hurry. When Ivan did slow down, Surri glanced over his shoulder and urged him to step lively. When the shed was in sight, Surri took Ivan behind a large tree.

"I want to show you one thing more," Surri whispered.

"Show me how you visit Sarah."

Ivan sat down, lifted his left front paw, and made three counter-clockwise circles while saying, "Sarah, Sarah, Sarah." Instantly, her image appeared. She still sat at her computer, typing and humming along to a song on the radio. Ivan looked hard. *Why is she still up? She should have gone to bed hours ago.* "This is where she was yesterday. She hasn't moved."

Surri asked, "Listen carefully. Is this the same song that was playing on the radio the other times you visited her?"

Ivan listened hard. He had never fancied himself skilled at human music, but he did recognize this song because it had some unusual howling tones in the background. "Yes! Yes, I think it is!"

"Now look at her computer screen. Did you notice yesterday what she was working on? Does this look the same or different?"

Ivan squinted to see what she was writing. It was the same as yesterday—the outline of a lecture on Tolstoy. "Oh! It is. It's the same thing. She wouldn't still be working on the same thing, the same page and everything." He turned to Surri. "What does this mean?"

"What do you think it means?"

Ivan stared at the image more closely. "I think it means that . . . that . . . that this isn't real. I've been betrayed again. Oh my gosh." He looked at Surri. "I can't go through with the initiation. I don't want to stay here. Garmr lied to me. He tricked me. I can't trust him."

"I'm afraid that's an understatement. Your problem now is to get out of here." Surri pointed toward the shed. "He's here."

Chapter Six

"Why is that a problem?" asked Ivan. "I'll just tell him I've decided not to stay."

"How do you think he'll feel about that?" The expression in Surri's eyes was very intense.

"I would expect him to understand."

"Get serious," said Surri.

Ivan looked toward the shed and saw Garmr walking in their direction. Ivan thought he had a few moments to discuss this further with Surri, but in an instant, Garmr stood next to him, and Surri had vanished.

"Good morning," said Garmr. "Out for an early morning stroll? Getting warmed up for some more herding games today—after the initiation?"

Ivan realized then that Garmr couldn't see Surri. Ivan joked, "Just out here having a conversation with my imaginary friend." He flinched inside and thought, *Oh boy, was that a stupid thing to say.*

"Why was that stupid, Ivan?" Garmr asked.

Ivan remembered that Garmr could read his mind. He'd forgotten about this after a week of fun and games. He froze.

"What's the problem, Ivan?"

Ivan knew he couldn't secretly process any of his own thoughts. He might as well speak them out loud. He knew he had to get away from Garmr, get out of this strange land, but he didn't know how, and he couldn't let himself think about it. He couldn't plan an escape, because Garmr would read his mind. He'd have to play it out as it came.

"Nothing. No problem," said Ivan. He struggled fiercely with his mind's desire to think ahead. He wanted to simply tell Garmr of his change of heart.

"Okay then. Let's proceed with the initiation. Then we can go herd those sheep again. Follow me." Garmr led Ivan to a dense, dark area of the forest. A small, red campfire burned low. It did not have the friendly orange licks of flames with blue tips that Surri's campfires had, and it made a low, humming sound. A large sheep appeared to be sleeping near the fire. Next to it was an old, domed trunk made of wood with rusted metal strapping and strange symbols carved on the top. Through the foliage, Ivan thought he saw hints of yellow eyes like those of cats. Fearful, jittery sensations arose in his chest, but he dared not allow himself to think about them. He concentrated instead on keeping his mind blank.

"Ivan, I'm so pleased you've decided to stay. I know you'll enjoy it here, and I'm going to enjoy your presence. You have chosen wisely. In our realm, we . . . ." Garmr went on talking, but his voice became a drone in Ivan's ears, a tone with no words. Ivan watched him talk, watched his facial expressions and gestures, but no words came through. The drone gradually became louder until it combined with the hum of the campfire in a dissonant, evil sound that caused his ears to burn. His heart felt frenzied. Before long, the sound entered every ounce of his being. He no longer had control of his physical self, his emotions, nor his mind. He couldn't tell whether his feet touched the ground. The sound vibrations governed every cell of his body.

When he looked into Garmr's eyes he saw they had become yellow, just like the cats' eyes that now emerged from the foliage. These giant-sized, black felines purred loudly and drew closer to him. The purring sound merged with the other two to become a clashing, demonic chord that nearly shattered Ivan's soul. He felt he was on the verge of exploding into a million tiny fragments that would fly apart, disappear into space, and never find their way back together.

Garmr brought his face close to Ivan's and smiled. His neon-yellow eyes seemed to reach out and take hold of Ivan's. Garmr stepped backwards very slowly, drawing Ivan with him toward the sleeping sheep. Garmr reached down and grabbed the nape of the sheep's neck in his teeth, and Ivan saw that the sheep was hollow. It was not a real sheep at all, only its hide, head, and feet. It dangled dreadfully in Garmr's mouth until he stepped over to Ivan and draped it over his back, adjusting its head to sit on top of Ivan's head and its legs to hang down over Ivan's legs.

Ivan's heart pounded. His head seemed to swell. His brain cried out to function, but the horrible chord was too loud, too dominant. Ivan watched Garmr lift the lid of the wooden chest. It fell open with a loud crack that startled Ivan and, for a moment, made his spirit sparkle with life. But immediately, the cloak of sheep hide began to draw his spirit away until it was no more, leaving Ivan a hollow shell of himself.

Garmr reached into the chest and pulled out a black dog bowl filled with sheep's blood that splashed across his face as he moved. As Garmr stepped close to Ivan with the bowl, he waved it under Ivan's nose, enticing him to take a drink. He held the liquid to Ivan's lips and began to chant,

> You become the sheep.
> You become the sheep.
> You give your soul to the sheep.
> You give your soul to the sheep.
> The sheep will carry you away
> Will carry you away
> Will carry you away.

He repeated these words over and over until Ivan lost control of his tongue and lapped at the sweet-tasting blood. The cats marched around them in a circle, their feet beating like drums as each paw hit the ground. They marched in unison to the tempo of Garmr's song. Around and around they marched. The fire, Garmr, the trunk, and Ivan were encircled by the cats as they paced in rhythm. Gradually, the tempo increased. Garmr's chant became faster, the cats marched faster, and Ivan's ability to focus on anything dissolved into the darkness.

Ivan felt he no longer belonged to himself. The sheep blood filled his entire being, and the hide had absorbed his soul into itself. Garmr spoke again, and his voice echoed from under the ground. It came up under their feet and surrounded everything in this forest enclosure. "As you give your soul to the sheep, so shall the sheep die, and Ivan will be born anew in the Realm of Garmr. Ivan, do you give your soul over to the sheep so that you may enjoy an eternity of pleasure? Say 'yes,' Ivan. Ivan, do you say 'yes?'" Garmr paused, then repeated, "Say 'yes,' Ivan. Say 'yes.'"

Ivan felt no control as his lips and tongue began to form the word 'yes.' In a flash in front of him, Surri appeared, although Garmr could not see him. "No!" shouted

Surri. "Ivan, you still have the choice. You can say 'no.'"

The "Y" poised itself on the middle of Ivan's tongue, but the rest of the word did not form. Ivan still could not think, but an impulse deep within him turned the "Y" into an "N." Still without thinking, Ivan whispered, "No."

Garmr's voice bellowed all around, "I cannot hear you. Speak louder, my son. Say 'yes.'"

Ivan looked at Surri. Surri stood with his palms and fingers together, pointed upward like a Hindu offering a blessing. Surri looked deep into Ivan's eyes. Hope radiated out of them like two separate suns. The warmth from these sun-filled eyes emanated love to Ivan. Ivan felt it enter his heart and warm it. He felt the slightest glimmer of life spark in his chest as he focused his whole attention on Surri's eyes. As he did, he felt some life pull back into himself from the sheep hide. Although he still could not think, he was aware of his own effort to reclaim himself as more and more of his old energy flowed out of the sheep and back into his body.

Louder now, Garmr demanded, "Say 'yes,' Ivan!"

Ivan took a deep breath. As he did, he pulled the remainder of his life force out of the sheep hide and back into his heart. "No!" he screamed at Garmr. He shook off the sheep hide and dashed out of the dark glen. He saw Surri's hind end in front of him, dashing away like a rabbit's. Fueled by the energy of his soul's re-entrance into himself, Ivan flew after Surri, never losing sight of the little tan butt and skinny tail. In a bolt of lightening, Garmr was huge and surrounded Ivan from above, from behind, from both sides, and from in front of him. His yellow eyes now burned with fury, and his blue merle coat and white face had turned dark orange. Ivan feared he would be overpowered by him but didn't allow himself to focus on anything but Surri's tail.

Garmr roared. The hideous sound engulfed Ivan. It chilled him and made him glowing hot at the same time. Fear resonated through every cell of his being. Yet, he kept going. He refused to lose his visual grip on Surri's rear end as they dashed between thick stands of ferns, over fallen logs, between thousands of trees, up hills, through valleys and through meadows. Ivan still didn't allow himself any thoughts despite Garmr's evil threats as he continued to surround Ivan. "You will not escape, Ivan. You are mine! You think you'll find your way out, but you will not!" And like flashing electric signs, Garmr's angry visage followed Ivan, appearing on one side, then the other, then in front, but Ivan kept going.

Garmr screamed, "I will have you!" but each time he appeared directly in front of Ivan, Surri made a quick turn, and Ivan followed. Ivan knew he could not think his way out of this nightmare. He knew his only chance was to follow every move that Surri made.

"NOOOOOOOOOO!!!" Garmr screamed at the top of his voice, and suddenly he was gone. In the instant that Ivan crossed the apex of the mountain onto the side with the waterfall, Garmr fell away. The evil roaring was instantly replaced with the sweet sounds of singing birds. The fiery visions stopped. Butterflies glided in the air, and tree frogs chirped as they clung to nearby tree trunks.

Ivan collapsed. He fell with a thud onto the ground, his chin flat on the grass, all four legs splayed apart. He panted, his head whirled, and he went into a swoon. He fell nearly unconscious with an ache of peace and safety. Surri stood nearby and waited patiently. Ivan sensed his presence, although he didn't have the strength to acknowledge it.

For several days, Ivan would awaken slightly and feel how his body was scorched and ravaged. His mind was still not clear, though his heart was filled with love. Each time he partially awakened, he sensed he wasn't yet healed and fell back into unconsciousness. He had a faint awareness of Surri walking around him, waving his hand-like paws over his body and resting them on his head, his back, his sides, and his legs. One morning, his brain began to awaken as he heard Surri's voice quietly calling, "Ivan, you best wake up. Time is running out. You must return to the waterfall."

Ivan raised his head and blinked dry, scratchy eyes as a blurred vision of Surri stood in front of him, shaking his head with a grim expression. "You almost didn't make it, Ivan. You really almost didn't." Ivan blinked a few more times until Surri became clear.

"What?" asked Ivan.

"I said, you almost didn't make it. Now you must get up and make your way down to the waterfall. Murphy arrives tomorrow. Can you stand up?"

Ivan tried to stand but collapsed under his own weight. "What's wrong with me?" he asked.

"You almost didn't make it," Surri said again.

"What do you mean?"

"Look at your fur."

Ivan looked at his body. His beautiful black and white fur was charred to a crisp, all grey and cracked. Much of it had fallen off, leaving bald patches of pink skin. His toenails were worn to tiny nubs. "Garmr did this?"

"Yes."

Ivan managed to sit up, and the images rolled back into his mind. "My god."

"Yes," said Surri.

Ivan considered the meerkat standing before him. He'd never known a friend like this. He wanted to draw him close and lick his face. "Surri" was all he could say as he beheld him. Surri nodded with his special, wise expression, eyes half shut. "I couldn't have gotten out without you," Ivan said.

"You almost didn't get out *with* me."

"What would have happened?"

"Not only would you have remained there forever like the others, you would never have herded another sheep, and you would never have seen Sarah again. The horrors you would have endured for trying to leave are not worth describing."

"I can't imagine."

"Don't try."

"You said Murphy arrives tomorrow? How do you know? Have that many days gone by? How do you know tomorrow's the day? I stopped tossing stones into the pool."

"I did it for you."

"Aw. Wow. Surri, you're something."

Surri nodded slowly. "Yes, I am."

Ivan grinned. On trembling legs, he stood up. Once he felt steady, he shook. He was sorry he did, because most of the rest of his burnt fur flew off in clumps and wisps that hung in the air like seeds in autumn, the ones with white, tendril-like parachutes that carry them to distant places. He stood and watched the cloud of grey fur particles float away. "I must look very ugly."

"Yes," said Surri. "You do. But it won't last long. It will help you understand where you've been. Once you integrate that experience into your new way of thinking, your former good looks will return." Ivan was sure he saw a smirk on the meerkat's face.

"Ready to head down to the waterfall?" Surri asked.

"I think so," said Ivan, afraid to walk. As the two started down the path, Ivan's body felt it had aged ten years. His joints were stiff, his muscles ached, and he was thirsty for the first time. "Surri, the whole time I've been here, I've been aware that I no longer have hunger or thirst, I guess because I'm just a spirit. Until now. Right now I'm very thirsty. If I'm still just a spirit, why do I feel physical again?"

"Just like the burnt fur—to help you fully realize where you've been, what you've been through. It should pass, too."

"'Should?' Not 'will'?"

"It's up to you."

"Tell me more, please," said Ivan.

"It's a good thing we've become better at communicating, because we have a lot of it to do."

Ivan didn't respond but waited for Surri to honor his request. As they padded down the path, Ivan stayed as close to Surri as he could, glad he didn't have to traverse this alone. He felt shaky, wondering if Garmr would sneak up behind him. He glanced behind them every few seconds, but no sign of Garmr appeared. "Are we completely safe from Garmr now? Can he follow us?"

"No, he cannot follow us here."

Ivan knew Surri was waiting for him to speak next.

"I suppose you want me to talk about what I learned back there."

"That would be good."

"I learned that I can't trust everyone."

"You already knew that."

"Surri, you're too honest sometimes," Ivan chuckled. He knew the subject Surri was waiting for was one Ivan preferred to avoid. *Well, what the heck,* he thought. *I may as well jump right in, get it over with.* "I suppose you think I was selfish to want to spend the rest of my existence herding sheep instead of helping other dogs."

"I never said that."

"But you were thinking it," said Ivan.

"You can't read my mind."

"Well, maybe I can," Ivan retorted. "Or maybe I'm just a good guesser."

"One and the same."

"What? You just said I can't read your mind. Now you're saying I can." Ivan tensed as the two teetered on fouled communication again.

"That is not what I said," said Surri.

"Whatever. The point is, I guess, that I need to think about why I became so enthralled with Garmr and what he offered."

"Excellent start."

"I really do love to herd sheep."

"No one said you shouldn't. It's what you chose to do in your last lifetime."

"I did?"

"You don't remember? Why were you an Australian Shepherd?"

"I'm still an Australian Shepherd."

"Are you sure?"

"I thought I was."

"Go back to why you became one."

"Huh?"

"Remember, when you first arrived in canine heaven, what Boy told you about recalling all your previous lives? Remember how you did that?"

"Oh yeah," said Ivan, and he visualized again the moving picture-like parade of dogs he had been. "But I don't think I *chose* to be a sheep-herding dog."

"You think it just happened all by itself, that it was an accident?"

"I guess so. I don't really know."

"Think harder."

Ivan thought hard as he hobbled along behind Surri. Slowly, an image of himself sitting in a small group of dogs emerged. These were dogs who looked familiar to him, although they weren't Jolly, Stealth, Beauregard, Murphy, and Carl. It didn't matter now who they were. What mattered was seeing himself tell them he believed he hadn't fully learned the concept of guilt. One of the dogs, a German Shepherd, suggested he reincarnate as a herding dog, and he would surely learn this concept. Ivan remembered deciding that Australian Shepherds were especially attractive and lively, and he would like to be this breed of herding dog.

He detached himself from the reverie and said to Surri, "Guilt."

"What about guilt?"

"I chose to learn more about it."

"Excellent. Things are coming back to you."

"So . . . why is that important? How will that make me feel and look like my old self?"

"This may take a few steps. Be patient and listen."

"I'm listening," said Ivan.

"To yourself?"

"No, to you."

Surri was silent, so Ivan went on thinking. Soon, though, they reached the bottom of the trail, and Ivan heard the friendly sound of his waterfall. He trotted over to the pool, reached to take a drink but glanced first at his reflection and nearly vomited. "Oh my god!" he exclaimed. He looked like an old dog who'd barely survived a dog fight. Both ears were torn, his whiskers were missing, his nose leather was scraped off, and the fur that remained was burnt beyond recognition.

"Come," said Surri. "I'll make you a campfire. We'll sit and talk—all night if we need to."

Ivan felt terribly rickety as he turned his body around, step by small step. There in front of him burned a lovely campfire that danced with the friendly, blue-tipped orange flames. "Oh, thank you, Surri. It's beautiful." He eased his body down onto the ground and groaned. "This is no fun. Let's get on with the conversation."

"I'm ready," said Surri.

Ivan sighed deeply and went back to "guilt." "Okay," he said, "so I realized before my last lifetime that I hadn't yet learned how to feel guilty. I don't know if that's entirely true, though, because even retrievers feel guilt, maybe not when they're puppies, but when they get to be young adults, don't you think?"

"I'm not an expert on dogs."

"You must be. Why are you here then?"

"I'm here because you need me."

"Oh." Ivan decided not to push him on the issue. "And I'm grateful for that, Surri. You know I am."

"Yes, I do. Thank you."

"Okay, so I'm guessing here that I need to understand why I chose to be a herding dog and feel guilt, why being a retriever didn't quite do it. Right?"

"I imagine so."

"You just imagine so? Then why am I doing this?"

"Just go on, Ivan," Surri said and impatiently waved his hand at him.

"Mmm! Sometimes you frustrate me, Surri."

Surri smiled.

Ivan took a deep breath. "Okay, so being a retriever taught me many things—devotion, service, playfulness, right?" He didn't bother to wait for an answer. "And if it's true that we keep recycling ourselves until we become a 'whole' dog, then I must have decided that there was a void. Am I on the right track, Surri?"

"I'm very impressed."

"You are? Great." Ivan felt a spark of energy rush through him. "I'll continue, then. So . . . let's see. What is it retrievers don't have? Um, I guess they're generally not great at guarding their herds—their people. They bark and carry on, but some of them don't even do that. A few do more, but generally speaking, if I needed to learn guilt and maybe protectiveness, being all those retriever breeds just wasn't doing it for me. I needed more." He looked at Surri, and Surri nodded. "But what I don't understand is how guilt and protectiveness go together."

"You just said that playfulness and devotion go hand in hand in retrievers, so why not guilt and protectiveness in herding dogs?"

"Hmm. You're right. And all dogs have all of these attributes to some extent. As an Aussie I learned to retrieve for Obedience titles, and I liked to play games with Sarah . . . ."

"Yes. Go on."

"But, my main drive, my main urge, was to herd sheep or geese or cows and to protect Sarah."

"Yes."

"So where does guilt come in? Why do herding dogs as a group experience more guilt than other types of dogs?" He looked at Surri.

Surri stared into the fire and didn't answer.

"Okay. You think I already know the answer, right?"

Surri looked at Ivan and winked softly.

"Oh boy. Hmm. What would Carl say? I'll try to be Carl. Let's see . . . if I were Carl, I would probably point out that because herding dogs have . . . um . . . such a strong sense of duty to protect . . . um . . . that they . . . um . . . I don't know . . . they have such a strong need to do the right thing for their people, that they worry about doing something wrong, . . . so, . . . when they *do* do something wrong, they can't stand it." He paused to glance at Surri again, who had a pleased expression on his face. "And . . . um . . . I guess that's what guilt is, right? You want so badly to do the right thing, you can't bear it when you're wrong." Ivan waited, because he thought there must be more, but he couldn't think of any more. "I guess that's it." He looked at Surri.

"Keep going."

"Keep going?" He took a deep breath. "Okay. There

must be more. Let's see. I did experience guilt as Sarah's dog. Whenever I thought I'd done something wrong, I couldn't stand it. I'd want to shrivel up and crawl under the bed, I was so ashamed." Ivan paused and thought of the first time they attended an Agility trial that was held outside rather than indoors. He'd smelled the scent of a rabbit that had hopped through the course earlier, and there was no fence. The open field where the rabbit had gone was right there. In that instant, finding that rabbit was much more important than scrambling through tunnels and jumping jumps, so he followed his nose into the field. Sarah came running after him, calling, "Ivan, here!" but he ignored her. The rabbit's scent kept getting stronger. It was very exciting, and nothing else mattered. When he reached the rabbit hole, Sarah caught up with him, grabbed him by the scruff of his neck, and scolded him. When he realized how he'd let her down, he was so overcome with guilt, he peed all over himself while they walked back to the car. She told him what a bad dog he was, and he hid in his crate for two days, even though the door was wide open.

Now, however, he needed to understand why herding dogs feel more guilt than others. Suddenly, a light flashed on. "Oh, I know! Herding dogs have more guilt, because the humans who bred us for certain qualities planned it that way. A long time ago, when shepherds relied on dogs to keep their herds together, they only bred those dogs who tried very hard to do the right thing. It was human selection! Herds of sheep were the shepherds' currency. The sheep were their whole lives, and they relied on their dogs to care for them. If the dogs didn't care, they were no good to the shepherds. Ahhhh, so it's not just how we evolved, it's how we were chosen to serve humans. If a retriever didn't retrieve a bird, then the worst thing that happened is the hunter had to walk into the field and pick it up himself. But, if a herding dog allowed sheep to escape or wolves to attack them, the owners suffered greatly. I think I'm catching on, Surri."

Surri said, "Yes, you are, Ivan. I thought you might."

"Might?"

"Okay, would. I thought you would. I *knew* you would, actually."

Ivan grinned. He thought he was done and shifted into a more comfortable position. "Is my fur back to normal now?" he asked.

"Look down at yourself. Unless you want to walk over to the pool."

Ivan looked down at his legs and his sides, expecting to see shiny, new, black and white fur. Instead, he was still half bald, and a lot of burnt fur still clung to him. He frowned and looked at Surri. "So I'm not done?"

Surri shook his head ever so slightly. "You have a ways to go."

"Oh." Ivan thought back through all they'd talked about since his escape from Garmr. "Oh!" he said. "I know! I must figure out why I was so attracted to what Garmr offered. That's the whole point of this, isn't it?"

"One of the major points, yes."

"Just one?" Ivan began to understand what Surri meant when he said they'd be up all night. He took a deep breath and felt that old queasy feeling return to his stomach, the one that suggested he'd have to confront his own selfishness. He thought back on the discussion with Jolly and the others about self*less*ness. He immediately felt ashamed. He'd betrayed not only the other dogs but himself as well. He felt guilty for being selfish.

"I feel guilty," Ivan said.

"What a surprise."

"Oh, come on, Surri. I really do. I think I was so enthralled with Garmr, because he offered me the two things I love best—herding sheep and being with Sarah. I wanted those things very much," and then Ivan sat up as though a gong had gone off, ". . . but the reason, dear Surri, is because I was *bred* to want those things. It wasn't my fault. Ha! See? I'm not so bad after all. I couldn't help it, because Man bred me that way. So, I'm not as selfish as I thought." He sat up and smiled at Surri.

Surri said, "Get real, Ivan."

"What? I am real. We just finished talking about that—that men bred herding dogs precisely for those reasons, to love herding sheep and to protect the sheep. So there. I think I'm off the hook." Ivan lay back down again, feeling very satisfied. "Harrumph! So there."

"You've forgotten one key factor."

"What?"

"Think about it Ivan. What's different between the Aussie you are now and the Aussie you were on Earth?"

Ivan thought a moment. "I don't have Sarah."

"You're almost on the right track."

"I . . . I . . . I . . . um . . . I don't know."

"Yes, you do. It's very obvious." Surri looked at Ivan earnestly. "What's the main difference?"

"Oh." Ivan felt stupid. "I'm dead."

"Re-phrase that."

"I'm . . . I'm . . . still dead."

"Are you really? Then why are you here talking to me?"

"Oh! My physical self died, but my spirit is still alive."

"Bingo. Now go on."

"This is hard, Surri. Do we have to talk about this now? I'm tired. I'd like to sleep a while."

"Take a nap, Ivan. I'll wake you."

Ivan instantly dropped off to sleep, his aching, ugly body grateful for the rest. Awhile later, Surri poked at Ivan's shoulder with his toes and whispered, "Psst. Wake up, Ivan. Wake up." Ivan stirred, then drifted back to sleep. Surri kicked lightly at him and called again, but Ivan refused to awaken. "Screeeeech, screeeech!"

"AAAAAH!" Ivan cried, bolted up, and ran several steps. As soon as he saw Surri he stopped. "Oh my god, Surri, I thought you were Garmr. It was a nightmare. Oh, that was horrible!"

"Just a dream, Ivan. Calm yourself and sit down here. We have a lot to do before daybreak."

"Why did you frighten me like that?" Ivan demanded. "My heart is racing."

"Calm yourself. You're fine. Come. Sit." Surri patted the ground next to him. The campfire still burned.

"Geez," said Ivan. "I was so sound asleep." He eased his sore body down next to Surri.

Surri said, "Selfishness and being dead. Are you really still an Aussie? These are the issues you were debating."

Ivan felt groggy. "I'd really rather sleep some more."

"This is ultimately your choice. But, if you sleep, you won't be ready when Murphy arrives."

Ivan's mind sizzled to life. "Oh, Murphy. Tomorrow. Okay."

Surri watched Ivan, then repeated, "Selfishness and death and am I really still an Aussie?"

Ivan dug in. "I thought I was still an Aussie. I acted and looked like an Aussie. I wanted to do Aussie things. Which is why I was so attracted to Garmr. But, if I'm dead, then I'm really no longer an Aussie. I'm just a dog spirit. Right?"

"I think you're on to something."

"But, *because* I thought I was still an Aussie, I wanted to do Aussie things, and these desires made me selfish. I thought I would be most fulfilled by herding."

"Bravo. Continue."

"But now that I realize I'm not an Aussie anymore, maybe I can start seeing other things that would be fulfilling besides herding."

Surri grinned.

"But, if I'm no longer an Aussie, why do I look like one?"

"It takes a while to shed one's identity from Earth. It happens more quickly for some than for others."

Ivan didn't understand but let it go. "Well, that explains the selfishness. I understand now why I was. Funny. I don't feel guilty about it. It makes sense. I did what was natural. Any other dog in my shoes would have done the same thing, don't you think?"

"Maybe now you see why there are so many dogs in Garmr's realm."

Ivan reflected on all the dogs he'd seen and met there, and his heart ached for them. "Yes, I do see."

"Go on."

"Okay." Ivan was eager but not sure where to go from here. "Um. So, I was attracted to Garmr because I thought I was still an Aussie who needed to herd and protect, which was selfish, but only because Man bred Aussies to want this, and now that I'm no longer an Aussie, I can want to do other things."

"Ta da!"

"Cool." Ivan felt a strange new energy. He felt lighter, brighter, more in tune with himself.

"Go take a gander at yourself in the pool."

Ivan forced himself to not cheat and look down at his legs while he scrambled over to the water's edge. A full moon high in the sky bathed the pool in crystalline, white light. He looked at his reflection and expected to see his old self mostly restored. He expected to see a few patches of grey, burnt fur and maybe a few remaining bald patches. Instead, his image was partially his old self and partially a glowing, golden-white aura that was more a general dog shape. The Aussie shape and colors were there, but the glowing, general shape surrounded them, merged with them, and made them more beautiful than before. And he felt the way he looked—as though a new, more powerful energy had entered his being. He shimmered and glowed inside, and he shimmered and glowed on the outside. Feeling rather jaunty, he watched his reflection turn and head back to Surri.

Surri asked, "So how do you feel, Ivan?"

"Wow," said Ivan. "Sort of va-va-va-voom!"

"Va-va-va-voom? What does that mean?"

"Energized. Super-good. On top of the world."

"A human idiom."

"Maybe so." Ivan became more serious. "Okay, Surri. I think what you're asking is what should I do now? That is, am I ready to go back to my group? Do I feel more able to lead them now? Is that what you're asking?"

Surri nodded, his eyes half shut again. Ivan worried that Surri was getting tired. It had been an awfully long day for him, too.

"Why did Boy choose me for this job?" Ivan asked.

"Because he believes you're ready."

"Am I?"

"Are you?"

Ivan sat down and gazed up at the stars. A slight breeze caused the tops of the pine trees to sway slightly. The stars twinkled with extra sparkle.

"I don't know. Why don't I know? Why don't I fully believe it's the right thing for me?"

"Maybe you're thinking too much," said Surri.

"One can never think too much."

"I don't agree with you."

Ivan had felt so good, and now he felt his stomach tighten once again. "So many obstacles," he muttered.

"The best things in life—or death—are not easy to come by," said Surri.

"And now I'm supposed to stop thinking? Where will that get me—or the dogs in my group? I have to think. I have to plan. I have to consider what's best for each dog. I have to figure out how to get Stealth to talk."

"You're becoming agitated," said Surri.

"Rrrrr. Why are you always right?" Ivan demanded. He paced around the campfire. He walked close to the pool to catch another glimpse of himself. He feared that the new energy had left him, but it was still there, the semi-formless luminescence around his Aussie shape.

Surri asked, "Have you ever heard humans discuss intuition?"

"Intuition. I suppose so. I've never been sure what it means, though. 'Women's intuition.' Why do women have it and not men? No, I don't know what it is."

"This is something we must talk about."

"Before Murphy arrives?"

"Yes."

"Oh boy." Ivan sighed and sat down. "Another challenge."

"Indeed." Surri paused to see if Ivan was ready. "Do you recall all the times that Sarah was away from home, and as she was coming back and approaching your house, you knew it?"

"Yes. Of course. It happened all the time."

"Was that thinking?"

"Um. I guess not. No."

"Was it emotion or feeling?"

"Mmm. I don't think so. Certainly not emotion."

"Was it a physical sensation?"

Ivan thought. "Nnno, I can't say I was aware of a physical sensation—you mean like a tingling or a tickle?"

"Yes."

"No. Not physical."

"Then what was it?" Surri asked, looking directly at Ivan.

"I-I-I don't know. I just knew. It was a knowing."

"That's what intuition is."

"Oh."

"And do you recall how you knew that you needed to come here—get away from Jolly and the others?"

"That was utter frustration."

"I mean, more deeply than that. Didn't you sense on some deeper level, like in your heart, that coming here would benefit you?"

Ivan thought back on how he did know, somewhere inside, that he needed to come to the mountains, even when it meant that Murphy would have to walk through the snow field. Yes, he knew at that time that he must do this. He answered, "Yes."

"That was your intuition."

"Oh. What is it exactly?"

"It's an ability to perceive other than with your mind, your physical senses, or your emotions."

"Okay. But where do the messages come from?"

"Ahhh, there's a question." Surri looked at Ivan hard. "I want you to use your mind for a moment. Think about where these messages might come from."

Ivan thought, *If they aren't from my mind, my emotions, or my physical self, then they must be from my spirit.* "Surri, has my spirit been inside of me my whole life? Has it always been inside here?"

Surri nodded. "Yes."

"So, I've been sending myself messages?"

"Sometimes it works like that. Often it does. Your spirit is aware of things that your mind isn't, like when Sarah was approaching home. Your spirit saw her coming and alerted you."

"Wow. Cool. Hey, thanks, Spirit!" Ivan chuckled.

Surri smiled and went on. "Did you notice that Garmr

could not see me? Did you notice that you've never seen me until you came here?"

"Yes, I did notice that Garmr couldn't see you. Is that because you're good, and he's evil?"

"Yes."

"But, wait. What did you mean that I couldn't see you until I came here? What do you mean?"

"I've been with you all of your existence, Ivan. When you get a hunch about something, like when you knew you should come here, I was sending you a message. I knew that it would be best for you to have this experience, and the only way I could convince you was to send what you perceived as a small inner voice—a hunch, your intuition. You and I have met in person, so to speak, many times before. You just don't remember."

Ivan stood up and paced around the campfire. He thought about this and tried to remember meeting Surri before. He thought hard and paced a long time while Surri waited. He thought back to Don, Sarah's friend. He and Sarah had had many conversations, along with other people that had come to their house, about death and angels and a hereafter. He recalled Don talking about guardian angels. Sarah and her other friends weren't sure they believed in angels, spirit guides, or spirits of any kind, but Don did. Ivan recalled being captivated by the idea; something in Don's words had rung true. He looked at Surri and asked, "Are you my guardian angel?"

Surri smiled from ear to ear. "Yes."

Chapter Seven

"Are you just like the guardian angels humans have?" Ivan asked.

"Yes," said Surri.

"Are all guardian angels meerkats?"

"No. Many meerkats serve as guardian angels, but other animal spirits do as well."

"Sarah's friend Don said that humans have additional angels—or spirit guides—who help them. Do I have more?"

"Yes."

"Are they all meerkats?"

"Some are. Some take other shapes."

"Like what?"

"See for yourself."

"How?"

"Turn around. Look."

Ivan turned around and saw eight animals—four meerkats, a mouse, a bear, an eagle, and a hippopotamus. They stood in a group and smiled at him. Each one had an aura of shimmery mist around it, and each one, as it looked into Ivan's eyes, emanated love. Ivan felt his heart would melt. Tears welled up, and his throat constricted. He wanted to sob with joy, so he let himself do that. He felt somewhat foolish but was so overcome with emotion he couldn't stop himself. The love they directed toward him was too big to take in. "You're so beautiful," he said, sniffing.

"Each one has a name and a particular purpose," Surri explained. "The meerkats assist me in watching over you, send messages as intuition, and generally serve to protect you. They are Kit, Mia, Sunny, and Hom."

The four meerkats bowed and said in unison, "Hello, Ivan."

Surri continued, "The mouse is Samuel, and he has reassured you when you've doubted yourself."

Samuel stood up on his back legs and saluted Ivan. Ivan bowed to him and said, "Hello, Samuel. Thank you."

Surri introduced the bear as Humphrey. "Humphrey has helped you feel strong and fierce when you needed to be."

"Really?" said Ivan. "Thank you, Humphrey. Here I thought I did that all on my own." Humphrey bowed to Ivan.

"The golden eagle there is Isotope. She has helped you guide Sarah, understand things better for yourself, and achieve goals."

Isotope spread her huge wings, flapped them once, and blinked at Ivan. Ivan could find no words. He bowed to her, and she nodded back.

"The hippopotamus is Esmerelda. She has helped you appreciate the earth, to feel solid and reliable, and to be a stable element in Sarah's life."

Ivan bowed to Esmerelda and said, "Thank you. Thank you very much." He turned to Surri and said, "I had no idea I was being helped so much. I thought I had been such a good dog for Sarah all on my own."

"Most dogs think that."

"Most, but not all?"

"There are a few highly-evolved dogs who sense our presence and learn to depend on it."

"Do these guides help all dogs or just me?"

"All dogs have their own sets of guides, but these here mostly have helped you, though some others came into your life when you needed them, then they went on to help others. These eight are the ones who have spent the most time with just you—since your initial existence."

Ivan was astounded. "I feel so blessed. I never thought I'd use that word, but I can't think of anything else to describe this. It's like being given a great big, juicy bone—a huge, wonderful gift."

"I thought you'd be pleased."

"Wow," said Ivan. He studied each of the eight animals. The four meerkats were similar, but he could see variations in their body shapes and facial expressions. *Kit, Mia, Sunny, and Hom*, he said silently to himself. Samuel, the mouse, looked so strong and proud for such a little guy. Humphrey was cinnamon-colored with a tan snout. Beneath his angelic glow, Ivan could see his ability to be fierce. Isotope's feathers were a hundred different shades of brown. Her eyes were keenly intense beneath their kind exterior. And Esmerelda, clownish in her huge roundness, showed a depth of character that was earthy and solid. Ivan teared up again at the sight of them. He finally looked at Surri and asked, "Now what?"

"We need to work with you before Murphy arrives. The sun will rise soon."

Ivan heard a bird chirp the first notes of its morning song, though he couldn't see any light on the horizon yet. Surri led them all to sit around the campfire. Ivan sat at attention, sensing this would be a very important discussion. Surri began. "Ivan, I presume you've decided to go back with Murphy."

"Yes, Surri."

"You will do your best work if you understand some things, and we're here to enlighten you."

"Okay," said Ivan. He felt wide awake and sharp-minded.

"Do you understand your duties with the other dogs?"

"Well," said Ivan, thinking back on Boy's words, "I think I'm supposed to help them recall their past lives, realize what they learned, and figure out what they still need to learn in order to become whole—become complete dogs. But everything fell apart."

"I will help you stay grounded," said Esmerelda, "level-headed, unemotional."

"And I'll help you stay focused," said Isotope as she lifted her wings away from her body slightly.

"Thanks," said Ivan. "I know I'll need your help. This is the hardest thing I've ever done."

"Your escape from Garmr might challenge that," said Humphrey, shaking his head.

"Oh, I'm sure," Ivan said with a little laugh. "Were you there for that?"

Humphrey nodded emphatically.

"We all were," said Sunny. "You needed all of us."

Ivan imagined how each may have helped in his or her own way. "And I thought it was just Surri."

"Oh no," said Mia. "We actually called in several additional meerkats. They've gone on to help others, so they couldn't be here."

"So Garmr tries constantly to recruit new dogs, huh?"

They all nodded hard. Hom said, "Boy was counting on you to go there and come back, but he never knows for sure. It was really up to you, even with our help."

"Does Boy know I'm coming back?"

"Yes," said Kit. "We let him know. He's extremely happy."

Ivan glowed.

Surri said, "Now, you need clarity about your mission. Each of your dogs is difficult in his or her own way. You've seen Jolly's personality at its worst. You know Stealth doesn't want to talk. You know Beauregard is self-aggrandizing, but you don't yet realize that Carl can be narrow-minded and Murphy too timid for his own good. However, Boy knows you can manage them but must understand the process." Ivan sat stock still with his full attention on Surri. "After each dog has figured out what he or she learned and still needs to learn, you must help them plan their next lives. You have been through more lives than any of the others. Many more. This is why Boy chose you. You probably have only one more life to live on Earth. Then you will remain up here to help others. This is why you're considered to be 'in training' as a spirit guide. Boy has been a spirit guide for a very long time. Before long, he will move to a higher level."

"How many levels are there?" Ivan asked.

"Seven," said Surri. "And when you, Ivan, move on to become a spirit guide, I, too, will move to my next level."

"Wow," said Ivan. "This is amazing. There's so much order to it. What happens after the seventh level?"

"We go back to The Source, who some call The Creator or God, who created and issued us. When we go back to our ultimate home, The Source learns from us—a beautiful process."

"Then why is there evil, like Garmr?"

"Earth is a planet of polarity. Not all existences are. Polarity is difficult. One cannot escape it on Earth. Evil helps us appreciate Good. Without it, there would be no comparison. Since all your incarnations are on Earth, you carry those experiences and values with you here."

"Whoa," said Ivan. "My head's spinning."

"Understandably," said Surri. "You'll need time to digest it all. What we're stressing right now is your responsibility to direct the other dogs. All decisions are their own, but you must help them make the wisest ones, especially when it comes to choosing their next lives. We'll be with you through the process in which *you* choose *your* last incarnation on Earth. And we'll be with you during your last incarnation. You'll need us more then than ever."

"Why?"

"Because it will be difficult."

"Haven't I had enough difficulty?"

"You may think so now, but the rewards for that difficult life will be magnificent, better than you can imagine. You will comprehend your true nature as a result. There is nothing like it. You won't regret it. Trust me."

Ivan felt as though he just graduated from college. He felt wiser, braver, and bolder than he could have imagined. He surveyed his angels. Their faces were aglow in the light of the campfire. Ivan turned to Surri and said, "I feel determined, prepared, ready. When will Murphy arrive?"

"It may be later in the day. He doesn't want to walk through that snow, you know, and he'll have to summon Reva and Sebastian again. Occasionally those two get so caught up in playing, they don't see a dog waiting. It could be mid-day before he arrives."

"Is there anything else I should know?"

Esmerelda spoke. "Did we tell Ivan we're always with him, and he can feel our presence anytime he chooses?"

"How will I do that?" Ivan asked.

"Just know we're there," Esmerelda explained. "If you have a question, ask it in your mind and then listen. We won't speak in voices that you'll hear with your ears the way you're doing now. Instead, our replies will come to you like thoughts. With practice, you'll distinguish the difference between one of your own thoughts and messages from us. You'll feel differently when one of us is speaking to you. You'll just know. You'll feel positive emotion."

Ivan worried. "I hope so. What if I can't tell?"

"Listen hard," said Hom. "It's like when you knew Sarah was about to come home. That was different than if you'd thought to yourself, 'I wonder if Sarah is coming home.' Do you see what I mean?"

"Yes," Ivan said quickly. "Yes."

Sunny spoke. "We should tell him about nudges."

"Nudges?" Ivan asked.

"Yes," said Sunny. "They're different than verbal answers from us. Sometimes we want you to do something we know is best for you, so we give a little nudge. To you, it feels like you're being drawn in a certain direction, but you don't know why. It's kind of like intuition. We can't make you do anything, because we don't have that power. However, we can give you little nudges, and you'll feel them. You've always felt them. You just didn't know they were coming from us."

"Can you give me an example?"

"Yes," said Sunny. "Remember when Boy gave you the choice between going back to the group or coming to the mountains?" Ivan nodded. "We were the ones who nudged you to choose the mountains. We knew you needed this experience. We didn't know you'd have such a close call with Garmr, but we knew you needed to come here to find yourself."

"Wow." Ivan said. "Yes, I remember how I felt compelled to come here. So that was you, huh?"

"Yes."

"Thank you."

"Any more questions?" Surri asked.

Ivan thought a moment. "Yes. Just one."

"Okay."

"Why do you and I have no trouble communicating now? Remember how it was when I first arrived?"

"It was difficult. We each needed to learn the other's language, that's all. I was good at listening and creating intuition but not speaking to you directly. You weren't very good at hearing me, but you learned."

Ivan thought about that. "Yes, I think you're right." They smiled at one another.

"I imagine you're still a bit tired, Ivan, so I suggest you take a nap until Murphy arrives. We'll be here. We're always here."

Ivan felt terribly drowsy. He barely had time to nod to Surri when he drifted off into a deep, peaceful sleep. When he awoke, the sun was high in the sky. He took a few moments to fully awaken as memories of the early morning surfaced. He looked around, but his spirit guides were gone. The campfire had vanished. He chilled at the aloneness. Inside his head, a voice said, "You're not alone. Remember, we're all here." He thought it sounded like Mia. His chest warmed, and he knew he could, in fact, hear his new-found friends.

He walked over to the waterfall. Rainbow colors danced throughout the water as it fell into the pool and sent forth perfect, concentric ripples. His image, still filled with iridescent light, swayed with grace as each ring waved through it. He admired his reflection, not for his physical good looks but for how good he felt about himself. He felt mature, as though he'd been here for years, not weeks.

"Ivan! Ivan!" Murphy shouted from a distance. Ivan looked at the snow field to see Reva and Sebastian plowing a deep path with their bodies. Ivan could hear Murphy but couldn't see him behind the large dogs.

"I'm here!" Ivan shouted back.

"We're coming!" Murphy called. Ivan felt giddy as he bounced up and down.

In unison, the two working dogs said, "Hi, Ivan. Here's Murphy."

Murphy waited until Reva and Sebastian had stepped far enough onto dry land so he could scoot around their rear ends without stepping in snow. Once on grass, he darted up to Ivan, then stopped abruptly, his eyes wide. "My goodness, Ivan. You look so different!"

"I thought I might," said Ivan. "I've been through a lot here. You look good yourself, Murphy. Getting used to that snow?"

Murphy giggled. "Maybe. But you—you look—gosh, I don't know—bigger, brighter—older, maybe—in a good way."

"It's great to see you, Murphy. I missed you. How *was* the snow today?"

"Not so bad. But still cold." His countenance changed as he glanced at the ground, then back at Ivan. "Did you—are you—what happened here? Are you staying here longer?"

"A great deal happened here, and no, I'm not staying. Will you lead the way back?"

Murphy stammered. "Oh, l-l-lead the way? Through the snow? I—I—I think Reva and Sebastian are better at that."

Mildly disappointed, Ivan said, "I'm sure they are. I'm ready whenever they are."

"We're ready!" said Reva and Sebastian. They turned to head back down their snow path. Ivan stopped for one last look at the waterfall, the pool, the spot where Surri's campfires had been, the trailhead, and the trail where it began its ascent to Garmr's realm. He shuddered at what he'd experienced there, all the deceit, the fascination, the horror, and all the poor dogs who'd been duped. Then he thought of Surri and the other eight animal guides, and he imagined them hovering above him, watching. With a warmth in his heart, he followed behind Sebastian, who followed Reva. Murphy waited to follow Ivan.

Ivan turned his head over his shoulder and called back to Murphy, "How did things go with Carl?"

"Oh gosh," said Murphy. "It's been a long three weeks. At first Carl seemed like a good leader. But then he started analyzing everyone. And he was often wrong, but he insisted he was right, and he gave long explanations for why someone behaved a certain way, and I think we all began to miss you pretty quickly. Except Carl. He was happy.

Stealth would fall asleep while Carl talked. Jolly played games with her toes. Beauregard argued with Carl. I tried to pay attention, but he lost me with all his big words."

"Did you accomplish anything? Did Boy ever stop by?"

"Boy visited every day, but he didn't say much. We talked a lot about what motivated us to choose the owners we did. That's what took up all three weeks."

Ivan smiled to himself. "I missed you a lot, Murphy."

"Thank you, Ivan. I missed you, too." Murphy paused, then asked, "How did you change your looks so much?"

"I didn't do anything. It happened all by itself. I learned some very hard lessons. And I almost didn't make it back. I had a very close call with a devil dog named Garmr. I'll tell you and the others when we're all together. It's a long story."

"Okay, Ivan. Whatever you want." Murphy was quiet for the rest of the trip, stepping quickly this way and that to avoid places where the snow wasn't packed.

When they reached the end of the snow field, Reva and Sebastian said good-bye. Murphy hurried to step onto the grass and thanked the two big dogs. They said, "Our pleasure," in their shared voice and trotted away. Ivan took a deep breath as he surveyed the vast grassy and wooded areas filled with dogs. He spotted their living room off in the distance and turned to Murphy. "How do the others feel about my return?"

"We didn't know whether you were coming back or not. I think everyone will be glad except Carl. Not that he doesn't like you. He just enjoyed being the leader."

"How long did Jolly and the others stay angry at you and me?"

"They seemed to forget about it immediately, probably because you left and Carl took over."

"Well, that's good. I hoped they wouldn't hold grudges."

As they approached the living room, Ivan saw Jolly, Stealth, Beauregard, and Carl sitting at the edge of the room, watching. He tried to read their faces. They looked expectant. As he and Murphy stepped up in front of them, their expressions went from awe to reverence. *Wow,* thought Ivan. *I must have changed more dramatically than I thought.* Jolly and Beauregard took a couple steps backward.

"Hi, Jolly. Hi, Beauregard. Carl. Stealth. I've returned."

"Hi, Ivan," they said.

"You look so different," said Jolly.

"That's what Murphy tells me. In what way?" he asked, looking down at his body and legs.

"You're bigger," said Stealth.

"And lighter. Or brighter. Shimmery," said Beauregard.

"There's more," said Carl. "There's something in your whole presentation. You seem grounded, more confident."

"Is this good?" Ivan asked, teasing them just a bit. "Or is it bad?"

"It's beautiful!" said Jolly. "You were handsome before, and now you're beautiful."

"Well, thank you, Ma'am," Ivan said and bowed with a chuckle. "It's good to be back. It's great to see you all. I feel like I've been gone for months."

"What'd you do dere?" Stealth asked.

"It's a long story," said Ivan. "Do you want to hear it?"

"Yes, yes!" they said.

So, Ivan told them his story from beginning to end. When he was finished, Jolly looked above her head and said, "I must have spirit guides, too. I wonder what they look like." Stealth, Beauregard, and Murphy looked up. "When will we get to see ours?" Jolly asked.

Ivan didn't know the answer to that question. He tensed, aware that he didn't, as he hoped, miraculously have all the answers but said, "I suppose you'll see them when you need to. Maybe I'll never see mine again. I don't know."

"Will they speak to me now like yours speak to you?" Jolly asked.

Ivan still didn't know for sure, but he listened for a moment and heard Mia say, "Yes, of course. Just tell her to ask and then listen."

He said, "Jolly, some time when you're alone and quiet, try asking them a question and then listen inside your head. I bet you'll hear an answer." Jolly's eyes became round with wonderment as she nodded.

Ivan took a breath and asked the group, "So, how did things go? I've told you my story. Now I'd like to hear yours. I understand Carl took over for me. Thank you, Carl." Carl nodded politely. "Who would like to tell me about it?"

No one spoke at first. Murphy and Jolly sat still with fixed eyes, and Beauregard and Stealth clenched their jaws. Ivan watched Carl, who seemed oblivious to the others' reactions, and said, "We embarked on a rather lengthy discourse formulating motivations for selecting the owner or owners that we did—in this past life, of course, as per yourself and the honorable Master Anubis."

"And how did that go?" Ivan asked. "Does everyone have a full understanding now?"

"Splendidly, if I do say so myself," Carl said as he gazed off into the sky. The other four rolled their eyes.

Ivan thought, *Nothing like a challenge right off the bat.* He surveyed them all and realized he didn't have a clue how to handle this. *Okay, meerkats and other guides, I need your help.*

A voice inside his head spoke. Ivan thought it was Isotope. "Take each one aside and have a private conversation. You'll learn a great deal this way."

Ivan brightened immediately. "Excellent!" he said.

"What's excellent?" asked Jolly.

"Um. It's excellent that you explored this concept. And I have an idea—well, she has an idea—never mind. How about if you all sort of take the day off. Go out and play, except that I would like to meet with each of you alone. While you're out playing, keep an eye on the room here and watch for me to motion you in. You know, it's just been so long, I'd like to spend a little time with each of you individually. Beauregard, you can be first. We'll go in alphabetical order. Carl's next, then Jolly, Murphy, and Stealth. Okay? Out you go, except for Beauregard." Happy, they all hurried out onto the lawn, each deciding what to do with this free time. Ivan smiled as he watched Jolly head for the snow, Carl for the park, Murphy for the beach, and Stealth for another living room.

Chapter Eight

Beauregard hopped onto the leather sofa and stretched out his legs. Ivan sprang up onto the easy chair across from him. Beauregard yawned, licked his lips casually, leaned back against the sofa, and asked, "So are we to address you as Master now?"

Ivan decided to pretend Beauregard was kidding and chuckled, "Oh yes, and you shall be called Sir Beauregard, Royal Knight of my kingdom."

Beauregard smiled, though he seemed tense. "There is that sort of quality about you now," he insisted. "You *have* changed. Quite dramatically."

"And I feel different, as though I've gone through a sort of metamorphosis, like a butterfly out of its cocoon. And how about you? What have these three weeks brought you? Did you gain any insights into yourself? I believe you all worked on why you chose your particular owner or owners in this past life."

"Carl's a pain in the butt. I think I could have done a better job. He talks way too much. He thinks he knows *every*thing, and let me tell you, he doesn't."

"I'm sorry." Ivan paused. "So the discussions weren't helpful?"

Beauregard thought. "Oh, I suppose they were somewhat helpful. Listening to the others' stories was more interesting than I would have imagined. I didn't realize how varied a dog's life can be. I thought all dogs' lives were like mine. And really, how could you want anything but what

141

I had? I was gorgeous at all times, loved at all times, pampered, petted. I did lots of travelling, saw all parts of this country plus Canada, Mexico, and England. I was idolized. And the romance! I doubt there are many dogs in history who mated as often as I did. And such beauties that came for my services! Such lovely ladies. Often two in the same day. Once, there were three visiting me at the same time. Ah. Heaven." He paused. "I guess this is Heaven, so my life on Earth was better than Heaven."

Ivan nodded as he listened. "And what surprised you about the others' lives?"

Beauregard started to relax. "Oh my goodness. The work, the difficulty, the limitations. Did you know Stealth's sole purpose was to fight? And poor Murphy only knew one owner his whole life? And Jolly never got to be in a conformation competition? Carl could have, but his owners chose not to take him. I can't imagine." Beauregard shook his head, sniffed arrogantly, and looked at the fireplace.

"So, you believe your life was the best it could have been."

Beauregard nodded. "Yes, without a doubt."

"Well . . . , I have a question," Ivan said. "Do you know what Standard Poodles were bred to do, and did you ever feel urges to perform those activities?"

"Bred to do? You mean other than show?" He sat up straighter, tucked in his chin, and pulled his legs closer to his body. He closed his eyes a moment, then said, "I believe Poodles were bred to be gorgeous and be good companions to humans. And, of course I felt urges to perform these activities. It came naturally to me. All the time."

Ivan smiled slightly. "Did you know that Poodles were originally bred to retrieve waterfowl out of icy cold water, which is why you have such dense coats and long snouts with which to carry geese?"

Beauregard shot Ivan a hard, suspicious look. He had no words. Ivan wondered if he were even breathing, because he was fixed in this position for a very long time. Finally, he blinked once and shook his head ever so slowly. "That can't be," he finally whispered. "Retrieving? Birds? Dead birds? With feathers? And blood?"

Ivan nodded.

"It can't be. Are you sure?"

"I'm very sure," said Ivan.

Beauregard gazed out into the distance. Ivan began to worry about him and wondered if he'd made a mistake in sharing this information.

"We're fancy French dogs," Beauregard insisted, his eyes still glazed.

"Actually, your breed originated in Germany," Ivan said frankly.

"Nooooo!" said Beauregard. "Then why are we known as 'French Poodles?'"

"I believe you were known in Germany as the *Pudel* or *Canis Familiaris Aquatius*. Aquatius means water. Later, the French adopted you."

Beauregard sat up and demanded, "How do you know this? Where did you learn it?"

"Mmm," Ivan thought. "I'm not sure. These kinds of things just come to me now."

Beauregard didn't question him further. Apparently, Ivan's new self-assured demeanor was enough, and the Poodle mumbled, "Well, I don't know what to say. This will take awhile to sink in."

"I'm sure it will," said Ivan. "Beauregard, have you ever gone swimming?"

"Never!" he replied, pushing his snout upwards.

"Ever felt the urge to?"

Beauregard looked at him in horror. "I never even became accustomed to baths. It messes so with one's coat. And those were really showers. I was never—oh—immersed, Heaven forbid. And to think of actually jumping into a body of water? Oh my. Never." Then, Beauregard was struck by a thought and gazed ahead without focusing. After a few moments, he said, "Wait." He looked at Ivan. "I just remembered something."

"Yes? What is it?" Ivan asked, leaning forward.

"I was young, maybe an adolescent—fifteen months old or so." Beauregard gazed further into the distance. "My handler had brought me to a party with him. It was summer. Lots of people in bathing suits. There was a pool, a huge one, shaped strangely, like the number nine. Some children were tossing around a large rubber duck that quacked. It was a game like football, I think. And every time the duck landed in the water, I had a strange urge to jump in and fetch it. I remember my handler scolding me, 'No, no, Beauregard. Bad dog. You may not go swimming.' I think I was jumping around a lot and pulling on the leash. I really *did* want to jump into that water. Gosh, now that I think about it, I recall that I couldn't stand *not* jumping in." He looked at Ivan. "Oh boy, Ivan! Then it's true. I *do* have retriever instincts." Beauregard gave Ivan an apprehensive smile, one that gradually became triumphant, almost smug.

Ivan expected Beauregard to come to his senses and disapprove of his own enthusiasm, but his eyes remained bright, his face animated. Even his legs moved around under him with the idea. Suddenly, his face fell, and he said, "Then, I wasn't fulfilling my true purpose, was I? I thought I was, but I see now that I didn't get to do real dog things." He paused. "Well, that's rather sad, isn't it? I was actually unfulfilled and didn't know it. Well, how about that?" His shoulders slumped as he sank against the back of the sofa.

"Beauregard! I have an idea. Follow me. Quick. Right now! Run! Follow me!" Ivan dashed out the door, glancing over his shoulder to make sure Beauregard followed, which he did, at a full gallop. Ivan grinned at the anticipation on Beauregard's face. Ivan raced across the lawns, past the park and the beach, and headed straight for the closest retriever pond. Here, an angel stood on the bank and threw balls, field bumpers, and sticks for retrievers to fetch. Ivan stepped up to the angel and told him what he and Beauregard were about to do. The angel nodded his head and chuckled.

"This way, Beauregard," said Ivan as he cantered halfway around the pond. He stopped, turned to Beauregard, and said, "Ready to go for a swim? Let's go!" and leaped into the water. Swimming was not his favorite activity, but, carried by his mission, he decided to enjoy it. He swam several yards toward the middle, listening for the splashing of Beauregard's body. When he didn't hear it, he turned and saw Beauregard standing on the shore.

What? I've gotten all wet for nothing? Ugh. He treaded water and yelled, "Come on in, Beauregard. It's lovely! I know it's what you want. Come on!"

Beauregard pranced in place and paced back and forth. He started to leap in, then seemed unable to do it and pranced in place some more. His face still showed enthusiasm, but it was quickly being replaced with anxiety.

"Come on, Beauregard. You've been wanting to do this all your life. Here's your big chance. You'll love it. It feels so good—just the right temperature."

"But my coat!"

"Oh geez," Ivan muttered under his breath. "Remember, you're in Heaven. Your coat will go back exactly the way it was when you get out. Come on! Don't worry about your coat."

Beauregard stopped prancing, and his face drooped sharply. "I can't," he called out meekly. "I really can't. I'm sorry."

"Oh geez," Ivan muttered again and swam back to shore. He pulled himself out of the water and shook several times, spraying water at Beauregard, who leaped back. When Ivan had shaken off as much water as he could, he looked at Beauregard, whose head hung. He wouldn't look at Ivan.

"I'm sorry to make you get wet," Beauregard said, wincing.

"That's okay," said Ivan and began to lead the way back around the pond. Ivan couldn't help but feel somewhat disgusted with the spoiled Poodle, but as they approached the angel, he had an idea. He walked up to the angel, who was waiting for a Golden making her last retrieve. Ivan took the angel aside and spoke with him. The angel smiled and nodded his head.

Ivan stepped over to Beauregard. "Let's hold on a second, okay? I'd like you to see something."

Beauregard murmured, "Yeah, okay." His head hung lower than before.

They watched as the Golden brought in her last bumper, shook, and trotted off to wherever she needed to go. Magically, the angel stood holding a whole armful of squeaky, yellow, plastic ducks. He squeezed one several times, making it quack. He waved it at Beauregard. "Hey, Beauregard, wanna fetch?" He quacked it some more, then tossed it a short distance into the water.

Beauregard leaped to the water's edge and looked as though he were about to jump in but at the last instant pulled back. So the angel squeaked another and tossed it in. Beauregard began whining, prancing, and pacing but still didn't go in. The angel, with perfect timing, squeaked the third, tossed it, and Beauregard made a beautiful, arced leap into the water. He paddled awkwardly, splashing the water with his front paws like a puppy on its first swim. He reached the duck, grabbed it in his mouth, carefully made a small circle, and headed back toward the shore.

Ivan was gleeful as he watched Beauregard's face. It was as though Beauregard had discovered the source of pure joy. His eyes lit up like candles as he delicately carried the yellow duck between his teeth. The angel clapped his hands and said, "Good boy! What a fellow you are!" Ivan jumped up and down with happiness, and Beauregard beamed as he climbed out of the water.

"Ohhhhhh, Ivan," he said without even shaking the water out of his coat, "That was wonderful!" He turned to the angel. "May I do it again?"

"Of course," said the angel and threw the duck farther this time. Beauregard retrieved it and asked for more. After that, he asked for more. Before long, Ivan began to feel he was back in Garmr's realm. Beauregard showed no signs of wanting to stop, and the angel was tirelessly obliging. Ivan was torn between being patient and wanting to continue their conversation. He realized they had all the time in the world, however, and lay down to take a nap. When Beauregard spotted Ivan's loss of enthusiasm, being the show dog he was, he came out of the water, stepped over to Ivan, and shook.

"AAAH!" screamed Ivan and jumped up.

"You're not watching me," Beauregard said.

"I'm sorry," said Ivan. "Say, how about we head back to the living room and continue talking?"

"Ohhhhh," Beauregard whined. "I'm having so much fun."

"You can come back later. The others are waiting, remember? When their turns come, you can do this all day."

"Really?" He brightened and looked at the angel for confirmation.

"Any time you like," said the angel. "This *is* Heaven, after all."

"Oh, thank you, thank you, thank you," said Beauregard. "What is your name?"

"Spruce," said the angel.

"Well, it's a real pleasure to meet you, Spruce. I'll be back as soon as I can."

"Okay, Beauregard. See you soon."

"Thanks, Spruce!" Ivan called and began walking.

Beauregard trotted beside Ivan with a bounce in his step. As if Ivan didn't know, he asked, "So, how was that, Beauregard? How do you feel?"

"Oh my gaaaaawd, I had no idea. My head is spinning. I can barely think. How could something so foreign be so sweet?" he asked, then looked into the distance, searching for the answer.

"And look at your coat. It's all back to normal."

Beauregard looked down at himself, trotting along, amazed to see that he was already dry and coifed to perfection. "Ah! Just like you said, Ivan. Amazing. Though I don't really care anymore." He paused. "How can that be! It's like my whole insides have changed. This is so weird. What used to matter doesn't, and what didn't now does." He chuckled. "I don't know whether to thank you or not!" He laughed.

Ivan laughed along with him and reflected on his own transformation in Garmr's realm, though his process was a far cry from Beauregard's. As they approached the living room, Ivan focused on the next step in their conversation. They entered the room, snuggled back into the furniture, and Ivan asked, "Did Carl direct the group to think about all of your past lives or only this most recent one?"

"Just the most recent one. But we talked about it until everyone was sick with boredom."

"Mmm," said Ivan, reminding himself of Surri. He grinned at his little friend's image and hoped he was watching all this. "So, may I ask, what did you learn about yourself in your most recent life?"

"Nothing that I didn't already know: I love to be admired, love being a show dog, love having people fuss over me, and love to make love," he chuckled deeply. "That's about it. No surprises. I think I know myself pretty well." He paused. "Or at least I did. I'm feeling a little fuzzy right now about who I really am . . . ." He looked to Ivan for guidance.

"I think it might be a good idea for you to remember lives beyond this last one. Do you have any sense about them?"

Beauregard stared into space again, then shook his head "no."

Ivan said, "I think I can help. Are you comfortable?" Beauregard nodded. "Good. Okay, then, sit back, relax, and allow your mind to be open. Take some slow, deep breaths, then ask yourself, 'Beauregard, show me my lives before this last one' and see what comes to mind. Try closing your eyes first."

The Poodle did so, and Ivan watched him. After a while, Ivan thought Beauregard had fallen asleep sitting up. He waited a bit longer, then very softly cleared his throat and shifted in his seat, but Beauregard still didn't stir. Ivan was unsure what to do, then remembered he could ask his spirit guides. In his mind, he called, "Surri, Hom, Isotope, are any of you there who could help me? Has Beauregard fallen asleep, and should I wake him?"

It was Sunny who spoke. "No, Ivan. Let him be. He's had a long series of lives. Be patient."

"Thank you!" Ivan called silently. Relieved, he sat back and waited. He tried to imagine all the lives that Beauregard might have had and why he had chosen a show career this time. Although he himself had been shown in Conformation and finished his championship, there wasn't much to it. He didn't particularly like the baths and brushing beforehand. He didn't like having his nails trimmed or chalk put in his white fur. Gaiting around the ring and standing stretched out to show the judge his good bones seemed silly, and he hated having the judges look in his mouth, feel his body all over, and do the goosy-feeling "ball check." He hated that.

But, he'd done his best for Sarah, and she was happy whenever he won. Being the star like Beauregard with all his ladies may have made a difference. Still, he couldn't imagine a whole lifetime of doing only that.

So, what, Ivan wondered, *inspired Beauregard to choose such a life? Perhaps he was homely and unloved before, which might have caused him to choose the opposite the next time.*

Beauregard eventually stirred, fluttered his eyelids open, and gazed about as if he were lost. He looked directly at Ivan but didn't seem to recognize him.

Ivan waited. "Beauregard? Do you know where you are?"

"Mmm? No, not really. Where am I? Who are you?"

Uh oh. What's happened here? "You really don't know who I am?"

Beauregard blinked and looked at Ivan hard. "No, I'm sorry, sir, I don't know who you are. Where am I?"

Ivan froze momentarily. "This is dog heaven. Do you remember coming here? Do you remember the others—Jolly . . . Murphy? Boy?"

"Mm, no, I can't say I do."

"What *do* you recall?" Ivan asked gently.

"I-I—I remember being a lot of different dogs."

A voice whispered inside Ivan's head, "Let him go on with this. Ask about those lives," said Isotope.

"I would like to hear about those dogs. Can you tell me about them?"

"Yyyeaaaah, sssurrrrre," Beauregard responded dreamily.

"The first one was two thousand years ago. I was a wolf on the plains of what is now known as North America. I led an average wolf's life—I hunted, mated, and died.

"Then, I was a wolf again, but this time on the continent known as Europe. This life was similar to the previous one. Actually, I had several lives as wolves. Many. Maybe fifty or more. And then one day I was a dog in Siberia. I was taught to pull a sled and had a nice man as an owner. I worked hard and died in middle age . . . ."

Beauregard went on describing nearly a hundred different lives. As Ivan predicted, the one before this last was troublesome. "I was a cute puppy out of a mixed-breed litter in New Mexico. A nice little girl picked me out. Her mother thought I was cute, too, but the father didn't want a dog at all. They kept me chained in the back yard. The father was mean. He beat the mother and the daughter, and I was helpless. I wanted to protect them, and I tried and tried to break the chain, but I never could. One time, it was really bad, and I was barking up a storm. The father got so angry, he came out, poured gasoline on me, and set me on fire. Then he kicked me so hard, some of my ribs broke. I was in terrible pain, but I managed to roll in the sandy soil and put the fire out, but not before it had burned all the fur off my head, my neck and all down one side. I guess I had barked so loudly the neighbors called the police, and they came and took the man away. He had badly hurt both the mother and the daughter. I was beside myself, because I loved that little girl so much. An ambulance came and took them away.

"The next day, a lady I didn't know showed up and delivered me to an animal shelter. Those people took me to a vet where I was medicated and bandaged, and then I was taken back to the shelter. It was a shelter where they never put dogs to sleep, but I heard them talking about putting me to sleep anyway because they were sure no one would ever adopt me. They said they couldn't believe how ugly I was. Whenever prospective adopters came to look at the dogs, everyone pointed at me and said, 'Oh my gosh. Look how ugly he is. Poor thing. I sure wouldn't want to touch him. Oooo. Poor thing. Poor, ugly dog.' And they hurried away to choose a different one.

"I was passed over for old dogs, blind dogs, dogs even I thought were ugly, and no one ever considered me. Even the people who worked there didn't want to pet me. I used to pray that I would wake up beautiful one day, but it never happened. For years. And then I started praying that I would just die. I never was petted or held. They did take me out and throw a ball once in awhile, and I loved that.

"Finally, I think I died of a broken heart. What a relief.

"And my last life was grand. I was a gorgeous show Poodle, loved and admired by all." Beauregard stopped and nodded his head once.

"Sadly, I developed cancer and was put to sleep. And now I'm here." He looked around, then back at Ivan. "Oh! I'm here! Oh yes! Of course! I'm in Heaven. And you're Ivan. I'm so sorry, Ivan. I guess I was spaced-out for awhile."

"That's okay, that's okay. It was worth it. My goodness, what an interesting series of lives you've lived," Ivan said with sincerity. Beauregard sighed deeply. Ivan continued, "Now I understand why you loved your last life so much."

Beauregard looked at him blankly. "Why?"

"Because the one before was so painful—because you were ugly and unloved."

Beauregard nodded his head but still looked confused. "What did that have to do with it?"

In that instant, Ivan realized that none of the dogs

understood that each time they died, they got to choose a subsequent life. Most chose a next life based on what happened in the previous one. If it was bad, they tended to compensate by choosing the opposite. Ivan tried to remember how it was that he understood this and the others didn't. Had Boy told him this from the beginning? He thought so. Or was it something Surri said? Regardless, he knew this to be true. Eventually, they would all be asked to choose the circumstances for their next lives. The wise would choose based on *all* previous lives, while the impulsive would choose based only on the most recent one.

"Beauregard, each time you die, you spend time here in Heaven. Part of being here and doing what we're doing is to enable you to choose your next life on Earth. Did you realize that?"

Beauregard thought a minute. "No, I don't think so."

"Well, it's true. Do you now see why you chose to be a gorgeous show dog—because you were so ugly and unwanted in your previous life? It makes sense that, because you suffered before, you would choose the opposite the next time."

"Choose? But how do we choose?"

The gears in Ivan's head shuddered to a halt. *Oh my gosh,* he thought. *I don't know the answer. I know we choose, but I don't know how.* He relaxed and said with honesty, "Beauregard, I don't know, but I do know we get to choose and always have in the past, but Boy hasn't told me yet how we do it. I'll find out, though."

Beauregard pondered this. "It does make sense, Ivan. Thank you." He sat and looked around. "I'm grateful to remember all I've been through. And I'm grateful to understand my Poodle retrieving heritage. It gives me a better perspective on my whole self." He seemed to have nothing more to say. "Are we done?"

"I think so. Carl's next. I bet I know what you're going to do with your free time. Tell Spruce 'hi' for me."

Beauregard grinned, said, "Okay," and leaped off the sofa.

"Wait!" Ivan called, and Beauregard stopped. "Tell Carl to wait till I call him, okay?" Ivan realized what hard work this had been and felt he needed a little break. "Tell him I'll find him in the park." Beauregard nodded and dashed toward the retriever pond.

Chapter Nine

After Ivan awakened from a nap under a big shade tree in the park, he yawned, stretched, and stepped down to the edge of the lake where he lapped a drink. He wasn't thirsty but wanted to feel the cool water in his mouth. He was delighted to find that it was as sweet as the water in the waterfall pool by the mountains. As he looked across the lake, he observed various dogs wading in the water, napping under trees, strolling around the park, or basking in the sun. He figured they were all members of groups like his, and each was taking a break or working on a personal issue. With a sense of satisfaction, he thought about Beauregard and how much they had accomplished. Now, on to Carl.

Carl makes me nervous. Beauregard was easy, because he isn't very self-aware. Carl, however, has spent his life with two people whose entire quest was self-awareness, both for themselves and others. How can I be a mentor to this dog? He probably has more to offer me than I to him.

"Why don't you raise this problem with him from the beginning?" a small voice spoke within Ivan's head.

"Surri!" Ivan cried out. "You're here. Where are you? I can't see you."

"You don't need to see me, Ivan. Remember?"

"Oh, but I want to see you. I miss you!"

"I'll reappear when you really need me to. For now, all you need is my voice."

Ivan paused to digest what Surri had just said, then smiled as he pictured the meerkat. He loved that face, those ears, and his wise, squinty eyes. "Thanks, Surri. I'll do as you suggested."

Carl the Genius. Ivan took a great big breath and decided he would not let himself be intimidated. Carl was, after all, just another dog, probably no more intelligent than himself. Carl had simply received a different education. *And come to think of it, Sarah's Russian literature material was just as lofty as Carl's Jungian psychoanalysts'.* "Yeah," he said to himself. "Dostoyevsky, after all, was considered by many as the western world's first psychologist, even before Sigmund Freud." He lifted his chin and felt more confident.

He scanned the park, looking for Carl. It took a while, but he finally located the small mop of a dog strolling along the walkway on the other side of the lake. Ivan trotted around the other way. He stood in the middle of the walkway, expecting Carl to see him, but the little dog nearly ran into Ivan, bumping Ivan's leg with his shoulder.

"Carl!" Ivan said.

Carl looked up. "Oh my goodness. It's you. So sorry to bump you there. I was deep in thought."

"I can see that," said Ivan. "I'm finished with Beauregard. Are you ready to join me?"

"Oh yes, of course, of course."

Ivan walked slower than normal so Carl could keep up. "Lovely day," he offered.

"Every day is lovely here," Carl mused, "although I find I actually miss the rain at times. There's a coziness to a rainy day, don't you think?"

"Mmm. I guess so." Ivan thought once again of the rainy days with Sarah in their house. "What did Dora and Siegfried do on rainy days?"

"Their clients came whether it rained or not. But on rainy Sundays, when no clients came, they often taught me a new trick."

"Like what? Do you have a favorite trick?"

"I'll tell you, it sure isn't the one where they balanced a dog biscuit on my snout and made me wait until they said 'eat' before I could eat it."

"Oooo, yeah, that's a bad one. I don't know any dog who likes that trick."

"I did like a game where they hid five or more items that I could identify—Dora's glove, Siegfried's slipper, my stuffed mouse, my squeaky cat, maybe a fresh rawhide—and then they'd tell me which item to fetch. I'd have to run all through the house to find that exact one, ignore the others, and present it to them. They always changed the order and the hiding place, so it was a challenge I enjoyed. How about you?"

"Wow," said Ivan. "Sarah had a similar game for me. Actually, the same game—exactly—but she used different items: her winter hat, one of her socks, a tennis ball, my stuffed octopus, and a dog biscuit. It was always hard to let the biscuit sit there and fetch the item she told me to. She always saved the biscuit for last."

"Why do humans do that? Dora and Siegfried did the same thing. They think they're tricking us. If they only knew how smart we really are."

"Yes! I always thought Sarah, as much as she loved me, never quite understood how much I knew."

"Mm hm. I think it's a problem for all of us."

"I wonder why they think we're dumb."

"Probably because we can't talk," Carl said.

"Oh, you're right. I never thought of that. That makes so much sense!"

Carl nodded, unaffected by Ivan's surprise at his thinking power. At this, Ivan realized he'd set himself up to feel inferior to Carl again. And things had been going so well, so equally. Without further thought, Ivan jumped right in. "Carl, sometimes I wonder how you feel about me as your leader. To be honest, I often feel intimidated by your intelligence."

Carl stopped in his tracks with his lower jaw agape. "You must be kidding, Ivan! After what Boy said about you, and with that incredible experience you had in Garmr's realm, and with how well-rounded and worldly you are, how can you possibly feel inferior to me? I lived with two stuffy intellectuals who couldn't see beyond their noses, and you have lived in the mountains, herded sheep, Sarah probably talked to you about Russian literature, you've been a show dog, earned obedience titles, and were selected to do this very special job. You're the special one!"

Ivan felt his ears drop low on his skull. He didn't know what to say. He had never thought of himself as anything special. He looked down at Carl, whose eyes showed the deepest respect. "Gosh, Carl. I had no idea how you felt. I figured that with your fine way of speaking and your un-derstanding of human psychology, you probably had little respect for a—sheep-herdin' dog like me."

Carl began walking again. "Not at all, Ivan. Put it out of your mind."

Carl's words were kind, but Ivan still wondered. "Okay, Carl. Thank you."

They walked along silently until they reached the living room. Ivan waited for Carl to choose a seat. He chose the smaller leather chair, so Ivan chose the sofa across from it. He stretched out and leaned against the back. *Wow,* he thought. *This is comfortable. I can see why Beauregard always grabs it.*

As Ivan began to address Carl, he felt better than before, but not one hundred percent confident. "So, Carl, even though you were leading the discussions with the others, were you able to figure out why *you* chose the owners and life you did this last time?"

Without having to think, Carl said, "Actually, no. Certain thoughts passed through my mind as I listened to the others, but I didn't have time to adequately go within."

Whoa. Now this is a surprise. I expected him to have it all figured out. "Well then, what did you learn about the concept from helping the others?"

"I really don't believe it—in the concept of multiple lives. I think we live once, die once, and that's it."

Ivan was at a loss for words. He wanted to challenge Carl but had a hunch this would be the wrong approach. He took a deep breath before speaking. He wanted to say, "So, then . . . you don't even believe what Boy has told us?" but he held his tongue. "One shot at getting it right, and then we come here?"

"Exactly. We must live our one life to the best of our ability and know that we'll then come to this lovely resting place. Multiple lives, going back, figuring out what situations will be best for the further development of our souls—it suggests that one never gets to rest and be rewarded for good deeds. As far as who we get for owners and what our life situation will be is all a game of chance. I don't believe we have control in any way."

"Interesting," said Ivan. "If this is the case, then how do you explain the fact that we have souls at all? It seems to me that it would be simpler if we didn't—that we be biological accidents that simply die. What purpose does this afterlife serve?"

"Reward. If we were good dogs, we come here as a reward. If we were bad dogs, then we go to Hell. All those dogs in Garmr's realm were bad dogs. They bit children, tore up their owners' furniture, ran away, attacked other dogs, etcetera. Much simpler than this system you believe in. I mean, if we know we keep getting more and more chances to get it right, why try hard the first time?"

Ivan had to agree with Carl's logic to some extent. *Why try hard if you know you keep getting more chances?* Ivan now realized why Carl's leading the group discussions may have felt forced to the others. "So, you really saw no sense in discussing with the others what they learned in their past lives."

"No, I didn't. Sorry."

Ivan blanked. *Where to go from here?*

"Ask him," Sunny's voice suggested.

Carl looked at Ivan with a wry smile. Ivan asked, "How do you think you can best spend your time in this group?"

"I really don't mind helping the others. If they want to believe that all this rigmarole will pay off, then let them believe it. My assistance can only aid in their ultimate well-being, and perhaps they'll see the light by the time it's all over."

Ivan felt like a snuffed-out candle. He felt empty. He had no idea what to say next. "Let him go," Sunny said.

"Sounds like you're very comfortable with things as they are," said Ivan.

"Indeed, I am. I'm pleased to go for walks in the park. It's what I love best."

Ivan almost began telling Carl about Beauregard's past lives as well as his own, but he didn't. Maybe somewhere down the road Carl would see the truth. "Is there anything you want to ask me or tell me?" Ivan asked.

Carl thought a moment. "No, I don't think so, but I will if anything surfaces."

"Okay," said Ivan.

Carl hopped off the chair and trotted to the doorway. He turned back as he stepped outside. "I believe Jolly is still in the snow field. Would you like me to fetch her for you?"

"That's awfully nice of you, Carl, but I think I'd enjoy walking out there myself. Have a great day in the park." Carl nodded and left.

Ivan's insides were knotted up. He hadn't anticipated this obstinacy from Carl. *Maybe I shouldn't label it "obstinacy." It's simply his own set of beliefs.* He recalled Surri's saying Carl could be "narrow-minded." *Well, that's okay to have one's own opinions. I just wonder how these opinions will affect the others. Maybe Carl will keep them to himself. He seems to have so far.* He sighed once, hard, and trotted towards the snow field.

As he approached the huge expanse of snow, he searched for Jolly. She was difficult to spot with her pure white coat. The Newfoundlands stood out, as did the St. Bernards, Bernese Mountains dogs, Siberian Huskies, and Malamutes, and there were quite a few Samoyeds and

Great Pyrenees, so Ivan had to watch for a long time before he spotted Jolly playing tag with a Norwegian Elkhound. Ivan pushed through the snow until he was within shouting distance. "Jolly! Jolly!" he called. She didn't hear him at first, but with the third "Jolly!" she perked her ears and looked at him. He leaped up and down so she would see him better. Her ears dropped, she said something to the Elkhound, then headed toward Ivan.

When she reached him, she said, "Do I really have to leave now? Can't you take someone else? I'm having so much fun." She wagged her tail low and looked hopeful.

"Oh, Jolly, you know we agreed to go in alphabetical order. This won't take that long. Why don't you tell the Elkhound you'll be back shortly, maybe an hour or so."

Jolly wiggled and tried to look cute. "But, Ivan, we're having so much fun now. Pleeeeeeeease?"

"Oh, Jolly, I don't want to change things. I think the Elkhound can wait awhile."

"But, he might find someone else to play with, and when I come back, he won't be available. Pleeeeeeeease?"

Ivan was losing patience and recalled Surri's saying that Ivan had seen Jolly's personality at its worst. *I'm not so sure. I think she's terribly spoiled. I best stand firm.* He paused a moment to listen for commentary from his spirits, but he heard none. "What's the Elkhound's name?"

"Lars. Why?"

"Laaaaaars!" Ivan called. The Norwegian Elkhound looked at Ivan. Ivan motioned him to come over, and Lars did. "Hi," he said. "I'm Ivan, Jolly's group leader. She says the two of you are having a great time."

"Oh, we are," said the Elkhound. "Does she have to leave now? I was hoping she could stay awhile."

"I need to talk with her for a short time. Will you be here all day?"

"Yes, I think so."

"Would you reserve time for her in about an hour?"

"Sure. I'd be happy to. She's great fun. There's a group game over there that anyone can join. I'll play with them till she comes back."

"Thank you for understanding, Lars."

Jolly frowned and said, "Bye, Lars. See you in a while."

Ivan began briskly walking, but Jolly lagged behind him, pouting. Ivan said over his shoulder, "He seems very nice."

"He is. I like him a lot."

They were silent all the way back to the living room. Jolly walked into the room and stood, waiting for instructions. "Choose a spot, any spot," said Ivan. Jolly ambled around the room, started to get onto the leather sofa, then changed her mind and sat in front of it. Ivan hopped onto the chair across from her.

"Comfortable?"

"Yep. How long will this take?"

"I don't know for sure. I want to know how things are going for you. Did you find any value in Carl's discussions about your past lives?"

"No. I don't think he believes we've had past lives."

Whoa. How did she pick up on that? "What makes you think so?"

"Ohhhhh, I don't know. I think he said it once." She

thought a moment. "Yes, he did. He said outright, 'I don't believe in all this stuff.'"

"He did? He wasn't supposed to say that."

"Why not?"

"Because it's not true!"

"Yeaaaaah, I suppose you're right. I mean, why would we all be here otherwise? And with what you experienced with Garmr and your angel guides." She started tapping one foot and craned her neck to look toward the snow field.

"Have you remembered any of your past lives?" Ivan asked.

"I haven't tried. I'm just having a good time. Are we done yet?"

"No. Come on, Jolly. We really have work to do."

"But, I don't want to work. I want to play."

"You can't just be here and play. You get to play a lot. But there is work to do."

Jolly looked straight at Ivan. "Okay, so what do you want to know?"

Ivan mustered his thoughts and said, "I don't need to know anything as much as I'd like you to do some reflecting. I'd like you to think about your next life. But you can't chose a next one until you understand this last one and ones before it."

"That sounds too hard," she said seriously, still eyeing him straight on.

"It's not so hard, really," said Ivan.

She tapped her foot some more. "Okay. So what do I have to do?"

"Hop up onto the sofa there and get comfortable."

She hopped up, sat, but didn't want to lie down. She craned her neck to get a glimpse of the snow field again.

"Stop that, Jolly. Just forget about playing for a while. The sooner you pay attention to this, the sooner you can go back to Lars."

"Ooooookay." She leaned back. "Okay, I'm comfortable."

"Please lie down. Good. Now close your eyes. Relax. Imagine that you've just come indoors after playing with the children in the snow in the back yard. You played for hours. You're tired and cold. Now, the whole family has gone off to a movie, and you're all alone to lie on the sofa undisturbed. Warm sunlight is shining through the large window and warming your whole body. Your mind is awake, but your body is soooooo mellow, so relaxed. You can barely even feel your body now, because it's so relaxed. You're safe, you're secure, no one will bother you for hours." Ivan watched as Jolly's breathing slowed to a soft, even rhythm.

"Now, I want you to think about your life as an old dog, a year or two before you died. Watch different scenes come in and pass out of your mind." He waited a few moments, then went on. "Now imagine scenes from your middle adult life. Just let different scenes come out of your memory, into your mind, then float out again . . . . Good. You're doing great, Jolly.

"Now, think about your young adult life and let some of those scenes sort of march through your mind and out again . . . .

"Now do the same with your adolescence . . . . Good.

"Now, with your puppyhood." He waited a bit, then

carefully went on. "Now, Jolly, remaining totally relaxed and feeling good, imagine where you were before you were a puppy. Allow yourself to see that you were a different kind of dog before that. Just relax and allow an image to come into your mind. Leave your mind open and allow any image that wants to come in do so." Ivan waited.

Almost immediately Jolly bared her teeth and snarled. *Oh my gosh! What's this?* Jolly bared her teeth harder and growled. She growled so hard that foam began to form around her lips. Her eyes opened but were glazed and unseeing. She sat up and growled harder. She barked at Ivan, got off the sofa, and walked toward him. He pushed back in his chair, then climbed down to get away from her.

"Quick," said Isotope's voice. "Give her directions to feel calm again and imagine herself back on the sofa—in the sunlight—in her most recent home. Hurry!"

As he stepped back from her, Ivan forced his voice to sound soothing. "Jolly, now quietly go back to your old self back on the sofa in your home. You're tired after a day of playing in the snow. The sun is warming and calming your whole body. You feel no tension at all. You're very, very calm and relaxed." Ivan heard himself rushing the words but tried not to.

Instantly, Jolly backed up, eased herself onto the sofa, and went back to a meditative state, breathing quietly as she lay back down. Ivan's heart pounded in his chest. His mouth was dry. He didn't know what to do next and felt like he'd done something very, very bad. "What now?" he whispered.

Isotope answered. "Tell her she will awaken when you

tell her to and that she'll remember this past life but will not feel the emotions that accompanied it. She will remain calm after she awakens. She needs to remember that past life. She's been shutting it out, because it was unpleasant. You'll need to help her through this, Ivan. Take your time."

Ivan proceeded, "Okay, Jolly, now that you're feeling so very relaxed and calm, I'd like you to wake up slowly. When you do awaken, you will remember what we talked about but will not feel the emotions. You may awaken now." He watched Jolly paddle her feet, shift her legs, and then stretch gently. She lay still with her eyes open. Then she scratched her right ear with a back leg. Finally, she lifted her head and said, "Hi, Ivan. Have I been asleep a long time?" She propped herself up on her elbows and looked at him with her normal, innocent expression.

"Actually, Jolly, you weren't really asleep. How did it feel to you? What do you remember?"

Jolly leaned her head against the back of the sofa and closed her eyes. "I remember being back home. The kids and I had played in the snow all afternoon, and now they'd gone to the mall and left me to sleep in the sun on the couch. It was lovely. Quiet. Relaxed."

"Do you remember anything else?"

She gasped air into her lungs, "Uuuuuuuhhh! Oh my gosh! Oh no!"

"What, Jolly? What?"

"Oh, I was a very different kind of dog!"

"Say more. What do you mean? What kind of dog? " Ivan urged her.

"Oh, I hope not! But . . . oh, dear, I'm afraid so. Could that be?" Jolly's face showed horror.

"I don't know," said Ivan. "Your demeanor did change while you were meditating."

"Is *that* what I was doing?"

"Well, you were going back in time, trying to remember your past lives."

"I didn't WANT to remember that life! But now I do! How dare you do this to me!" she yelled. She scrambled up, jumped off the sofa, and rushed out of the room. Ivan followed her to the doorway and watched her canter back to the snow field.

"Well, darn!" he whispered. "It's just as I thought in the first place. I'm bad at this." He looked up at his invisible Isotope and cried, "I told her she wouldn't feel the emotions! What went wrong?" He waited for Isotope's answer.

She said, "You did the right thing, Ivan. You did it all correctly. Some things can't be helped. The feelings she has about that life were just too overwhelming. This approach doesn't always work, but it's not your fault. There may actually be a positive outcome to this," she assured him.

"Oh, Anubis! Can't you find someone else?" Ivan called out.

Boy appeared suddenly and faced Ivan. "Ivan, you must be patient with yourself. Remember how I said you would be 'in training' with me? This is part of the training. You're going to face difficulties. This is how you learn."

"Well, I don't understand what I should have done differently. Isotope said Jolly really does need to remember that lifetime. And now she does. But, she stormed off. So, I've failed, but I don't know why."

"Ivan, you have not failed. Jolly had a normal reaction. You did everything correctly. You simply don't know what to do now. So, let me help you."

Ivan took a deep breath and sighed. His shoulders sank, and he turned his attention to Boy.

Boy continued. "She's very upset to learn what she did. Her running off is her way of trying to escape from herself. Can you blame her? Rather than face her dark side, she's trying to leave it here with you. Playing is much easier than facing something bad. Don't you agree?"

"Of course, of course. But, I couldn't think of anything to say to keep her here, so I've failed."

"Ah, but you haven't failed. She did precisely what she needed to do. Do you think that playing will erase the memory she just uncovered?"

"No, I don't think it will."

"Of course it won't. She'll play for awhile and try to forget, but the memory will come back to her. Your job is to be patient. She won't be able to erase that memory. It will keep looming in front of her. Soon, she'll want to address it. She may choose to talk to Lars, but she'll be more comfortable talking to you, because you already know. Remember, be patient."

"We all thought Heaven was supposed to be a place of beauty and rest," Ivan whined.

"That's a misconception. But, is there not beauty here?"

"Of course," Ivan said reverently.

"The canine soul never stops growing. Whether we're in a physical body or in this non-physical realm, we continue to learn and grow."

Ivan nodded. He had nothing else to say. Boy motioned his snout toward the snow field, and Ivan headed in that direction.

Chapter Ten

Ivan stood chest-deep in snow, gazed toward the mountains beyond, then focused on Jolly and Lars playing with three other dogs. He pushed toward them, stood a short distance away, and waited for Jolly to notice him. After awhile, she lifted her head and looked at him, then quickly shifted her eyes down and back to her playmates.

Ivan decided to wait. He sat down, surprised that the snow wasn't particularly cold and didn't melt where his body touched it. Boy's suggestion to be patient felt right. He believed Jolly would eventually come and talk with him.

However, she was in no hurry. Ivan wanted to lie down, but he was afraid he wouldn't be as visible to her, so he stayed in the "sit" position for what felt like hours. He thought of moving closer, but something told him to stay put. The sun was now low in the sky, and most of the snow dogs had left. Lars, Jolly, and their playmates didn't seem to care and continued playing. Ivan wondered what stage of work they were in. Maybe they were done working and had nothing better to do. Ivan wondered how long a dog could stay here before choosing a new life on Earth. Maybe these dogs had already processed their past lives and were waiting to reincarnate. *There's so much I don't know yet. I wish Boy would tell me more. I guess I could ask him, yet that seems rather impolite, as if I don't trust his one-step-at-a-time instructions.* "Rrrrrr," Ivan sighed softly. *I wonder how long they're going to play. It'll be dark soon.* He shifted around on his hindquarters and waited.

The sun just disappeared beneath the horizon when Lars and the others suddenly dashed away. Jolly stood alone and watched them. She glanced at Ivan, then ambled in his direction, her head down.

"Hi, Jolly," said Ivan. "Looks like you were having a wonderful time. Why did they all leave?"

She said, without looking at him, "Play time is over. It's night now. Time to go to sleep."

"Oh. Okay," Ivan said brightly. "Let's head back together. I imagine the others are in the living room waiting."

"Mm hm," she hummed and kept walking. Ivan walked alongside her and didn't say anything else. They were silent until she blurted, "Why did you sit there and watch me that whole time? Don't you have other dogs to talk to?"

"You and I weren't done, Jolly. And I'm taking one at a time. In alpha- . . ."

"-betical order, I know," Jolly interrupted. "Well, I thought we were done."

"Mm. I didn't."

Jolly didn't respond. Ivan wanted to prompt her, but he resisted. He believed Boy was right, that she'd want to talk to no one about this but Ivan.

Just before they reached the living room, she stopped abruptly. "Ivan," she said with a serious expression. "I now understand why I chose this last life."

Ivan felt his chest swell. He looked at her but didn't speak. She continued. "I was an attack dog in the life before this last one. I was trained to attack humans, and I grew to feel worthwhile doing so. To make up for that, I became Jolly. Lovable, harmless Jolly."

"It makes perfect sense," Ivan said.

"Yes." She paused and looked directly into his eyes. "And I will never choose to be an attack dog again. I will always choose to be Jolly."

As though she'd vacuumed all the fears out of his belly, Ivan felt his work with her was done. It was clear as a bell. "I . . . I . . . I believe you're correct, Jolly. That was . . . well . . . easy."

Jolly was no longer her daffy, silly self but newly level-headed, intelligent, and serious. "Yes. Easy," she said and glanced toward the inside of their living room. "Now may I go to sleep?"

"Of course, Jolly. And . . ." she'd started to walk away from him. ". . . thank you."

"No, Ivan. Thank *you*." She walked into the living room, leaving Ivan standing speechless outside.

He watched as the others greeted her and glanced out the door at him, then back at her. Jolly found a comfortable spot in front of the sofa, curled into a big ball with her back against it, and fell asleep. Ivan could see that the others wondered what had happened to her. They must have seen the change in her manner. Ivan walked in and said, "I hope you all had a pleasant day. I believe it's bedtime." Carl yawned, Stealth stretched, Beauregard watched Ivan carefully, and Murphy quickly made his way to the rug in front of the fire. "In the morning, I'll begin with Murphy. Just like today, the rest of you can play or sleep or do whatever pleases you. Stealth, when I'm done with Murphy, you'll be next. Where do you think you'll be?"

"I stays right here in dis room, if dat's okay."

"That's fine. Murphy and I will probably go to the beach."

Within moments, all but Ivan were asleep. He was too wound up. He thought about this day, beginning with Beauregard and what a wonderful adventure it had been for both of them. Then he thought about his frustrations with Carl and wondered how things would shake out. *Maybe Carl will just stay here in dog heaven forever. I wonder if that's an option. Gosh, there's so much I don't know. I think I'll try to find Boy. Ha! And will he be surprised that I'm not in some kind of crisis!* He chuckled to himself.

He tiptoed out of the living room, stood in the cool, dark air, and breathed in the fragrance of the nighttime flora. There was something invigorating about the subtle messages carried into his nose, an excitement he recalled from his late evening walks with Sarah. He recalled Sarah's explaining to him that many plants don't emit their fragrances until after dark so they can attract nocturnal insects. Breathing in deeply to digest these lovely odors, he set out in search of Boy.

In a whisper, he called, "Boy! Anubis! Where are you? Will you come talk with me?"

Off a few feet to Ivan's left, Boy appeared. "I'm here, Ivan." He yawned and stretched, then with a jolly wag of his tail and a grin, he said, "Can't let a fellow get some sleep, eh?"

Ivan became instantly serious but recalled Surri greeting him like this a couple times. "Oh, I'm sorry. I thought it was still early enough. Never mind. I'll find you in the morning." He started to walk away.

"Just kidding, Ivan. Dogs don't really need to sleep here. They just think they do and are so used to it, we don't tell them otherwise. Just like you no longer need to eat or drink. However, many wish to continue those earthly pleasures. Remember how sweet the water in the pond tasted?"

"Oh, yes. But, it's true I wasn't thirsty. I simply enjoyed the cool wetness."

"Precisely." He smiled at Ivan again.

Ivan chuckled, still unsure.

"You haven't discovered humor here yet, have you?"

"Humor? No. It seems we have such serious work to do—nothing to laugh at."

"Well, the truth is that humor is a big part of your spiritual existence."

"You mean having fun?"

"Oh, having fun is easy, like playing games with Sarah, running an agility course, fetching balls, that sort of thing. Humor is a little different. Like just now when I pretended I'd been asleep. It was a joke. I was trying to make you laugh. But, you took it seriously. In time, you'll get the hang of it. You might call it a 'higher art form.'"

"Art? Dogs can do art?"

"Of course. It's more subtle in dogs than in humans, but it's there, as when Beauregard strutted himself around a show ring. That was artful compared to others who plod around. Or the way some retrievers display a flashiness in the field. Some are prettier doing it than others. That's art. Or herding sheep. Some herding dogs do it with a finesse and flair that others don't. See what I mean?"

"Oh yes, I understand that." Ivan thought a moment. "But humor. I don't know."

"It will come. You'll see. Look for opportunities."

Ivan flashed on one time that Sarah asked him to go fetch his squeaky toy. When he went searching in her bedroom, he spotted one of her brassieres on the floor, and he brought that out instead. He thought that would be funny. She knew he knew the difference, and they had a good laugh. "Yes, I think I understand," said Ivan. "Okay, I'll try to be more humorous. It feels good."

"Absolutely, it does," said Boy, then paused. "So, what's on your mind this evening?"

"Well, I'm not in a crisis for once," Ivan grinned.

Boy laughed. "Okay, good."

Ivan felt himself lighten up. "Can we walk while we talk? It smells so good out here tonight."

"Every night. Yes, it's delightful. I usually go walking about this time anyway."

Ivan felt the most secure he'd felt so far with Boy, almost like they were friends, as they strolled into the night. "I called for you because I have some questions. I spent today helping Beauregard, C . . ."

"Splendid work!" Boy interrupted.

"Oh, well, thank you. I felt pretty good about it."

"You should, though I know you had some problems with Carl."

"How do you know?"

"It's a type of awareness I've developed over time. Humans would call it 'psychic powers,' but it's just a knowing. I simply know things others cannot yet perceive. Much like the intuition that Surri explained to you."

"Oh." Ivan wondered if he, too, would develop 'psychic powers' some day. "So, I don't know what to do with Carl. He believes we don't go back to Earth, that we have only one lifetime and then come here to stay."

"This is true for some dogs."

"Really? I thought we all kept going back until we became like you."

"For most, that is so. Only extremely rarely does a dog make it to this level in just one lifetime. It has happened a few times. And, some get stuck. They cease moving and never develop beyond a certain point. Carl might be one of those. They're somewhat rare. Some get stuck for a while but eventually decide to proceed. Others want to evolve as quickly as possible. In fact, I got stuck for awhile. I had had a delightful life as a Jack Russell Terrier. I felt fully satisfied with who I'd been and saw no reason to become anything else. I was in that mode for quite some time."

"Gosh. What made you move on?"

"I was put in charge of a group of new arrivals, like you."

"But you hadn't been before?"

"No. The governor of this level at the time, who has since moved on, decided to put me in charge of a group, and that did the trick. It forced me to delve into issues I had avoided."

"Wow."

"You, however, show no signs of being stuck. You're one of the eager ones."

Ivan felt suddenly giddy. He was pleased with himself. "So, what do you suggest I do with Carl?"

"Nothing. Just let him be part of the group discussions. He may cause some confusion in the others, because he's smart and may present some convincing arguments, but just let things unfold as they will. You're doing a fine job."

"So the next step is to bring everyone back together to choose our next lives?"

"You've got it. See how insightful you are?"

Ivan felt himself flush. "Oh, I don't know about that."

"Humility is a fine trait, too. You're a fine, humble dog spirit, Ivan. I'm pleased that you've reached this stage in your development." Ivan flushed again and didn't know what to say. "Anything else you want to know?" Boy asked.

Ivan searched his mind. He had had so many questions, but now he felt complete, at least for the time being. "Not right now, but I probably will before long."

"You really are doing a fine job. I admire that you went to Garmr's realm and returned to do your work."

"Gosh," said Ivan. "Thank you. I admire you, too."

Boy's golden aura brightened as he faked another yawn. "Gotta get some sleep now." He winked. "Call me any time." He turned and vanished.

Ivan stood and grinned. His step felt light as he decided to take a stroll around the lake. The stars shone brightly, his olfactory sensors were primed with nocturnal perfume, and he felt a happy energy fill his being. He walked around the lake three times, then headed back to the living room where he entered quietly, careful to step around the five sleeping dogs. He slid onto his favorite spot in front of the fireplace next to Murphy and let himself fall asleep, even though he didn't need to.

In the morning, Ivan awakened before the others and, as a joke, decided to howl like a wolf. "Aaaaah Whoooooo!" Instantly all five jumped to their feet, their hackles up and their eyes wide. Ivan grinned. "Wake-up call," he said cheerily and glanced at each dog. Murphy trembled, Carl shook, Beauregard darted his eyes around the room, Stealth bared his teeth, and Jolly cringed behind the sofa. "Hey! Relax. That was a joke!" he continued with cheer. Jolly peeked around the side of the sofa. Stealth let his lips down. Beauregard looked at Ivan with a quizzical expression. Carl stopped shaking, and Murphy stopped trembling. "Come on, you guys. We've been so serious all this time. Boy told me last night that humor is something we should develop. It makes us feel good."

"*That* did not make me feel good," said Jolly.

That old, crummy, I'm-not-good-enough feeling hit Ivan in the stomach. Once again, self-doubt crept into his soul, and he felt like running out and never coming back.

"No, Ivan. Don't run," said Surri's voice inside Ivan's head. "Admit your error and ask their forgiveness."

Ivan sat down and gulped once. "Hey," he said softly. "I'm sorry. I meant that to be funny. You see, last night after you fell asleep, I went out and talked with Boy. He explained 'humor' to me. He said we've all been too serious and should bring more fun and jokes into our lives, that humor makes us feel good. He also said that it's not an easy thing to do—as you just witnessed. I apologize. It was my first attempt. Obviously, I need to work on it. I'm sorry."

Carl grinned. "Ivan, how did you do that? I've never tried howling before. Have any of you?"

As though someone had flipped a switch, they all chattered at once. Jolly said, "Oh yes, I always howled at sirens. The kids thought it was funny."

Stealth said, "I howled at the full moon to keep burglars away."

Beauregard said, "Oh no. Never. I would never howl. What a disgrace that would have been."

Murphy said, "I tried it once or twice to see if I could. Mostly, I just squeaked."

Jolly said, "It's easy, Murphy. Just tilt your head back, take a deep breath, make an O with your lips, and let it go. Like this." And Jolly howled.

Murphy did exactly as Jolly instructed—tilted his little head back, formed an O with his lips, took a deep breath, and let out the most perfect, high-pitched coyote-howl imaginable. Carl joined in and sounded much like Murphy. Stealth let loose with a deep, mournful howl, and Beauregard finally gave in, followed Jolly's instructions, and sent forth a most-lovely, musical, alto-howl. Ivan joined in, and the whole living room reverberated with the sound. Soon, laughing between breaths, they howled their hearts out.

"Look," said Jolly. She pointed her snout at the opening of their living room. An audience of two hundred dogs stood watching, their heads cocked and their ears perked. The howlers stopped howling and looked at the curious bunch.

"Is everything okay?" a Beagle from the crowd asked.

Ivan and his group started giggling. Ivan said, "I guess we were pretty loud. Sorry. Yes, everything's okay. We were just having some fun."

"Hope we didn't wake anyone up," Beauregard added.

The members of the audience stood wide-eyed for a few moments, then dispersed, mumbling to one another under their breaths. As they walked away, several dogs glanced back over their shoulders.

"Oh boy, I bet we have a reputation now," said Beauregard. "Imagine what they think of us."

"Oh pooey on them" said Carl, and the others giggled.

"Aaaaah Whoooo," Murphy added, and they all giggled again.

When things settled down, Ivan announced, "Today, most of you are on your own again. Do whatever you want. I'll be meeting with Murphy and then Stealth. I don't know how long this will take, but once I've met with all of you individually, we need to have another group discussion. Okay?"

"Okay," they said as Beauregard, Carl, and Jolly trotted out of the room. Stealth made himself comfortable on a fluffy rug, and Murphy sat at attention in front of Ivan.

"Where would you like to go?" Ivan asked.

"How about the beach?" asked Murphy.

"What a surprise," said Ivan, winking at the little dog. "Let's go. Can we go for a swim, too?"

"I suppose," said Murphy, hesitating. "The water might be cold."

Ivan just smiled and trotted toward the lake, Murphy at his side. When they reached the beach, Murphy said, "How about if we sit in the sun. It's so nice and warm."

Ivan knew he would get too hot, but he said, "Sure. Fine. Do you have a favorite spot?"

"Over here," said Murphy and led Ivan to a sunny area far away from the water. "This seems to be one of the warmest spots."

Oh boy, thought Ivan. *I'm gonna cook.* He could already feel the heat penetrating the black areas of his coat—his back, his sides, and the top of his head. "Mind if I take a quick dip first?"

"No. Go right ahead. I'll wait here for you."

Ivan galloped down to the lake and waded in. He

pushed off and let his body coast through the water, cooling his skin. He ducked his head under the surface and paddled around until he felt cool, then walked back to Murphy, being sure to shake before he reached him.

Murphy had been sitting up watching Ivan, but as Ivan approached, he lay down so as better to bask in the sun. Ivan lay down as well and stretched his front legs out so his toe nails nearly touched Murphy's. Murphy asked brightly, "So what are we talking about, Ivan?"

Ivan spoke carefully. "We're talking about what you remember about lives before this last one—to understand why you chose this last one—and ultimately to better choose the next. Do you remember lives before the one with Helga?"

Murphy thought, his held tilted to one side. "Gosh, Ivan, no. I'm sorry. I don't."

"That's okay, Murphy. Most dogs don't remember. But, I helped Beauregard and Jolly remember theirs."

"Not Carl?"

"No, not Carl. At least not for the time being."

"He doesn't believe we go back," said Murphy.

"He told you that?"

"Not directly. He implied it, though, many times. I think he thought he was fooling us, but he wasn't."

"Did he tell you what he does believe?"

"Only that he knows he'll be here forever and how happy he is."

"Yes, that's what he conveyed to me as well. What do you believe, Murphy?"

"I'm not positive I believe anything for sure, but when I visited Helga up here, she said that when she goes back to

Earth she wants me to be with her again. I told her I would. I hope I can keep that promise. Can I?"

"I believe so, Murphy. I don't know if being with Helga again will be the best choice for you. We have to figure that out. Remember, she'll be different in her next life. She won't likely need a dog to answer the door and help her with a bad heart. She could be a young marathon runner for all we know." Ivan realized he was entering unfamiliar territory and wished he had asked Boy last night how dogs can rejoin their owners.

"Well, if she is a runner, she'll need a dog to run alongside her, and I'd like to be that dog."

Ivan felt tempted to argue with Murphy but said, "Well, let's see if you still believe that after we figure out who you were before this last time, okay? Are you willing to experiment a little?"

"Sure, Ivan. Whatever you want."

"Are you comfortable? Lie back and relax. Feel the warmth of the sun as it enters your body and chases out any last molecules of coldness that you have felt since leaving Greenland. Every last little, cold molecule has warmed and melted. You will never feel cold ever again. Feel how wonderful this is, how happy your body is, and how free you feel from that experience. You are totally warm and relaxed.

"Now think back to your life with Helga when she was old and you cared for her." He paused. "Now think back to her middle years when you were just a puppy. Recall how loved you felt and how well Helga took care of you." Ivan paused again. "Now imagine being a fetus inside your mother's uterus, how warm and protected you felt. You're doing very well, Murphy." Another pause. "And now, think back to where you were before you were that fetus. Go ahead and let yourself go back in time to the dog you were before you were Murphy. Let any scenes from that experience come forth into your present-day mind. Just allow them to flow in, remember them, and flow out again." Ivan paused while he watched Murphy's eyelids flutter softly, his body move a little this way and that, his front paws twitch, and his back legs run in place.

"When you think that you have recalled all the scenes from that life, bring your awareness back into the fetus that became Murphy, then Murphy as a puppy, then Murphy as he assisted Helga, and then slowly bring your consciousness back here as we lie on this warm, sandy beach. Begin to wiggle your toes, wag your tail, and slowly, in your own time, open your eyes."

Murphy wiggled his toes, wagged his tail, and sleepily opened his eyes. "Hi, Ivan." He yawned. "Oh, that was nice."

"Really? Tell me what you saw."

"I was a Bernese Mountain Dog, and Helga was my owner, except she wasn't Helga. She was Helga's soul, but her name was Erna, and she lived in Switzerland. She was a ski instructor. I came to her when she was in her mid-twenties. She used me to rescue stranded skiers in the winter. It was a wonderful life, and even then, she said we would always be together. I had to wait until her later years as Helga to join her again. In between I was here—here in dog heaven, waiting for just the right time when she would need me."

"Wow," said Ivan. "That's lovely. So, do you think that you and she will always have lifetimes together?"

"Yes, yes I do," Murphy said.

Oh gosh, thought Ivan. *I wonder if that's possible.* "Murphy, would you mind waiting here while I go talk to Boy? You're happy here in the sun, aren't you?"

"Sure, Ivan. Why? Did I do something wrong?"

"Oh no, not at all, Murphy. You're wonderful. I just need to find out if you should be with Helga always—if that's how it is for lots of dogs, or if your case is unusual. I just don't know."

"Well, I hope it's true. I don't want to be with anyone else. And she did say we'd always be together." He stood up with his tail tucked between his legs. He began to shiver.

"Oh, no, Murphy, don't worry. I just want to find out from Boy if we all go back to our previous owners like you have. I think it's beautiful—the bond you and Helga have. I wonder if I'll go back to Sarah, too. I'd love to. I hope I will. Sometimes, as I lead the group, I run into questions. This is just one of them. Relax. Okay? Just lie down and enjoy the sun. Remember how it entered your body before and chased away all those cold molecules? Try doing that again. I'll be right back."

Murphy lay back down, though apprehension remained on his little face. "Don't worry, Murphy. I just need to know this for myself." Ivan dashed across the beach, calling "Boy! Anubis! I have a question!" As he sprinted across a lawn, Boy appeared.

"What's the matter, Ivan?"

"Oh. Thank you for coming. I'm working with Murphy, and he claims that he'll always be the dog of Helga, his past owner. He recalled a lifetime with her before this one and says they have a sort of pact to always be together.

Is that possible? Is it good? Should I encourage him to find a different owner next time? Can I go back to Sarah?"

"This has you very excited, Ivan. Calm down. The answer is simple: if it's in a dog's best interest and the owner's best interest to reunite, then by all means, a dog should choose that."

"But, can they go on forever like that?"

"No. One or the other will eventually evolve to the next higher level where they won't need each other."

"But then what!" Ivan exclaimed a little too strongly.

"Then the dog will find a way to further his growth—a different owner or situation that needs him more, or the human will outgrow the dog, and the dog will find another human whom he can love just as much. There's nothing unpleasant about this. It's always about love and growth. Always."

"But Murphy insists he'll always be with Helga. How can I tell him otherwise?"

"Don't tell him. He'll find out for himself when the time is right. Ivan, you don't need to know all the answers right now. Just trust that love and growth lead the way. Let those two principles guide you. Don't make it so hard."

Ivan calmed down.

"And remember to tune in to Surri, Isotope, Humphrey, and the others. I think you forget about them sometimes."

"Oh, you're right. I do. I find it easier to come running to you."

"Part of your training is learning not to depend on me but to listen to your own, personal helpers. That's what they're there for, and they love to assist. Nothing makes them happier than helping you. And once you get the hang of how to converse with them, you can teach the others to do so."

"Oh yes. Right. I see. Okay. Yes, I'll do that." An image of Murphy's worried face appeared in Ivan's mind, and he felt he should hurry back. He turned to go.

"And Ivan . . . ," said Boy.

"Yes?"

"Calm down. Don't be such a perfectionist. Trust your intuition. Your guides are waiting for you to talk with them."

Ivan's ears dropped. He lowered his head. "Oh, I know you're right. And they're so wonderful." He lifted his eyes to meet the golden Collie's. "Thank you."

Boy nodded. "Oh, and Ivan . . . ."

"Yes?"

"They have senses of humor, too." He winked at Ivan and vanished.

Ivan grinned as he trotted back to Murphy. He realized, though, that he would much rather go off by himself now and converse with Surri and the others.

"Then that's what you should do," said Samuel's voice inside Ivan's head. "Murphy can wait. There's no rush for any of this."

"Ahhhhh, yes," whispered Ivan. "Thank you, Samuel. I'll do that."

When Ivan reached Murphy, he said, "Murphy, good news. You can keep being Helga's dog as long as you and she want that."

Murphy sat up and smiled. "Oh, I'm so relieved, Ivan. You had me worried."

"I'm sorry. I didn't mean to." Ivan paused. "Murphy,

while I was talking with Boy, I realized that I need to spend some time talking with Surri and the others."

"Oh yes," said Murphy. "Go ahead. They sound delightful. I'd like to meet mine some time."

"I think you should. Everyone should. But right now, I need to spend some time alone with them. Then I'll be back. Is this where you want to hang out for the day?" Murphy nodded. "I'll come back in a little while."

"Sure, Ivan. Thank you. See you later."

Ivan felt deliciously free. He cantered away from Murphy, not having any idea where he was going. It just felt good to be free from his responsibilities. He picked up the pace until he was in a full gallop. He whizzed past one group of dogs after another, some sitting on lawns under big shade trees, some huddled in groups in garages, kitchens, dining rooms, bedrooms, and living rooms, some having casual conversations at the edges of ponds or in fields. All of these dogs lifted their heads as Ivan sped by. He glanced at them and smiled as they wagged their tales at his joy.

He galloped to the edge of the snow field and stopped to gaze at the mountains. They were so beautiful. At least this side of them was beautiful. He shuddered at what lay on the other side. He started to turn back but stopped as he recalled the lovely waterfall at the base of the mountains. "Ah! Perfect!" he shouted and dove into the snow. The pond and the waterfall would be a peaceful place to reconvene with his guides. He tried to gallop through the deep snow, but the going was slow as he rabbit-hopped his way. *Gosh. I should have called Sebastian and Reva to break trail for me.* Instead he summoned incredible stamina and leaped his way to the other side. When he spotted the waterfall, he sighed deeply. "Ohhhh, how lovely." The water in the pond sat still as a mirror. He stood at the edge and peered in to see his reflection. There he was, handsome as ever with the shimmery aura around him. He lifted his head and called, "Oh Surri! Can you come and bring the others? Oh please?" he sang out. "I know you're here. I'd sure like to see you all again. Can you come? Please?" He searched the area in front of him, then heard the familiar scritching sound in the bushes behind him. He turned and saw Surri saunter out into the open.

The meerkat sat back on his haunches and rubbed his eyes with both front paws. "Always gotta wake a guy up, don'cha?"

"Oh, I'm sorry, Surri."

Surri grinned. "I'm kidding, Ivan. We knew you were coming." He motioned a paw behind Ivan. Ivan turned around, and there, in their glowing splendor, stood all his guides.

"Oh!" gasped Ivan. "I'd forgotten how beautiful you are. Oh my goodness. Look at you. Thank you for coming. Oh my gosh, this is so special. Oh my, oh my."

"You have some questions for us?" Surri asked.

"Questions?" Ivan could think of no questions at all. He felt stunned, overcome with the animal spirits' beauty, and grateful beyond words. "I don't think I have questions. I did in the last few days, and some of you helped me out. Sunny, you did, and Isotope and Samuel. Gosh. Thank you so much. Of course, Boy answered some questions, questions I guess I could have gone to you with. I'm sorry. He was so handy . . . ."

"We're even handier," said Mia. "You don't even have

to go looking. We're always with you. Remember?"

"Oh no. I didn't mean to hurt your feelings. Really, I didn't."

"We know that," said Hom. "You're in training. Not only with Boy but with us. We understand that. We're not hurt. We just want to help. It's our purpose, you know?"

"And once you learn to listen to us while you're here in heaven, you'll be able to do it back on Earth as well," said Isotope.

"I'm sorry to be so stupid, but how can I learn to listen better? It seems that when something comes up, I naturally go searching for Boy. Maybe because I can see him?"

"That's probably true," said Surri. "On top of that, he's a dog, and you would naturally assume he'd be easier to communicate with."

"I suppose so," said Ivan. "How do I overcome this? I just love you guys—and gals," he added, bowing quickly to Sunny, Mia, Kit, Esmerelda, and Isotope. "Maybe I just need to train myself to stop and listen rather than run, huh?"

"That would be a good start," said Surri. "But maybe we can help remind you that we're here." He turned to the other eight spirits. "So, what do you think? What can we do to remind Ivan that we're here?"

"I could easily drop a feather now and then—right in his path," said Isotope.

"I could leave bits of fur clinging to bushes and tree branches," said Humphrey.

"I could leave footprints," said Esmerelda. "There would be no missing them," she said as everyone looked at her huge feet and giggled.

"I can yank on your belly fur," said Samuel. "—if you're lying down or sitting, that is."

"What about the meerkats?" Surri asked.

Kit said, "I think we've been pretty successful at just speaking in his head." The other four meerkats, including Surri, nodded their heads. "You seem to always hear us," Kit added.

"Or," added Hom, "we can appear as quick shadows scurrying around doorways and furniture."

"And trees and bushes," Mia added.

"Oh, yes, that would work," Ivan agreed.

"We could also emit some meerkat odor," Hom offered.

"Oh yes, that too. That's how I first discovered Surri—by his scent."

"Eventually, you won't need these sensory cues," said Surri. "You'll learn to listen to your intuition, which is really us trying to get your attention."

"Ahh, yes, my intuition. I have to admit I've sort of forgotten about it."

"Most Earth creatures—especially humans—," Surri added, "are more mental and emotional than intuitive. But they're learning, as you are."

Ivan nodded. "Well, then, I think we have a plan." They all agreed and started to leave. "But, wait! Don't go away, please. Can you stay awhile longer?"

"What's wrong, Ivan?" Surri asked.

"Nothing's wrong. I just want you to stay."

"We're always with you."

"I know. But I really like seeing you."

"Well, maybe we could practice. You know, sort of make a game of this."

"Okay," said Ivan eagerly.

"How about if we give you signs, and you guess which one of us left it? Maybe you could take a walk up the path there, and as you walk, we'll each give a hint. See how quickly you can name the guide who left it."

"Great," said Ivan and trotted toward the trailhead. He slowed to a fast walk and opened all his senses as widely as he could—his eyes, ears, nose, and sense of touch. He walked with zeal, turning this way and that, peering at every tree and bush, ears perked and sniffing the air.

He walked for a quarter mile or so and began to feel a little abandoned when suddenly he stumbled. "Oof!" he said as he turned a front ankle in the path. When he looked down, he saw a large rounded impression in the soil with four smaller indentations above it. "Esmerelda!" he shouted.

Inside his head, he heard her voice, "That's correct, Ivan. See," she giggled, "I didn't think you could miss my footprint."

"I had to fall into it, though," Ivan laughed. "I sure didn't see it."

"You were too busy looking for feathers, shadows, and bear fur," she teased.

"Maybe so. Oh! and look there! I just saw the shadow of a meerkat scoot around that tree stump."

"Which meerkat is it?" Esmerelda asked.

"Uh oh," said Ivan. "I don't know."

"You could ask." Ivan could hear the smile in Esmerelda's voice.

Ivan entered his own mind and asked, *Which meerkat was that?* He waited for an answer, trying hard to listen.

"That was I," a small, feminine voice giggled.

"Oh gosh," said Ivan. "Is that Mia, Sunny, or Kit? I can't tell you apart."

"It's Sunny," said Sunny. "Telling us apart will take some time. You'll have to get used to our voices. We're similar but not identical."

"Okay," said Ivan. "I'll work on that." He smiled at the air and started to walk again. Before long, he spotted something brown and fuzzy hanging low on a bush. He ran over and sniffed it. "Humphrey!"

"Yes!" said Humphrey's voice inside Ivan's head. "But, that wasn't difficult, was it?"

"No," Ivan said with a wag of his tail stub. He walked further when he saw, on the side of the path, something brown with golden flecks of sunlight. He hurried over and saw a beautiful eagle's feather. "Oh, Isotope, this could be no one but you."

"That's right," her beautiful, clear voice echoed in his head.

He picked up the feather in his teeth and walked on when he heard his favorite scritching sound, saw a small dark shadow disappear under a bush, and smelled the odor of meerkat. He tucked the feather into some deep fur on his rump, ran over to the bush, lay down, and poked his snout under it. Just then something tweaked his belly, and he leaped up. "Samuel! That's gotta be you!"

"Right again," said Samuel's sweet, high-pitched voice. "But which meerkat was that?"

Ivan lay down again, poked his nose back under the bush and thought the odor was just like Surri's. "Surri?" he asked the air.

"Hey, right-o, Ivan. You have a great sniffer," said Surri.

Ivan sat up and smiled when he got another tweak under his belly. "Hey, Samuel, stop tickling me," he laughed.

Surri himself emerged from under the bush. "I think you have the hang of this, Ivan. I think you're ready to go back and deal with Murphy and Stealth."

Ivan's body sagged. "Aw, come on. This is so much fun. Can we keep playing?"

"Games are fun, it's true, Ivan, but you have work to do."

"Ohhhh, okay," Ivan said. He felt like a pouting puppy but snapped out of it. "May I see you all once more before I go?"

"Sure," said Surri. "We'll meet you down at the waterfall."

Ivan snatched the feather in his teeth and galloped back down the path, surprised at how far he'd come. When he approached the waterfall pool, a huge, white globe of light glowed at its edge. Inside, he saw images of all his guides, all waving or nodding their heads. Feeling once more the overwhelming love, he waved at them with one paw. He gently set the feather on the ground for Isotope to reclaim. With renewed energy, he turned toward the snow field, plunged back into it, and bunny-hopped his way back to dry land. From there, he cantered back past all the other groups of dogs and found Murphy on the beach.

Chapter Eleven

"Hey, Murph, I'm back," Ivan said with cheer.

Murphy had been stretched out on his side to expose as much of his body as possible to the sun. He sat up with sleepiness on his face. "Oh, hi, Ivan. I must have dozed off. It's so pleasant here."

"I know you love it, Murphy."

"Did you find your spirit guides? Where did you go?" He sat up.

"I went back to the pond and waterfall, and they were all there. They taught me how to ask *them* questions instead of running off to Boy all the time."

"Sounds like a built-in committee," said Murphy.

"Yeah," chuckled Ivan, "and they're all right here in my head. Well, actually, they're all around me, but their answers are in my head."

"Can you help me find mine?" Murphy asked, looking hopeful.

"Only if you trek across the snow field by yourself and meet them at the pond," said Ivan. Murphy's face fell. "Just kidding," Ivan continued. "They're all around you all the time. You just have to tune in to them."

"How do I do that?"

Uh oh. I don't know how to teach this. I just sniffed out Surri, and he did the rest. Uh oh.

Humphrey spoke inside Ivan's head, "His are just like yours. He simply needs to go off by himself and call to them."

"Oh, thank you," said Ivan.

"For what?" asked Murphy.

"Oh, I was thanking Humphrey."

"Now which one is he—a meerkat?"

"No, he's the bear."

"Do I have a bear?"

"I don't know. I think you should go off by yourself and call for them. I found Surri by smelling him. Maybe if you go into that field and sniff around—and ask, they'll materialize."

"Oh, I don't know," said Murphy. "I'm a little scared."

"Of going into the field or of meeting your guides?"

Murphy gulped. "Both."

"Nothing bad can happen to you. The field's perfectly safe, and finding your spirit guides is . . . well . . . heavenly. They pour out so much love, it's almost unbearable. It's quite wonderful, Murphy. I'll wait under that big oak tree for you." He nodded at the first large tree beyond the beach. "Go on. I think you should do this."

Ivan noticed a slight tremble in Murphy's legs as the little dog stood up and gazed out toward the wheat field. A corn field stood right next to it. Murphy asked, "Which field? Corn or wheat?"

"I would choose the corn field, because it's more interesting to me, but I think you should choose the one that tugs at you."

"Well, I don't know . . . ," said Murphy as he slowly headed in that direction. Ivan watched him tip-toe all the way to the wheat field and disappear into it.

Ivan suddenly dashed across the beach, because the sand was too hot on his pads. Under the shade of the oak tree, he lay down, because he realized Murphy might be gone a long time. The sun was directly overhead, meaning the day was half gone. He wondered how Stealth was doing all by himself in the living room. *I'm sure he's content, and I must wait here for Murphy.* He gazed around at all that was going on—so many dogs doing so many activities. The air was a perfect temperature. A slight breeze rustled the leaves overhead, sweet aromas of ponds, flowers, grass, and other dogs filled his nose, and birds sang beautifully all around him. *What a splendid place. I don't know that I want to leave either,* he thought as an image of Carl entered his mind. *I wonder if Carl misses Dora and Siegfried.*

He thought of Sarah. *Gosh, just like Murphy with Helga, I'd like to be with Sarah. I wonder what I should do in my next life. It has to be something heroic, something extraordinary. I wonder if there's a way to do that with Sarah. I mean, how does one know what to choose?* Just then the odor of meerkat passed under Ivan's nose. *Of course! I can ask them. Okay, guides, just how does one choose one's next life?*

Surri spoke. "Ivan, there's a special place called the Room of Knowledge. Boy will direct you there when the time is right. You cannot go there on your own. The Room of Knowledge contains every detail about every human on Earth, every dog, and every life you've lived. You can learn about Sarah or anyone else. You can view predictions of events likely to occur on Earth, though that is not entirely reliable, because things that have been set in motion by the Creator don't always come to pass. But, the Room of Knowledge is where you will gather information in order to best plan your next life."

"When can I go there?"

"As soon as your work here is done, and we don't know when that will be. That depends on Jolly, Carl, Beauregard, Murphy, and Stealth, because you're their leader, and you can't go until they do."

"Oh," said Ivan. "That makes sense. But, wow, this Room of Knowledge sounds very cool. Where is it?"

"It just exists. It's nowhere, and it's everywhere. You'll understand when the time is right."

"Can I see it now?"

"You saw it each time you've been here before, but you cannot access it right now."

"Why not?"

"Because the time isn't right, Ivan. Trust me on this."

"But what harm would come if I saw it now? I'm very curious."

"Ivan, relax. This is just the way it is. I'm sorry now that I told you." Surri chuckled. "But, I guess this tenaciousness of yours is exactly why Boy chose you to lead a group. However, you must be patient. Okay?"

"Yeaaaaaah, I suppose." He sighed and paced a few steps under the tree. "But I'd sure like to at least see the Room. Can you tell me where to look?"

"No. Now stop asking, please. Besides, here comes Murphy."

Ivan looked toward the wheat field but didn't see his little charge. Within a few seconds, however, Murphy's small face pushed through the wheat, and the whole dog emerged surrounded by a whitish glow. Ivan smiled at the happy skip in Murphy's step as he trotted toward him.

"Oh, Ivan. How can I thank you enough? That was

wonderful. I met all my guides, and they are soooo beautiful—just like you said. The love they send out is fabulous. And they were humorous, too. I have a raven, a tiger, a chipmunk, a zebra, and four moose. Oh, and my guardian guide, the main one, is an orangutan."

"Wow. A primate. Like a human."

"I guess so," Murphy shrugged. "Her name is Dahlia. And she's very smart. She said she's been with me since I first emerged from the Creator. She knew everything about me."

"You look happy, Murphy. And remember how you were afraid?"

"Yeah. That was silly."

"Did they give you insight into what your next life should be?"

"They said I need to think about it some more, but I'll probably be with Helga again. She'll be a different person, and I'll be a different dog, but we'll be together."

"That's nice," said Ivan, feeling hopeful about a reunion with Sarah. "Is there anything you want to discuss with me? You seem pretty clear."

"I *am* clear," said Murphy. "I just can't conceive of doing anything else but being with Helga and helping her however she may need me."

"Great," said Ivan. "Do you want to go back to the beach, then, while I go talk with Stealth?"

"Yes, I'd like that. I can daydream of my next life."

Ivan smiled. "Okay. I'll see you back in the living room. It's been a pleasure, Murphy. I'm glad you're in my group."

Murphy wagged his wispy, little tail and smiled up at Ivan. "Thank you, Ivan. Me too."

When he entered their living room, Ivan found Stealth asleep on his back, rear legs hanging loosely to the sides and his front paws neatly folded over his chest. Ivan hated to awaken him. He stepped quietly up beside Stealth and whispered, "Stealth. Stealth. Wake up. It's me, Ivan. I'm back. Wake up, Stealth." The hefty terrier didn't move, though his eyelids stuttered this way and that. Ivan figured he was dreaming and decided to wait. He lay down next to Stealth and watched until his eyelids were still. "Stealth?" he called softly.

Stealth rolled over onto his side and looked at Ivan. "Oh, hi, Ivan," he whispered. "I was havin' da nicest dream."

"Really? What about?"

"I was cantering trough a field, and da nicest little boy was my friend. He kept trowin' a ball fer me, 'n' I'd run 'n' fetch it. It was a sunny day. Da sky was blue. Da little boy loved me cuz I kep' fetchin' dat ball. Over 'n' over 'n' over."

"Sounds delightful," said Ivan. "Do you think this was one of your past lives?"

"Geez, I dunno, Ivan. How in da world would I know dat?"

Ivan chuckled. "Well, you've asked the right question of the right dog. Would you like to remember some past lives?"

"If dey's good ones. Not bad ones. I remembers da last one plain 'nuf. An' I don't wanna 'member it no more."

"Well, good. It seems we all remember this last one. The ones before that are harder to recall. Do you think you may have been a retriever once?

"Ya, I kinda does."

"Well, I tell you what. Go ahead and get comfortable so you can relax."

Stealth shifted himself around and lay on his side, his legs bent slightly. "Okay. I be comfterble."

Ivan led Stealth through the same procedures he'd led the others until Stealth was breathing slowly and regularly. "Now, Stealth, I'd like you to skip past most of this last life. Think back to when you were a puppy, all warm and safe with your mother. Think of her licking your whole body with her warm tongue. You were so safe and so secure. Now think back to how it felt when you were still inside her womb—safe and warm. That's very nice." Ivan noticed how slowly Stealth breathed.

"Now, Stealth, go back to the dog you were before you were Stealth. Allow an image to come into your mind." Ivan saw that Stealth seemed to be smiling. "It was a very pleasant life. Go ahead and remember more of it." Ivan sat back and waited. "You're doing very well, Stealth. Now, I'd like you to fast-forward to the end of that life. Remember how you died." Ivan paused. "Once you've done that, go ahead and recall your spirit existence here in dog heaven, the time before this one. Try to visualize the process and the thinking that led you to choose your life as Stealth. What were the factors in the previous life that caused you to choose the body and life of Stealth?" Ivan paused and watched as Stealth's brow furrowed, and he seemed to tense a bit. His face became serious, almost rigid, and then his head hung lower, even though he was lying down.

"And now, Stealth, think through this last lifetime. Think about the various experiences you had, and I know some of them were unpleasant. But, as you think about them, see if you can understand what you learned from those experiences." Ivan waited longer now. "Shortly, you will wake up, and when you do, you will remember everything you just learned in this process. Now, wake up slowly, gently."

Stealth began to wiggle his toes and feet, then his long, spiky tail flapped twice on the floor. He shifted his body, opened his eyes, and looked around the room. He sat up, started nodding his head, then shook his head. He seemed to be deep in thought. "Dat was good, Ivan. I tink I unnerstan' now."

"What did you learn?" Ivan asked.

"When you told me to 'member dog heaven—da time b'fore dis one? Yeah, I did dat. And I saw dis scene where I was in a groupa dogs, sumptin' like dis one, and we was talkin' 'bout aggression. I realized I had never 'xperienced bein' aggressive b'fore. I was always da nice dog—da Golden Retriever-type, you knows? Always playful 'n' friendly, never bit no one, hardly barked, just played wit children and stuff. So when we was talkin' 'bout aggression, I could hardly tell what dey meant, so dat's when dey said maybe I should choose dat fer dis last lifetime, 'n' I guess dat's what I did." He looked at Ivan with wide, soulful, honest eyes.

Ivan found this idea very intriguing. "So, do you think that all dogs need to feel aggression—actually be an aggressive dog at least once?"

"Yeah, I guess I does."

"Well, I'm curious, Stealth. What do you think it did for you?"

Stealth thought for a moment. "I tink it done sev'ral

tings fer me. I tink . . . I tink it put me in touch wit da udder side-a dogs. Ya knows, not da friendly tail-waggin', kissie-face side but da darker side—da fightin' side—da side dat kep' dogs alive in da wild—ya knows—before we was domesticated—da scrappin' side—da side dat'll rip yer face off if ya steals my food." Stealth looked at Ivan with seriousness. "Ivan, maybe it ain't nunna my bizness, but is you in touch wit dat side-a yerself?"

Ivan was stunned. *Me have a dark side?* he thought and immediately rejected the idea. *Yet . . . , I must have, or I wouldn't be at this point in my development. Gosh, we all should have this awareness, but boy oh boy, I'm not aware of it in me. But . . . it must be in there . . . way back in some far distant life. Wow. I need to think about this.* He looked at Stealth and said, "To be honest with you, Stealth, I think I must have had the awareness at some time, but I can't remember it. Thank you for bringing it to my attention. I probably need to work on this. Maybe you can help me."

"Me helps you?" Stealth looked surprised and pleased at the same time. "Oh, I be happy ta do dat. I don't know how, but yes." His face looked brighter than Ivan had ever seen it. A faint yellow aura seemed to hover around him.

"Okay, Stealth. In a little while we'll work on me," he chuckled. "Boy said I am in training, you know, so I'd love your help." He smiled fondly at Stealth. "But, before we get off the track, what else do you think this awareness has done for you? You said there were several things."

"Ya, okay. Ya. I tink it maybe did one udder ting. I tink dat 'cause I was a aggressive dog, I can now 'preciate bettah da good tings 'bout dogs—'bout me."

"Say more about that," Ivan asked, curious.

"Wellll . . . let me see. I guess dat . . . Wellll, let me backs up a bit." He smiled and gave a slight, soft chuckle. "Its funny, Ivan. Now dat I know I was a nice dog before dis last time, I tink I can talk about da bad tings a little easier. Ya know what I mean?"

"Of course," said Ivan.

"Okay den. I tink I start by tellin' ya a bad ting I did dat's been weighin' heavy on me. Ya know? I been so 'shamed of it, I din't wanna even look at da udder dogs. I tought if I looked at 'em, dey'd know right away what I done. Like dey could read it in my eyes, ya know?"

Ivan nodded, engrossed.

"Da 'Merican Staffordshire Terrier was 'riginally a very noble dog dat helped da American farmers and settlers who developed deir country. But, I was bred ta be a serious, fightin' pit bull dog, da ones dat people bets monies on. My grandaddy was one a da best, an' my owner, his name was Judd, paid over two tousand dollers fer me. 'Cuz he knew I'd win it all back fer 'im. Judd, he loved me in his own kinda way. I knew it. But, he kep' me chained to a tree in da back yard, an' he paid kids ta go by 'n' taunt me. Dey teased me wit food an' called me names. Got me all riled up so's I wanned nuttin' more den ta break my chain and go chomp on 'em. An' I tried ta break dat chain. I chawwed on it 'n' yanked on it. 'N' when I was da mos' riled up, Judd, he'd come out and poke at me. He had some ole dog's dead head on a stick, an' he'd poke it at me, an' I'd tear inta it, tryin' ta kill it, even dough it was already dead.

"An' 'bout twice a week, Judd'd take me down ta da next block where dey had a fightin' ring in a big ole garage. People'd come from all over da city, an' Judd'd take deir money. Den, he'd come back where he had me in a cage, an' he'd poke at me and bang on da cage. He was tryin' ta git me all riled up like da kids did in da back yard. He'd bring me out and poke anudder, fresh-dead dog head on a stick at me, an' I'd bite at it. It felt so good ta sink my teeth inta anudder dog—dead or alive. It jus' felt good. So good, I din't wanna ever let go. I jus' sank my teeth in and hung on. An' I won all dem fights Judd put me in. I was da star, da top fightin' dog in da whole state. An' I loved it. I musta killed twenty, tirty dogs in my career. 'T's hard to 'xplain. 'T's like it was in my blood. I loved it. Yet, whenever I tought 'bout it, it made no sense to me." He looked at Ivan with hope in his eyes, as though Ivan would explain.

Ivan looked at Stealth with compassion, then cocked his head, unsure what to say. Surri, inside Ivan's head, said "Remember our conversation about the way Man has bred dogs to want to do certain things, like herding, retrieving, or digging for rodents? Man also bred dogs to want to fight. All the bull terriers were originally bred to grab hold of the snout of a bull and not let go. Man took this trait and bred it further so dogs would fight other dogs—and not let go. This is why it was so gratifying to him."

Ivan said to Stealth, "Just now, my guide, Surri—you know, the meerkat I met in the mountains—just explained that Man bred this desire into you." Stealth was eager to know more, and Ivan shared what Surri had said.

When Ivan was finished with his explanation, Stealth blurted, "But not a child!"

"What?" Ivan asked, afraid to know more.

Stealth hung his head. "Ohhhh, I tought I could tell you dis part, but I don't tinks I can. It's too awful." He turned his back on Ivan and walked out of the living room.

Ivan's heart felt leaden as he watched the defeated dog depart. *What should I do? I should probably run after him, but something's holding me back. Is it that I don't really want to know what he did—to a child? Oh my gosh. I really* don't *want to know.*

Isotope spoke gently, "Let him go for now, Ivan. He's made great progress. He'll tell you more when he's ready. Don't force him."

Ivan nodded. Yet, his heart felt broken as he watched the tough, brindle-coated dog slink across the lawn. His sad form walked towards the snow field and disappeared.

Ivan thought about all the details Stealth had shared. He mourned Stealth's very damaged sense of himself and longed to help him unleash his terrible burden. He allowed himself to imagine what it must have been like being Stealth on Earth with those inbred desires to rip things apart. He thought of Stealth's question about Ivan having experienced these same traits and that these traits are inherent, to one degree or another, in all dogs. Now that Ivan had had individual discussions with each of the dogs, he brightened at the idea of discussing the aggression concept with the whole group. *Maybe it will be helpful to all of us.* He glanced out at the snow field one more time to spot Stealth, but all he saw were the same, heavy-coated, snow dogs playing their games. He decided to go round up everyone else and bring them back to the living room.

Chapter Twelve

Ivan cantered throughout dog heaven—the beach to locate Murphy, the park to find Carl, and the retriever pond to get Beauregard. Once they were back in their living room, he headed to the snow field to pull Jolly away from Lars. While there, he searched for Stealth but couldn't find him. He told Jolly of his concern, and she said, "Maybe he's gone back to the living room. With that short coat of his, he was bound to get cold here. Let's go see," and she quickly trotted back with Ivan. When they entered the living room, Murphy, Carl, and Beauregard lay sleepily waiting, but Stealth wasn't there.

Ivan told them Stealth's story and how he'd walked away. Carl said, "If I were him, my self-esteem would be so low, I might want to give myself over to Garmr. It would bring internal justice to my situation."

A thunderclap of silence hit the room. Jolly said, "What if he does give himself to Garmr?"

Beauregard said, "If he gets initiated . . . ."

Jolly asked, "Oh, Ivan do you think . . . ?"

Murphy began to shiver, Beauregard's ears dropped low, and Carl pondered the situation. Jolly's jaw tightened as she looked at Ivan for direction. Ivan's heart clenched with guilt. He looked from one dog to another. "Wow," he said quietly. "We can't let him give himself over to an eternity of hell."

"And for him, that would mean an eternity of fighting other dogs," Carl added.

"We have to go rescue him," said Jolly and headed for the door.

"Wait," said Ivan. "Let's not just charge over there. Let's make a plan. Let's think this through. Garmr's realm is a very serious, dangerous place. I bet he has more tricks up his sleeve than the ones he used on me. We're going to need help."

"What kind of help?" Carl asked. "All we have to do is gallop over there, find Stealth, and drag him back."

Murphy said, "I know what Ivan means. Our spirit guides. I met mine earlier today, and I think they can help a lot."

"Oh pshaw," said Carl. "There's no such thing."

Beauregard, Murphy, and Jolly swung their heads back to see Ivan's response. Just then, the odor of meerkat filled the room, and an eagle's feather floated down from the ceiling. "Smell that odor?" Ivan asked them. "See that feather?"

They all nodded, even Carl.

Hom spoke inside Ivan's head, "It's true that Stealth has gone to Garmr, and you all must try to rescue him. You don't need to convince Murphy about your guides, but ask the others to manifest theirs. This is the time."

"Okay." He addressed his dogs, "Hom just told me that we *do* need to rescue Stealth from Garmr and that we all need our guides' help. Murphy has done this already, but now I'd like you, Beauregard, Jolly, and Carl, to go back outside. Find an appealing place where you can be alone. And then just ask . . . ask your guides to show themselves to you. And speak to you. Ask them to introduce themselves." He paused as he saw the looks of doubt on their faces. "Really. You can do this. Hom said you should.

It's beautiful. There's no need to be afraid. It's a wonderful experience. Relish this. Open yourselves to it. You'll be delighted." They still had doubt on their faces, so he said, "Go, now. Shoosh! Take all the time you need, though it won't take very long at all. Murphy and I will wait. We need their help. Go now. Off with you." He motioned his muzzle at them to get them to move.

Jolly was the first to slink out the door. Beauregard followed, and Carl, with an expression of disdain, ambled out slowly. Ivan looked at Murphy and asked, "What do you think? Do you think they'll be successful?"

"Yes, they will. It's so easy." Murphy paused. "Except for Carl. I don't think he'll even try."

Ivan sighed heavily. "You're probably right, but I can't force him." Murphy nodded, then the two sat still and silent, facing the doorway, eager for the return of their comrades. Neither dog moved until they perked their ears at footsteps entering. It was Beauregard. His face was elated, and he had a slight shimmer around him. His eyes were pleasantly wide, yet he was calm. He smiled at them as he entered.

"Do you know," he said, "that my main guide is a cat! Do you believe that? A wild cat, though—a cougar. He's here to teach me about hidden meanings. His name is Ollie. And I have three newts, a millipede, a fox, a buffalo, and an osprey. They're wonderful! Ollie said it's true that we need them on our journey to Garmr's realm. He said Garmr's cats are extremely evil."

Murphy and Ivan glowed along with Beauregard. As the three sat among each other's bliss, Carl came ambling back in. "Nothing," he said. "I asked, but nothing came. I knew it."

"Maybe because you were so sure you wouldn't see them," Murphy said with earnestness.

"I doubt that," said Carl. "Nonetheless, I will accompany you to retrieve Stealth. My keen observation and analytical skills will be assets."

Ivan took a short, deep breath and said, "Thank you, Carl. I'm sure they will."

After a few moments, Jolly galloped into the room with such speed, she nearly knocked everyone else over. She slid to a sitting stop, then stood up with her whole, big body wiggling from tail tip to nose leather. "Oh my gosh!" she exclaimed. "You were right! It's true! I love them! They love me! Thank you, thank you, thank you, Ivan. And Murphy. Oh my gosh! My main guide is a giraffe, of all things. He wants to teach me to reach high, reach for the stars. His name is Elbert, and I just love him." She whirled around in a circle three times while the others scooted backwards. Murphy got slapped in the face by her tail, but he didn't mind. She continued, "And I have a large black spider, a ferret, a cockatoo, a rattlesnake, and three ostriches. Each one has something to teach me, and I just love them all! I'm so happy." Then she became serious. "They said we need them to come along, that our mission is incredibly dangerous, but they think we, with our guides, can get Stealth out safely—if, and it's a big if—we can trick not just Garmr but his helpers, too. They said his helpers are very crafty." She glanced at Beauregard and saw him beaming. "You found yours too, didn't you?"

Beauregard glowed brighter and said, "Yes."

Then she looked at Carl and frowned. "You didn't, did you, Carl?"

He raised his snout and said, "As I've implied previously, I think these are all figments of your imaginations. However, I am going to accompany you to find Stealth."

Jolly realized there was nothing more to say, so she smiled and said, "Great, Carl. I'm glad you're coming. We need you."

Carl nodded in reply. "Well, then, let's not dally any longer."

"Yes," said Ivan. "Let's get going." He led the way at a fast trot, Beauregard right behind him, then Jolly, Carl, and Murphy. They made a beeline for the snow field. When they reached the edge, Ivan's concern for Murphy made him stop. He was about to say they would all make a nice path for him when Sebastian, Reva, and Lars came traipsing through the snow. The others sat back in surprise.

"We'll cut a path for you!" the three said in unison.

"Hi, Lars," Jolly said demurely. "Thank you."

"Of course," said Lars. "I feel privileged to help."

Sebastian led the way, followed by Reva and Lars and then Ivan's group. By the time the larger dogs had padded down the snow, the path was as flat as a concrete sidewalk for Murphy. Half-way to the mountains, Ivan glanced back at Murphy to see him skipping along with a smile on his face. Once they arrived at the end of the snow field, Reva, Sebastian, and Lars said a quick "Good-bye and good luck" and headed back.

Ivan turned to face the others. He motioned toward the waterfall with his snout. "That's the waterfall I told you about. And there's the trail head."

"The waterfall's lovely," said Jolly.

"Let's head up the trail," said Carl.

Ivan was at a loss about how to direct them. He didn't have a plan, despite his suggesting one. He allowed Carl to lead the way up the path, which left Ivan feeling somewhat ineffective. The scenery looked the same as before—spruce trees, ferns, wildflowers, and the soft, brown path with no overlooks. He wondered if the others would question the sameness, but none did, and they soon reached the top.

As they stood on the apex and peered into the valleys, a flood of exclamations poured out. "It's lovely," "It's magnificent," "It's breathtaking," "How beautiful," and "Look at those little turquoise lakes down there!" Ivan agreed, but he kept jerking around, looking for Garmr. Garmr's fury was fresh in his mind, and he shuddered as he stood there. Dread permeated his bones, and he felt edgy.

"Let's go down there and look for Stealth," said Jolly.

"Oh, I don't think we should," said Ivan, recalling Garmr's warning to never go down there without him. Yet, Ivan clearly didn't want Garmr to lead them anywhere. *I hope we can do this without encountering him at all.*

"Unlikely," Surri said inside his head.

Ivan's heart sank, and his bones trembled. *This is nuts. Yet . . . , we can't leave Stealth.* "Look," Ivan said to his group, "when I used to meet Garmr here, he told me never to go down there by myself. He said I should always wait for him. And the one time I forgot, he became very angry. Yet, I'd just as soon not see him. I don't know what he'll try to do to me."

A dark silence fell upon them, then Beauregard said, "I think we should just gallop down there, find Stealth, and then flee as fast as we can. Forget Garmr. Let's avoid him."

The others murmured agreement. Murphy said, "Ivan, I think you should lead the way. But go slowly enough so Carl and I can keep up."

Ivan still felt reluctant, yet this seemed the only strategy. He set off at a medium canter, looking back over his shoulder to make sure the two smaller dogs could keep up. Down and down they ran until they entered the first green valley. The evil flower field was gone and, instead, there was a large, serene park with a small lake, a quiet dirt path going around it, huge oak trees, park benches, fragrant flower beds, and birds singing. They all stopped and looked. It was so peaceful, they entered with no fear, not even for Ivan. When they'd walked a third of the way around the lake, enjoying the fragrances and bird songs, there, on the edge of the path, sat a well-groomed Lhasa Apso very much like Carl but a shade smaller.

"See," said Carl, before they were in hearing range of the dog, "Lhasa Apsos are meant to be in parks. She looks very happy, doesn't she? Let's talk to her." No one objected, so they approached her. Carl, in a soft voice, said "Hello, Madam. I'm Carl, and these are my friends Murphy, Beauregard, Jolly, and Ivan. Lovely day for a stroll in the park, isn't it?"

She looked off to one side, bowed her head, and said, "Yes, it is lovely."

"How long have you been here?" Carl asked.

"Not long," she said. "And you?"

"Oh, we just arrived, too. We're looking for our friend Stealth. He's a pit bull terrier. Brindle-colored. Have you seen him?"

"No, I haven't." She looked shyly at the ground. "But,

I hear that they hang out a couple miles away, just over that next hill." She pointed her nose in that direction. "I went past there once. I think I might be able to find them again. Would you like some company?" She turned one shoulder towards Carl and bowed her head again.

Gosh, she's sweet, thought Ivan. *I hope Garmr doesn't get a hold of her. Maybe we can get her out of here, too.* "What is your name?" Ivan asked.

"Charon," she said.

"Sha-rone?" Ivan asked.

"Yes, that's right."

"What a pretty name," Carl said, wagging his tail fast. Charon giggled and glanced away.

"So, you're willing to take us to where you think Stealth might be?"

"Uh huh," she said. "Come on, follow me. I think I remember where they are," and she headed off on the path.

Ivan wanted her to be specific about how long she'd been here and whether Boy had sent her. He worried that Garmr would trick her into staying, because she was so soft. He couldn't imagine Boy sending such a sweet dog to such a horrible place. It didn't make sense. Yet, he didn't know her story and sensed he should not be assertive. Maybe Carl would discover why she was here. Most likely, she, too, had been put in charge of a group and couldn't handle it.

Charon trotted gaily along with Carl at her side. Ivan had to admit they made an attractive couple. He wondered if dogs could mate here in heaven but realized there would be no purpose. *But, they could fall in love.* Charmed by the two together, Ivan, Beauregard, Jolly, and Murphy trotted along behind them, trying to overhear their quiet conversation.

They exited the park, and Ivan was a little sad to leave its peaceful security. Once they walked out into the grassy valley, the birds didn't sing, and the fragrance of the flowers was left behind. He was again aware of the chill in his bones and darted his eyes this way and that. He knew from Surri's and Hom's words that he *would* encounter Garmr. Where, when, and how were unknown. They trotted along for what seemed like forever to Ivan. *So, where is this place of the pit bulls?* He cringed at what the place would look like—dogs fighting to the death, shredded flesh, eyes ripped out, ears half torn off, and having to do that day after day for eternity. His heart quickened, his breath shortened, his head began to swim, and his legs weakened. He wanted to bolt back to the living room.

"Calm yourself," Kit whispered to him. Just then he stumbled into a depression in the ground. He looked down and saw a hippopotamus footprint. "Esmerelda," he whispered, then thought, *Yes, you're here to help me feel grounded.* He took a deep breath, thought of her huge roundness, her connection to the Earth, and he felt better.

He leaned into Beauregard's ear and asked, "How long have we been trotting behind Carl and Charon?"

"For a few minutes," said Beauregard. "The park is just back there."

Ivan looked back over his shoulder, and sure enough, the park was not far away. *Whew! I am not myself here.* "Jolly," he spoke in her ear, "what do you think of all this?"

"I think it's lovely. Charon is adorable. I'm hoping we can rescue her, too. And so far, it's not so bad. I thought it would be filled with ugly, evil things, but it's really quite nice."

"Just wait," Ivan said. "No, Jolly. I'm sorry. I hope you're right. It's just that I thought the same thing. You know. I told you my story."

"I know you did, Ivan, and we believe you. It's just that it's sooooo nice, it's hard to believe it can be awful."

"Yes, I know," Ivan said and decided to keep his mouth shut. He paid more attention to where they were going. As they headed up a hill, he knew they might almost be there. When they reached the top of the hill, Charon stopped. Carl stood close to her, his tail wagging like an egg beater.

"The place of the bull terriers is right down there. See?" Charon pointed with her little snout.

The scene below was of American farmland in the 1800s—farmhouses where American Staffordshire Terriers lay snoozing on front porches or accompanied children around the yard. Some barked at passersby, and some were out in the woods helping their owners hunt wild pigs. Several dug in the ground for vermin, and a few herded cows. Nowhere did they see dogs fighting.

"Do you see your friend Stealth?" Charon asked.

"I can't see from here," said Jolly. "May we go closer?"

"As far as I know, it's okay," said Charon. "Like I said, I haven't been here long."

Ivan didn't like the sound of that the first time she said it and liked it even less now. There were so many questions he wanted to ask her, but the time wasn't right.

"Let's go down there," Charon continued. "Maybe you can find your friend. And I think there might be another park down there, on the other side of that second farm," she said mostly to Carl. They trotted down the hill until they were close enough to see if any of these farm terriers was Stealth.

"I don't see him," said Murphy.

"I don't either," said Jolly. "Can we go further, maybe into those woods where they're hunting and down into that pasture where they're herding?"

"As far as I know it's okay," said Charon. "I'm not familiar with any rules here."

The others turned to Ivan for an answer. His thoughts spun, and he couldn't formulate a response.

"Maybe we should split up," said Beauregard. "We could each cover a different area and meet back here. Hopefully, one of us will find Stealth, so we can get out of here."

"Good idea!" said Murphy.

"That sounds like good, logical thinking," Charon said. "But, why do you want to get out of here? I think it's lovely."

Ivan ignored Charon's question and said, "No, I don't think that's wise. I think we should stick together."

"Carl and I could search the park over there," Charon suggested, "while you look through these farmlands."

Ivan felt instantly annoyed with her. *Why is she contradicting me?* "No," he said firmly. "We'll stay together in one group. Charon, do you know who Garmr is?"

"Garmr? No. I've never heard of him. But, like I said, I haven't been here long."

"Why are you here, anyway?" Ivan asked. "Did Anubis send you here? Were you put in charge of a new group of arrivals and found it too difficult?"

"Why yes," she said, surprised. "How did you know that?"

"I'll tell you later. Look, everyone. We mustn't get sidetracked. Let's find Stealth and high-tail it out of here. Charon, we'd like you to join us, and we'll explain why later. You don't want to stay here. I know. I've been here before.

"Now, this is what I think we should do. As a group, let's gallop past all these houses, through the woods, alongside the pastures, and keep a lookout for Stealth. If we don't find him here, I have a hunch there's another place where American Staffordshire Terriers work. We'll look for that place if we don't find him here. Okay?"

Murphy, Jolly, Beauregard, and Carl dropped their heads a little and nodded. Just as they were about to take off, Charon whispered something in Carl's ear. His eggbeater tail went into high gear, and a mischievous look came over his face. "Ivan," he said, "I want Charon to take me to that park to look for Stealth. We'll meet you back here. This is more efficient. It'll save time."

Ivan began to argue with him, then decided against it, and Carl did have a point. Maybe he and Charon would find Stealth in the park, although Stealth didn't gravitate to parks. Nonetheless, time was running out. "Okay, Carl. Good luck. We'll meet you back here." The Lhasa couple trotted away, and the other four took off for the yards, pastures, and woods. Murphy's legs were somewhat longer than Carl's, so Ivan ran a little faster than before. Beauregard ran at Ivan's side, and Jolly and Murphy followed.

They galloped down a packed-soil, residential street. Ivan and Murphy scanned all the porches and yards on the left, and Beauregard and Jolly scanned the ones on the right. At the end of the street, they turned and ran through acres of woods, using the same strategy but didn't find Stealth. When they ran through several pastures filled with cows, sheep, and goats, Ivan felt the familiar itch to herd them but kept going. When they finished searching every part of this farmland, they stopped, panting.

"He's not here," said Murphy. "Now what?"

Jolly eyed Ivan. "You think there's a fighting-dog area, don't you, Ivan? You think he's there."

Ivan, trying to catch his breath, said, "I'm afraid that's exactly what I think. I have from the beginning, but we had to look here, didn't we?" The others nodded with expressions of apprehension. "Let's go get Carl first." They ran back past the pastures, the woods, and the residential area, checking once more for Stealth.

When they reached the place where they and Carl and Charon had separated, the Lhasa Apsos weren't there. "Just as I suspected," said Ivan. "We can't spend time hunting down Carl. We'll come back later. Stealth is our top priority."

"But, we can't leave Carl here," said Beauregard.

Ivan sighed heavily. "I know. But, I think, at this moment, Stealth is in more danger than Carl, so I think we should find him first. Anyone disagree?" The others shook their heads. "Okay. Good. Did any of you notice a putrid odor coming from the far side of the pastures?"

Jolly piped up, "Yes! Yes, I did. What was that? It smelled like rotten meat. Like the ground beef Julie threw in the trash after she'd left it in the refrigerator too long. She used to try feeding it to me, but I got sick."

"Yeaaaah," Murphy said slowly. "I think I smelled it, too. Sometimes Helga didn't keep up with the food in her refrigerator, either."

Beauregard looked interested but puzzled. "I'm sorry. I don't know what you're talking about."

"That's okay," said Ivan. "Three out of four of us recognized it. I'm afraid that's where Stealth is."

"Why?" Beauregard asked.

"It will be easier to show you," said Ivan and dashed off again. The other three followed at a full gallop back again through the 1800s American farm community until they reached the end of the far pasture. Ivan and the others sniffed the air.

"Eeeeew," said Beauregard. "That stinks. What is it?"

"Come," said Ivan. He looked at them hard. "This may be unpleasant. Brace yourselves." He took off galloping toward the foul odor with the others close behind. They soon found themselves in an old, run-down area of a large city. The houses were in poor condition, windows were broken, fences were falling down, and yards were full of litter. Many of the back and front yards had pit bull terriers chained to trees. Few had bowls of water, and most were extremely thin. All of them growled and barked at Ivan's group.

"This is scary," said Murphy, scooting closer to Jolly.

"Look for Stealth," Ivan ordered as they trotted quickly from one yard to the next. They circled around the end of a block and back through the alley. The rotten meat smell became stronger.

"What *is* that?" asked Beauregard.

Ivan stopped alongside several large, metal garbage cans with lids perched loosely on top. He gingerly pushed one of the lids off, and it fell to the ground. They all peeked inside. There, stiff as wood, were two mangled, dead bodies of pit bull terriers. Each had an eye missing. One had no ears left at all, and both had huge, open gashes in their bodies and rear legs. The four spirit dogs jumped back. Murphy landed right in the lid of the can and made a loud racket.

"Shhhhh," scolded Jolly. "We don't want anyone to know we're here!"

Murphy's ears dropped, and he started shivering.

"Oh, I'm sorry, Murphy," she said and cuddled him against her large body.

He leaned against her with his eyes shut tightly. "Why did we have to come here? What if we find Stealth in one of these cans?" he sobbed and turned his face into Jolly's white fur.

"I don't think we *will* find Stealth in a can," said Ivan. "I think we'll find him—very much alive—in one of these garages." They looked around, up and down the alley. "That might be one down there," he added and led the way.

Negative energy emanated from a ramshackle, garage-type building as the four dogs sensed an evilness inside and stopped in their tracks. As though Satan himself were in there, nasty growling noises spiraled out to the dogs' ears. They slowly backed away, haunches tucked beneath them. Ivan thought to himself, *Oh boy. Not only are we going to find Stealth in here, I have a hunch Garmr's here, too. Can I handle this? Am I strong enough?* Magically, a choir of all nine of his guides sang, "Yes, Ivan, you can do this. You're very strong. You know what you're up against. And we're here to help. Go ahead. Do what you must do."

He turned to the others. "This would be a good time to connect with your guides. Take a moment. We're going to need them. I would bet that both Stealth and Garmr are in here."

The three looked at him, wide-eyed. "Both?" they all said together.

"I don't know for sure, but it's a strong feeling. Not only will we have to convince Stealth to come with us, we'll have to fight Garmr off as well. But, we can do it. I know we can." He paused. Jolly, Murphy, and Beauregard gave Ivan their full attention. "Now, close your eyes and take a few deep breaths. Feel your feet planted firmly on the ground. Try to relax just a moment and allow yourselves to see your guides." Ivan watched as each did what he asked. When he saw serene expressions come over each one's face, he said, "Now ask them to protect you." They kept their eyes closed while their lips made little speaking movements, then they opened their eyes and looked at him. "Let's try to sneak in quietly and see who's where. We may decide to come back out and talk before we take any action. Watch me for a cue. But let's not talk while we're in there, okay? Any questions?" As they shook their heads "no," Ivan began walking toward the hinged door of the garage. He touched it lightly with his nose, and it opened just a crack. He tried to peer in, but it was too dark. Sounds of humans cheering and booing flooded his ears. He poked the door open further and saw not individual human faces but a blur of human forms, many of whom shouted and raised their fists. "Just as I thought," said Ivan in a hushed voice. "It's dog fighting—so people can make bets and win money."

The human forms stood with their backs to the door, allowing the dogs to slip inside unnoticed. Ivan motioned the others to follow him, and they passed, one by one, into the building. The air smelled of cigarette smoke, old liquor, and blood. Ivan saw that the human forms were puppet-like, not actual human beings. *They must be for the dogs' benefit.* They walked in a large circle behind the humanoids until they came to a break in the crowd, a place where they could see into the pit—the fighting ring. They hid behind the closest human form. Jolly, being the tallest, peered around to look, Beauregard poked his head under hers, Ivan under Beauregard's, and Murphy, shivering, stood beneath Ivan and looked, too.

Two pit bull terriers, teeth bared, side-stepped across the ring while eyeing one another. One was Stealth, and the other, Ivan knew instantly, was Garmr disguised as a pit bull. Ivan recognized Garmr's voice as he coaxed Stealth in Stealth's own dialect. "C'mon, tough one. See if ye's c'n grab me. Ah hah!" he shouted as Stealth grabbed the front of Garmr's stifle in his teeth and wouldn't let go. "Ye luvs it, doncha? Don't dat feel good?" Garmr seemed to be in no pain at all but pretended to be. Swiftly, he whirled around, shoved his own snout under Stealth's and flung Stealth off to the side. Then, he grabbed Stealth by the throat and threw him to the ground. Ivan almost shouted out when Garmr dragged Stealth across the ring and back again, Stealth's feet flailing in the air. At just the right moment, he let go and allowed Stealth to grab him by the throat, and Stealth dragged Garmr across the ring.

"Does dis feel good?" Garmr bellowed.

Stealth, with a fierceness none of them had ever seen, shouted back, "Oh, you bet it does. I luvs dis!"

Garmr made another swift maneuver to free himself, jumped back, and said, "Okay, you're da winner of dis match. Go back to yer crate, tough one. Next!" he called out. Stealth jogged out of the ring and through a doorway to a back room, and a different pit bull terrier came out. Garmr repeated a similar set of maneuvers with him.

The shouting and cheering were so loud, Ivan realized he could whisper to the other dogs and not be heard by Garmr. He motioned for them to go back behind the humanoids where he gathered them in a tight circle and said, "Well, we know where Stealth is. We must get into that back room and talk to him."

Murphy asked, "Do you think he's been initiated yet?"

"No, I don't. That's why Garmr's still involved. Once a dog gives its soul to this place, Garmr leaves him and goes off to recruit new ones. We need to get to Stealth before Garmr convinces him to stay here. So . . . , we need to sneak back there."

"Wait," said Beauregard. "Only one of us needs to go back there, and I'm the logical one."

"Why?" they all asked.

"Because I'm the only pure black dog. The rest of you have a lot of white on you, and Garmr could spot you. I can slink back there among the shadows, and he won't see me."

"Wow," said Ivan. "That's very brave of you, Beauregard. Are you sure?"

Beauregard nodded his head. "It's the only thing that makes sense."

"You can't lead Stealth out right now. Find out if Garmr comes at night. He always left me alone to sleep. So, that's probably when we should come back."

"Okay, I'll find out," Beauregard said and slipped away before Ivan could give him more instructions. He had been about to say, "Be as quiet as a mouse." Just then, Ivan felt a tickle on his belly. He smiled and knew Samuel was telling him to stop worrying.

Ivan, Murphy, and Jolly stood stock still and waited. They clamped their ears close to their heads to shut out the shouting and growling, and they breathed shallowly to avoid the nasty odors. Ivan knew it was these very fragrances that agitated the fighting dogs. As he smelled the smells and listened to the sounds, he drifted into imagining himself in Stealth's place as he fought Garmr and how it must feel to dig one's teeth into the flesh of another dog, to clamp down, lock on, and not let go, to feel the muscle fibers tear under the pressure of his jaws, to taste the blood run though his mouth, to dig his toenails into the dirt and jerk his head this way and that, ripping the flesh even more, feeling the pressure of the bone under the torn muscles, and to allow the flood of adrenaline to course through his veins and make him want to hurt or kill his opponent.

When he emerged from his reverie, Jolly and Murphy were looking at him oddly. He dropped his ears, ashamed they might have read his mind. He wondered if Stealth was correct, that some part of all dogs enjoyed a good fight.

Chapter Thirteen

Louder cheering from the humanoids alerted them that this fight was over, and Garmr's "winning opponent" headed to the back room where Beauregard was talking to Stealth. Ivan tensed. He hadn't thought about the possibility of an encounter between this pit bull and the Poodle. He wondered if Beauregard was having any trouble convincing Stealth to come back with them. Was Beauregard capable of pressing his case and winning any argument Stealth would give him? Perhaps Stealth really loved fighting enough to want to stay here. That would be tragic, because they all could see his more positive, loving side.

Did Beauregard have a full enough understanding of Stealth to present the important points? *Oh gosh, I don't think I properly coached Beauregard for this conversation. Stealth may tell Beauregard that he's found what he truly loves to do and wants to stay here. Is Beauregard adequately convinced that although Man bred for certain instincts, the soul of the dog can rise above these?* Ivan thought back on Beauregard's realization about his own retrieving instincts. *Is this enough?* Now Ivan wished he'd gone back there himself.

Maybe I should run back there. Oh my gosh! How can Beauregard possibly fight off that other pit bull? Dogs bred to fight don't think first. They just attack. Oh my god, poor Beauregard. He won't know what hit him. That dog is all pumped up, and his fighting juices are flowing full strength after fighting Garmr. I must go rescue Beauregard.

Just then, shrieking, growling, yelping, and fiercer

229

growling from the back room caused them to perk their ears in alarm. Ivan bolted to Beauregard's aid, but Jolly grabbed him by the scruff of his neck just in time. "Wait!" she commanded in a loud, garbled whisper.

"Beauregard can't fight off a pit-pull!" Ivan choked. "Let go of my neck!" he scolded.

"Maybe he can," said Murphy. "It will be a mess if we all run in there."

Ivan fought a moment more, then relaxed, so Jolly loosened her grip. "You can let me go!" Ivan hissed.

"Promise to not run back there?" Jolly said, gagging on Ivan's neck fur.

"Yes! I promise! Now let go!"

Jolly loosened her grip a little more but not completely. When she sensed that Ivan spoke the truth, she released him. By then, they heard only snarling and growling, the kind one hears from a dog fight, and no yelping.

"That's either a very good sign or a very bad sign," said Ivan, his muscles fired, ready to fight.

Suddenly, there was silence. They held their breaths and listened harder. Just then a black mass of fur bolted past them, shouting, "Let's get out of here!" It was Beauregard. Jolly, Ivan, and Murphy followed him. Out the door they flew and ran at top speed for several blocks.

Ivan looked back to make sure Murphy was keeping up. The sight of those spindly little legs going so fast assured him. Ivan looked this way and that, in front and behind them, expecting Garmr to appear in angry, bellowing form as he did during Ivan's narrow escape. Finally, Beauregard slowed and then stopped. The others gasped when Beauregard turned to face them. One of his ears was sliced in half and dripping with blood. Two large wounds gaped open on his thigh, a tear in his neck revealed shredded muscle fibers, and a puncture wound on his snout oozed blood as well.

"What?" Beauregard asked. "What's wrong?"

"You!" said Jolly. "You're full of holes. You're bleeding! Doesn't it hurt?"

Beauregard looked down at himself. He saw the wounds on his thigh but couldn't see the others. He shrugged. "I'll be okay."

"What happened in there?" Jolly demanded.

Ivan kept looking around for Garmr. *How can Garmr not know we're here? Why isn't he confronting us?* This made the situation reek of greater things ahead.

"Well," said Beauregard. He took a few licks at the wounds on his thigh. "I talked with Stealth. He was locked in a crate. He was very glad to see me. He said he understood Ivan's story about herding sheep and how it had nearly convinced him to stay. He said he realizes that fighting feels good to him only because Man bred that desire into him, and he's ready to leave." Beauregard stopped as if he were done with his story. He licked his wounds some more.

"Then what?" Murphy asked. "Did you ask him whether Garmr leaves him alone at night?"

"Oh yeah. He said yes."

"Then what!!!!" Jolly shrieked. "Why are you all cut up?"

"Oh. That was that dog after Stealth. When he came into the back room, he saw me and attacked me," he said calmly. "At first I didn't know what to do, having never been in a—geez!—dog fight. The damned dog barely set eyes on me and just attacked. I didn't know what to do and heard myself crying out for help. Then Stealth coached me.

He yelled at me how to turn, how to get out of a locked jaw, how to spin and bite back. Then, it all sort of came naturally, and I nailed that pit bull. Then Stealth told me to run, so I did."

"Beauregard, you're awfully calm for all that," said Ivan.

Jolly and Murphy instinctively stepped up to Beauregard and began licking the wounds on his head and neck. Ivan joined in, and before long, Beauregard was miraculously healed.

This is such a strange place, Ivan thought, still feeling on edge, still glancing around for Garmr. *It's a bad place, but some good things happen here.* To Beauregard, he said, "So, Stealth's expecting us to come back for him tonight?"

"Yes, I said we would."

"Good," said Ivan. "It appears to be late afternoon. Nighttime will arrive before long. We better find Carl and Charon. They're probably wondering where we are." Without saying any more, they cantered out of the city, back through the valley, back through the 1800s American farmland, and found the entrance to the park. It looked identical to the one in which they'd first met Charon. Neither Carl nor Charon sat waiting for them, however, so they entered the park and once again were filled with feelings of peace and safety.

"Gosh, this feels good after being in that city," said Murphy.

"Yes, it's pleasant here," said Jolly, stopping for a stretch.

Ivan stretched, too, and said, "I suppose they're strolling around the lake."

"Well, let's go find them," said Beauregard and trotted off.

"He's certainly become quite the knight," said Jolly and followed.

The four dogs trotted all the way around the lake but never spotted the two Lhasas. Birds sang, flowers emitted sweet fragrances, and colorful butterflies hovered in the air. On the edges of the park were vast, extremely dense thickets of ornamental trees in full bloom with various shades of pink and orange. Ivan stopped and peered into the darkness. "I have a hunch we should go in there."

"Is it a nudge from one of your guides?" asked Murphy.

"Maybe so," said Ivan but didn't stop to tune in. He trotted several feet into the thicket, stopped, sniffed the air, and cocked his head one way and the other, listening for something. He continued walking, and the others followed, also sniffing and listening. "Go slowly," he whispered over his shoulder and took one careful step at a time. Then he heard it—the rhythmic drumming of cat paws and the terrible drone of Garmr's music. He stepped faster towards the sound.

"What is that?" Beauregard whispered.

"It's an initiation," Ivan whispered back.

Murphy and Jolly slammed on their brakes. "I'm not going there," said Murphy.

"Me neither," said Jolly. "Let's get out of here. Garmr might snatch us up and initiate us, too."

"No, no, you have to be willing," said Ivan. "I don't think we're in any danger of that. Come on. I hope he didn't get Carl. But how could he when he's been with the pit bulls?"

They tiptoed closer to the sound until they saw an evil, red glow through the trees. They crouched down and crawled on their bellies. A low berm allowed them to hide their bodies yet peer over the top. Their eyes widened at what they saw.

A large disc of ground burned reddish-orange with fire burning beneath it. Carl stood in the center. Around him marched the large, black cats, the ground shaking beneath their paws. They chanted a rhythmic song whose words the spirit dogs could not understand. Carl was draped in a robe of flowers, bird feathers, and butterflies' wings. In front of him stood Charon, who was now the size of a draft horse. Her coat glowed a fierce red and her eyes neon yellow.

"She's Garmr!" Ivan whispered under his breath. "My god, who would have guessed that!"

Murphy made a strange burping noise and bolted back toward the park's entrance. "No! Murphy! Get back here!" Ivan whispered as loudly as he dared, but Murphy was gone. "We have to stop him," he said, and the three took off. It was nearly dark, so Murphy was hard to see except for little flashes of white here and there as they gained on him. *Thank goodness he's just a little dog,* thought Ivan as he spurred himself to gallop faster. He knew Beauregard and Jolly would have no trouble keeping up. Yet, it wasn't until they were out of the park that Ivan caught up to Murphy. "Murphy! Stop!" Ivan shouted, breathless, and Murphy did. He turned to face Ivan, shivering so hard his teeth chattered like a box of old bones.

"This is too sc-sc-sc-scary, Ivan," said the little dog. "I'm going b-b-b-back home to our l-l-l-living room."

"We have to get Stealth," Ivan said firmly. "Besides, I don't think you should try to go home by yourself."

"What should we do about Carl?" Jolly asked.

Ivan paused, then said,"Let's see if we can interrupt the initiation. This will be extremely dangerous. But, we have to try." The others looked at him in disbelief. "Maybe," said Ivan, "if we can do what Surri did for me—emanate love to him with all our hearts—maybe he'll snap out of the spell. Come on. We have to try!" he said, hearing the urgency in his own voice. "Let's go!" He hurried off without waiting to see if they followed. He galloped back to the thicket. When he turned to tell the others that he intended to circle around to the far side so Carl could see him better, he saw them huddled together quite a distance back. *Oh, geez. I guess I have to do this by myself.*

He slinked to the far side of the initiation site where Carl, if he looked up, would see him. The fear in Ivan's bones was replaced with determination, and the demonic sounds, the beating of the cats' paws, and the evil light coming from the ground didn't phase him. He stood directly opposite Carl's mesmerized gaze and tried to make eye contact with him. He pushed love from his heart toward Carl and wished with all his might that Carl would respond. But, Carl's eyes couldn't see Ivan.

Charon asked Carl to say "yes," and when Carl did so without hesitation, Ivan felt the familiar pangs of guilt rip through his body.

Humphrey spoke into Ivan's head, "Ivan, you tried. It's no use. It's not your fault. It's what Carl wanted. Go now and take the others back to Stealth. We think you can rescue *him*."

"Thank you," Ivan whispered, his stomach hot with guilt. He sighed a huge sigh and bolted back to the others. He tried to shake the sickness in his belly, but the image of Carl saying "yes" to Charon wouldn't dissipate.

When he reached the others, he said, simply, "I was too late. Stealth is our main concern now."

"That Charon," said Jolly. "What a fooler she is."

Ivan looked at Jolly in disbelief. "Jolly, Charon is really Garmr. Didn't you see her just now?"

"Is that what that was? I didn't understand." Her jaw dropped as she thought about this. "How can that be?"

"He has all kinds of tricks, tricks I can't even imagine," said Ivan. "Charon fooled me too, though there was always something about her I didn't trust. Wow." He paused a moment, taking it all in. "But, let's hurry and get Stealth before anything happens to him. Garmr obviously knows we're here."

The four dogs raced back to the city, down the streets, and through the alley until they reached the garage again. It was all dark now, and no sounds came from inside. Ivan touched the door with his nose, and it opened easily. *Too easily,* he thought. He felt the trembling in his bones again. He poked his head through the doorway to find nothing but darkness. He sniffed the air. It smelled of cigarette smoke, liquor, and blood as before. The humanoids were there but unmoving, caught in mid-gesture like dozens of mannequins. *Creepy.*

He wondered if he and the others would be able to find their way to the back room. He took one cautious step at a time, trying to feel his way with his feet. He'd never experienced darkness this black, this leaden.

"You guys right behind me?" he turned and whispered.

"Yes," Murphy, Jolly, and Beauregard whispered back. He felt Murphy bump into his rump.

"Sorry. It's so dark in here," Murphy said.

"Use your nose," was all Ivan could think of to reply. Then he chuckled to himself, since that's what Murphy had just done.

"Want me to lead the way?" Beauregard whispered.

"Good idea," said Ivan. "Okay. Come on up here."

Beauregard had been at the end of the line. He nudged his body past Jolly, Murphy, and then Ivan. "Thanks," Ivan whispered as he felt the length of Beauregard's body sweep slowly past his own.

"Sure," said Beauregard.

Ivan kept his nose as close to Beauregard's rump as possible without goosing him, but, hard as he tried, he did bump him a couple times, each time whispering, "Sorry."

"It's okay," Beauregard whispered back. After they rounded a curve, he stopped, turned, and said, barely audibly, "We're at the door to the back room. I sure hope *all* the dogs are in crates, not just Stealth."

"How many are there?" Ivan asked.

"Six or seven."

"Yeah, they *better* be in crates," Ivan whispered.

Ivan heard Beauregard scratch lightly on the door and then the squeaking of the hinge. A strong odor of wet, bloody dogs flooded his nose. Beauregard stopped. Ivan ran into him again, Murphy ran into Ivan, and Ivan felt Murphy shove him again as Jolly ran into Murphy. They stood, silent, waiting, listening, sniffing, and straining their eyes to see something, any hint of light, but there was none. The blackness was even thicker and darker in here. Ivan could hear a number of dogs snoring softly. He started breathing easier, knowing the others were asleep. *What next?* he wondered. He hoped Beauregard would lead them to Stealth's crate, unlatch the door, and they would all tiptoe out. He felt Beauregard move ahead by one step. The rest followed, each keeping direct contact with the dog in front of him or her. And so they moved, one slow step at a time.

When Beauregard stopped, Ivan knew they had reached Stealth's crate. He heard Beauregard whisper to Stealth and felt his body jiggle as he fidgeted with the latch. Ivan heard Beauregard's teeth slide along metal, making little snapping noises as he failed to find the right spot, the right amount of pressure. One of the crated dogs stopped snoring. A few of the others stirred in their sleep. Ivan felt his bones tremble again. What if one or more were *not* in crates? He took some quiet, deep breaths to calm his racing heart. He wanted to step closer to the crate to make sure things were okay, but he resisted.

"Let Beauregard handle this," Humphrey's voice spoke softly inside Ivan's head.

Ivan took another quiet, deep breath. "Okay," he responded in his mind.

More snapping sounds and more teeth-on-metal sounds caused the remaining snoring dogs to awaken. For the longest moment, there was nothing but silence. Ivan couldn't even hear breathing. Then a low, rumbling growl came from one of the crates to Ivan's right. He held his breath, hoping the dog would go back to sleep. He heard Jolly and Murphy holding their breath as well. He wanted so badly to jump ahead and give Beauregard some help. Different kinds of crates had different kinds of latches. Maybe Beauregard was familiar with only one kind. As he started to move forward, he felt something like a bear paw on his chest. It held him back. At first he was startled and thought maybe this was Garmr, then realized it was Humphrey.

A sharp springing clack let them know the crate latch was now open, and they all turned to make a dash for the door, but the thick darkness forced them to freeze. A couple of the crated dogs growled again. Ivan relaxed a little as he realized none of the dogs was loose. Soon, he felt Stealth's body slither along his own as Stealth made his way along the line of dogs. They were so scrunched together, Ivan could feel Murphy's small body resist Stealth's as Stealth slid past him and could hear Stealth's body slide along Jolly's furry one. After a pause, the line began to move forward. Inch by inch they tiptoed their way out of the back room.

Ivan felt nothing but Murphy in front of him and Beauregard behind him as they baby-stepped their way from the back room, through the fighting ring, and over to the audience area. He felt suspended in nothingness, as his senses could detect little but his feet on the ground. The odors were no longer perceptible, perhaps because he was used to them. His bones still shook as he expected Garmr to appear in a huge bolt of light at any moment. Then, Ivan felt a small jerk as Stealth ran into something. The jerk smoothed as it rippled along Jolly's body, then Murphy's and into his own. He felt Beauregard respond to it as well. Ivan figured Stealth had run into one of the humanoids. Soon, they inched forward again with small steps.

Ivan's heart relaxed when he heard the creak of the door to the outside, and a flash of bluish street lights met his eyes. Stealth's dark form passed through the doorway and emerged into the street. Jolly's and Murphy's forms followed. When Ivan stepped out into the street, the air struck his nostrils with a fresh freedom. Behind him, the door slammed softly after Beauregard. They stood together, panting, and looked at one another with hesitant joy. Could it really have been this easy?

Stealth whispered, "We done it, you guys. We's out. I'm out. Tank you fer comin'."

"Let's get away from this garage," Ivan said and led the way, at a trot, out of the city and into the surrounding countryside. He still glanced uneasily this way and that for Garmr and stopped in a field under a large maple tree. Still not comfortable talking out loud, he whispered, "I can't believe Garmr didn't try to stop us. Maybe he really does just sleep at night. Whew!"

"Yeah, whew," said Jolly. "That was really tense."

Murphy nodded, a shiver passing through his body every few seconds.

"That crate latch!" whispered Beauregard. "I've never seen one like that."

"You didn't see it tonight, either!" joked Jolly.

"That's for sure. Have you ever experienced such darkness?"

"No, never, not me," they all mumbled together.

"How did you figure it out?" Murphy asked.

"I just kept feeling it with my lips and trying different angles."

"You're our hero," said Jolly, and the others nodded.

"Where's Carl?" Stealth asked.

"Carl," Ivan said sadly. "We tried to rescue him from

an initiation, but we were too late."

"'Nitiated? Carl's been 'nitiated? By Garmr? How'd dat happen?" Stealth asked.

"It's a long story," said Beauregard. "There was a female Lhasa named Charon. She was Garmr in disguise and wooed Carl into staying. Ivan tried to interrupt the initiation, but it didn't work."

"And you left him to come and get me?" Stealth asked, his eyes large with wonderment.

Ivan didn't know how to respond. Jolly simply said, "Yes," and that was enough. Ivan flashed Jolly a knowing glance.

"I'd like to see if there's any way to still get him out," said Ivan. The others agreed, Ivan led the way, and they cantered through the 1800s American settlement, and back to the park.

At the entrance, Murphy said, "I don't want to see Garmr again. I'll wait here."

"No," said Jolly. "We're staying together."

"I agree, Murphy," said Ivan. "It's too dangerous to leave you alone. All I want to do is try to talk to Carl. If it's fruitless, we'll leave."

Grim expressions came over their faces as they followed Ivan into the park. Ivan trotted cautiously, looking this way and that, to the edge of the thicket. He didn't hear anything but proceeded to pick his way through the small trees. He headed for the berm, and they crawled the last way to the little hill and peeked over. There was nothing but darkness. Without saying a word, they turned and headed back. They emerged from the thicket and stood, not knowing where to go next.

"Let's take a quick cruise around the lake and see if

we can spot him," said Ivan and led the way. The night was lighted by a gibbous moon that shone onto the dogs, the lake, the bushes, and the trees. Ivan scooted from one set of bushes that lined the path to another, looking for Carl. He lifted his head and peered down the path. He saw the short form of what looked like Carl as it trotted gaily along. The group hurried to get ahead of the dog by cantering around and behind a row of bushes that ran parallel to the path. This put them just ahead of the small dog. They peeked around the last bush, waiting to see whether or not this was Carl. It was.

Just as he was about to pass them, Ivan called out in a loud whisper, "Psst. Carl. It's me, Ivan, and the others. Are you okay?"

Carl stopped and looked at them. He lifted his nose in the air and kept trotting.

"Wait!" called Ivan. "We got Stealth. Are you ready to go back with us now?"

"You're all so pitiful," hissed Carl. "No! I'm staying here. And I'm very, very happy. Good riddance to you!" and he trotted away.

The others looked at one another. "How sad. How very, very sad," said Ivan. He hung his head, still aware of the guilt in his stomach.

"Maybe we should get out of here while the getting's good," said Jolly as she started to lead the way.

With a heaviness in his heart, Ivan stared at the trotting Lhasa Apso, then walked at a fast pace to catch up with the others. Once out of the park, he turned to them. "I know my way back. Let's just go quickly, okay?" They cantered together through the moonlight.

Chapter Fourteen

As the five dogs loped along, they enjoyed the night air and the pleasant moonglow on the grass. Ivan began to relax. *Garmr does seem to sleep at night. At least, when I was here before, I never saw him at night. I sure hope he remains true to form so we can make it out of here.* He heard the regular, easy panting of Beauregard next to him and Jolly, Murphy, and Stealth behind him as they ran. Leading the way, Ivan realized he was finally comfortable as their leader. He'd made good decisions about Stealth, and his intuition about Charon, sketchy as it was, had been accurate. No one but Carl had been hurt, and Carl didn't even realize it yet. *And just maybe, this is the best place for Carl. I don't believe there were any alternatives for him anyway. All he really wants to do is walk in parks. Maybe this is a happy ending to this adventure.*

As though a full set of floodlights in an outdoor sports arena had been switched on, the meadow through which they cantered lit up. Five scenes, like stage sets on a Broadway play, appeared before them. They halted abruptly. On the far left sat a cut-out view of a small house with an elderly woman sitting in a chair. To its right was the Best In Show ring at Madison Square Garden. Next was a back yard with four children playing. To its right was a field filled with grazing sheep, and on the far right end was a dog-fighting arena.

"Helga!" Murphy called out.

"Show time!" murmured Beauregard.

"Children!" said Jolly.

"Sheep," Ivan whispered flatly.

"Fighting," said Stealth, a little too enthusiastically.

"Uh oh," said Ivan out loud as a chill shot through his bones, and the trembling returned. *I should have known this was too good to be true.*

Murphy, Beauregard, and Jolly, like magnets drawn to bars of iron, glided as if on ice toward their respective scenes. "Uh oh," Ivan said aloud again. "Hey, you guys, don't go there," but they didn't hear him and slid like skaters toward the stage scenes.

"Fighting," said Stealth again, his head high and his ears perked. He began to move in that direction.

"Don't go," Ivan warned, and Stealth stopped. "Those sheep look awfully appealing, too, but something bad's going on here."

"I hears a bad sound," Stealth said and looked at Ivan.

Ivan perked his ears and felt, rather than heard, an uncomfortable, all-too-familiar beating in the ground. "Oh boy, I think we're in trouble," he said as he lifted each paw up in order to feel if the sensation were real. The ones on the ground felt the tremor with each low-pitched beat.

"You're staying here with me, aren't you?" Ivan asked Stealth.

Stealth took a deep breath, stepped back two steps, and sat down at Ivan's side. "Yes, sir. I ain't goin' nowhere. I be here wit you."

"We have to get Jolly, Murphy, and Beauregard back. Any ideas?" Ivan asked.

"Le's just go snatch 'em up," Stealth replied.

"Yeah, I think so," said Ivan as he started trotting towards Jolly. "Can you get both Murphy and Beauregard?"

"No problem," said Stealth and headed toward Beauregard.

Ivan ran up to Jolly, who was just stepping into the backyard scene. He cut in front of her and faced her. "Get out of my way, Ivan," she said. "Those are my children. I love them. I need to play with them."

"No. Those are not your children. This is a trick. They just look like your children. Remember how I told you Garmr made Sarah look like Sarah? She even felt like Sarah when I leaned against her. But she wasn't Sarah. Just like those humanoids in the dog-fighting garage. They looked human but weren't. It's a Garmr trick."

Jolly wouldn't take her eyes away from the children and nosed past Ivan. Ivan spun around and stood in front of her again. "Jolly, it's a trick. Garmr is tricking you!"

"They sure look real. There they are—Jennifer, Jane, Jack, and Joseph. It's really them. I know my own children when I see them." She looked hard at Ivan. "Get out of my way." She started to go around him again.

"Jolly, no! You have to believe me."

"I think you're wrong, Ivan. They even smell like my children. Look. They want me to play tag with them."

Ivan looked at Jolly's children as they jumped up and down and waved at her. Ivan agreed they looked real, but he knew better. "Jolly, if you go in there, you may be trapped in Garmr's realm forever. You don't want that, do you? Don't you want to be with them as another Jolly on Earth—not here in Garmr's Hell? Jolly, look at me."

She looked at him with a glassy gaze. *Damn him. He's put a spell on her. How can I break it?* Intuition nudged him to bite her on the snout. She jumped back and growled.

"Jolly! Wake up! It's me, Ivan. Wake up!" He bit her again, then grabbed her by the back of her neck and tried to shake her, but she was too much larger than he, and he had little effect. Still drawn to her children, she dragged him along, not even noticing how he clung to her. Ivan let go of her scruff and shouted to his guides and to Jolly's, "Help me!" Instantly, his guides and Jolly's materialized. There stood Surri, Mia, Kit, Hom, Sunny, Humphrey, Isotope, and Samuel. In the next instant, all of Jolly's guides appeared led by Elbert the giraffe. Ivan watched as Surri and Elbert spoke in fast words, then turned to the others. Suddenly, they all blew up like balloons, quadrupled in size, and moved close together to form a tall, dense barrier between the backyard scene and Jolly. It was like someone had drawn a heavy curtain, and the scene was replaced by darkness. The only light came from the other dogs' scenes on either side of them.

Jolly shook her head and blinked at Ivan. "What's going on?" she asked. "Why did my children disappear?"

"Because they're not really your children. Jolly, are you awake? Do you hear me?"

She shook her head again. "I think so."

"This is like the flower field I told you about. It makes your head all fuzzy."

"Yeah, I see," said Jolly. "So those weren't really my children?"

"No! This is a trick. Garmr's not asleep at all. Now, turn around and go back with me. She began to follow alongside him. "Wait," he added. "Did you recognize those animals?" He turned back to look at the barrier made by his and Jolly's guides. They were still blown-up so they could block the scene.

"Ohhhh," Jolly breathed. "There's Elbert. Hi!" she called to them and wagged her tail. They nodded their heads at her. They seemed to be straining to stay blown up to this size.

Surri called out. "Ivan, hurry and get her away from here. This is not easy for us."

"Come on, Jolly. Let's go help the others."

Jolly comprehended and quickly followed Ivan next door to Murphy and the Helga scene. Ivan stopped to look over at Beauregard and Stealth. Stealth had stopped Beauregard and was talking to him. Beauregard's guides, led by Ollie the cougar, were forming a barrier along with nine animals Ivan didn't know about. *Those must be Stealth's guides.* There was a sloth, a snowy owl, three great blue herons, a musk ox, a gila monster, a leopard, and a jack rabbit. Ivan smiled inside, happy that Stealth's angels had come forth without being asked. When he turned around, he heard struggling noises. There stood Jolly with Murphy in her mouth. He hung by the back of his neck like a helpless puppy. As he struggled, Ivan saw the glassy gaze in his eyes.

"Jolly, hold him towards the scene." He called out to Murphy's guides, "Murphy's angels, please cover this scene to break Garmr's spell!" Instantly, Murphy's orangutan, Dahlia, and his other guides made themselves large and covered the image of Helga. Jolly shook Murphy until Murphy blinked his eyes and looked at Ivan. "I think that did it," said Ivan. "Murphy, that wasn't really Helga. You were under a Garmr spell. It didn't work on Stealth and me. Your guides just saved you." To Jolly, he said, "I think you can put him down now."

She did, and Murphy shook himself all over, then sat trembling so hard, Ivan could barely focus his eyes on the little dog. "Th-th-that was incr-cr-credible. I had n-n-no c-c-c-c-control over myself at all. W-w-w-wow, Iv-v-v-van. Thank y-y-you."

"Thank your spirit guides." He motioned toward them as they continued to hold themselves up. Murphy looked, then beamed them a huge smile.

"Now, let's get out of here," Ivan commanded and headed for Stealth and Beauregard. Beauregard's spell was broken now, too. "Come on," he said to them, and the five dogs galloped as fast as they could. Ivan was sure he knew the way and sped through the darkness. The moon had mysteriously disappeared, and their way was lighted now only by some faint stars.

They sped past the park where they'd first met Charon and headed up the mountainside toward the safety of the summit. As they climbed higher and higher and were nearing the apex, Ivan felt his tension abate. His heart warmed as he thought of the many animal guides he knew were galloping above and around them. The top of the mountain was in view.

A fire ball burst from the ground, sending up a huge wall of flames. It was taller than the trees and stretched wider than the mountain itself. The dogs backed up as the flames threatened to burn them. So awestruck they couldn't speak, they kept backing up, eyes wide, taking in the sight. Ivan's heart plummeted. He knew they were captured and destined to stay in Garmr's realm. They were hopelessly trapped. Either that, or their very souls would turn to ash.

As if this weren't enough to stop them, Ivan heard an ominous hissing noise behind him. He turned and saw dozens of black cats, each taller than a man, their eyes piercing the dogs with yellow evilness, their coats aglow with the fire's reflection. They made a semi-circle behind the dogs, so there was no place for them to escape, not to the sides and certainly not into the fire.

The roar of the fire wall, the hissing of the cats, and the steady drumming from under the ground were all too loud for Ivan to speak to the others. The fire threatened to engulf them, and the cats closed in, driving them toward the fire.

"Surri!" Ivan yelled out. "What do we do? Help us! Please!" He glanced at the other dogs to see them frozen with fear, ears pressed close to their heads, eyes like saucers, and rear legs shaking beneath them.

Suddenly, Humphrey the bear, Beauregard's cougar, Murphy's tiger, Stealth's leopard, and Jolly's ferret appeared in front of the cats. They bared their teeth and growled from deep within their throats. They tried to intimidate the cats, but there weren't enough of them to do so, and the cats kept closing in. Ollie the cougar lunged at one of the cats as did Murphy's tiger and Stealth's leopard, but three good cats against the dozens of evil cats was insufficient. Ivan watched first with joy when the feline guides appeared, then his heart sank as he realized how outnumbered they were. Humphrey the bear took on three more cats, and the ferret took one on as well, but this still wasn't enough. Just then all the hoofed guides emerged and aimed flying hooves at the cats, sending many into oblivion. Yet, they were still outnumbered. Dahlia the orangutan, together with all the other, non-flying animal guides materialized and knocked out the rest of the cats.

The dogs stood, mouths open, eyes still wide, watching the horrendous battle. The cats' hissing ended, but the ground still beat, and the fire blazed higher and wider than before. It appeared that the dogs' only chance for survival was to run back down into Garmr's valley.

Ivan turned to study the wall of fire. It was growing closer to them, pushing them farther down the mountain. "Surri?" Ivan called out. "What now?" He felt guilty asking for more help.

Surri spoke inside Ivan's head. "Ivan, do you remember when you first met Garmr, and he told you that you, too, could appear and vanish at will like he can?"

"Yes," Ivan said out loud and nodded hard.

"This is called translocation, and now is the time for all of you to learn it."

"But how?"

"You'll have some help. Look above you."

Ivan looked up, as did the other dogs. Floating lightly above each dog were his or her spirit birds. Surri continued. "As I'm talking you through this, each dog's main guardian is talking to his or her own dog. I think we all have their attention." He paused. "Yes, we do. Okay, Ivan, this is going to take faith on all your parts as well as a sincere desire for it to happen. As you look up at your birds, the birds will lift higher. Imagine yourself lifting off the ground at the same time. But, you really need to believe it can happen."

"I've seen Garmr and Boy do it."

"Yes. Now it's your turn. I'm worried, however, that the others won't have the same degree of faith that you do, but it's all we have left. Are you ready?"

"Ready!" Ivan said as he looked up. Directly over him, Isotope hovered in the air, her wings stretched out in their seven-foot span, the flames of the fire wall reflecting off her brown feathers. Ivan had never seen her in flight and nearly fell over backwards at the sight. As she flapped her wings slightly, she rose a bit higher.

"Now, go with her Ivan. Follow her with your heart. Allow yourself to lift up with her."

Isotope flapped again. Ivan focused totally on her, extended his heart towards her, and felt his feet lift off the ground. She went a bit higher, and he followed. He felt secure in the process and trusted her completely. Before they got very high, he looked down at the other dogs to make sure they were being equally successful, but they still stood on the ground, looking up at their birds.

"Look, everyone!" he called down to them. "I'm doing it! You can do it, too. Go with your birds!"

With that, he saw Murphy float upwards with his raven, and Jolly, Beauregard, and Stealth lifted off the ground as well, their birds looming above them with outstretched, flapping wings. Ivan and Isotope led the way up and up, then over the wall of fire. The flames burst higher, trying to reach them, but they couldn't, and the dogs and their birds flew to the other side of the mountain. They floated above the waterfall pool, then landed softly at the edge of it. The birds vanished, leaving the dogs in such a state of mind they couldn't speak.

Ivan felt like an entirely different being than before—

ragged inside from the trauma yet lighter and more powerful. He also felt tuned into each of his guides in a way he
hadn't experienced until now, as though he knew each one
more intimately. The other dogs looked equally trauma-
tized and simultaneously euphoric. Ivan started to speak,
but it seemed improper.

After what must have been hours, Jolly began to wiggle
slowly. "Wow," she said softly to the others. "Just wow."

Beauregard, Murphy, and Stealth looked at her and
nodded. Surri spoke inside Ivan's head, "You might suggest
that you each go off by yourselves to commune with your
guides, get to know them better, thank them for all they
did, and ask for their continued guidance."

"Oh. Nice," said Ivan. "I'll do that." To the dogs he
made that exact suggestion and asked that they meet back
here at daybreak. They nodded, didn't say a word, and
headed off into the woods this way and that.

For Ivan, the time was spent just looking at his angel
guides, exuding love to them, thanking them for their help,
and asking that they remain with him in the future. They
acknowledged his gratitude and assured him they would
never leave. When the eastern sky began to glow and birds
began to sing, he wandered back to the waterfall. Beauregard, Jolly, Murphy, and Stealth all arrived about the same
time. They agreed to head back to their living room.

"Wait," Ivan said gently. "I think we should say a for-
mal good-bye to Carl. Even though *he* can't hear us, I think
we should ask his guides to look after him and hope that
some day, some how, he'll be able to leave Garmr's realm.
With that, they all stood with their eyes closed and asked
that this be so. When they were done, Ivan led the way

to the snow field. "Jolly, would you like to lead the way? Maybe Beauregard and Stealth should be next, then me, and Murphy can go last."

They agreed and began the trek through the snow. When they were nearly there, Ivan glanced back over his shoulder to see that Murphy was gone. "Hey, everyone!" he called. "Murphy's gone."

"No he's not," Jolly called back. "He's up ahead."

"What?" said Ivan.

"He's there already," Beauregard said.

Sure enough, when they reached the grass, there sat Murphy beaming. "How'd you get past us?" Ivan asked.

Murphy giggled. "I translocated." He smiled sheepishly.

The others laughed out loud and said, "Way to go, Murphy."

With joy in his heart, Ivan led the way back to the living room. Just as they were about to enter it, Boy appeared in the doorway. Ivan tightened. He felt instant, huge guilt about Carl. He lowered his head, feeling like a very bad dog. "I'm sorry about Carl," he said, summoning the courage to look Boy in the face. He was sure Boy would reprimand him.

Boy's face, however, was happy, not stern, as he said, "Ivan, you've done a most remarkable job. Not only did you find your own true self in Garmr's realm, you had the courage to lead your group to rescue Stealth, which is one of the bravest acts I've ever seen. On top of that, you helped the others discover their personal angels in such a way that you achieved a group cohesiveness that normally takes ten times longer. And on top of *that*, you all found the extensions of your spiritual selves and together created a force much stronger than Garmr. This is miraculous! I've not seen anything like it." His aura glowed much, much brighter as he smiled upon all of them and wagged his tail.

"Thank you," said Ivan, not quite believing all he'd heard. "But . . . Carl. We lost Carl."

Boy became serious. His tail stopped wagging. "Ivan, it's a fact of our existence that we all have free will—to make choices." He paused a moment. "Carl made his, and this is not something for you to feel guilty about. He was fully informed."

"But, he was tricked. I should have helped him see the truth."

"Carl is a very intelligent dog who was exposed to the many fine teachings of the famous human, Carl Gustav Jung. He couldn't have known more about the soul."

"But there must have been something we could have done."

"There wasn't, Ivan. Let it go. Focus on moving forward. You can't go back. You did so many good things. Think about those good things. Shed your herding-dog guilt. Think about the dog you want to be in your next and final incarnation." He looked at Jolly, Beauregard, Stealth, and Murphy. "Focus on the here and now. Continue to feel the joy of all the wondrous events that have brought you to this stage of your evolution."

They lifted radiant faces to meet Boy's eyes. "Now, you have two more tasks," he continued. "The first is to help one another choose a next life. The second is to go to the Room of Knowledge and plan that next life. Do you have any questions?"

Ivan turned to the others to see if they did.

"What's the Room of Knowledge?" Jolly asked.

Boy said, "It's a place that has records of every life you've lived. It also shows what is possible in the future, who the various humans are that you might choose to be with, their needs, their histories, and what shape your life is likely to take if you choose that person, although there are no guarantees. We make our best choices on what is *likely* to happen, not what necessarily will happen."

"Will I get to see who Helga will be so I can be with her again?" Murphy asked.

"Yes," said Boy. "Any other questions?"

"Where is it?" Stealth asked.

"That's hard to explain. It's nowhere and everywhere."

That sounds familiar, thought Ivan, recalling Surri's description.

"How can that be?" Jolly asked.

"It will become clear when the time comes," said Boy.

"And we get to go there after we decide what we want to be next?" asked Beauregard.

"That's correct," said Boy, "a task that may sound easier than it is. But," he said, looking at Ivan, "now is the time. I wish you the best. Don't forget to ask your guides for help." He gave Ivan a salutary smile and vanished.

"Translocation," said Stealth, looking above him. "I wonder where he goes all da time."

"Probably to help all the other dogs," said Murphy. "There are many groups like ours."

"Oh, no," joked Ivan. "There are *none* like ours." The others chuckled as he led the way into their living room.

Chapter Fifteen

As each dog settled into his or her favorite spot on the sofas, chairs, and rugs, Ivan wondered how they should address this next task. *Just how* does *one go about choosing a next life?* He stepped in front of the fireplace, in which burned a cozy, medium-sized fire with friendly blue tips. He smiled and whispered "thank you." He knew Surri heard him. The fire gave him the gentle impetus to begin. He faced Jolly, Murphy, Stealth, and Beauregard. As he scanned their faces, Carl's absence created a hollow ache in his stomach. "Ohhhh," he sighed loudly. "I feel so sad about Carl."

"Me too," said Jolly, hanging her head.

"He was a pain in the neck, but I miss him, too," said Beauregard. His lower eyelids drooped.

"He did his best," said Murphy. "I guess he couldn't help being arrogant."

"He'll be happy dere fer quite a while, I tink," said Stealth.

The others brightened. "I like that," said Ivan. "Yes, let's think positively about it. And who knows, maybe some day we'll find a way to get him out." He took a deep breath and felt the cloud lift. "Thank you, Stealth." Stealth nodded, his head higher and brighter than any time prior.

Ivan went on. "We certainly have been through a lot. My goodness. The transformations we've all gone through are incredible."

"Not to mention translocations!" Murphy said with brightness. They all chuckled.

"Yes, those too," said Ivan. "And now that we've come so far and discovered so much about our selves, we can begin to see whom we should become next." He paused. "But, I really don't know how to go about this. Any ideas?"

Beauregard spoke. "I think we began doing this in the beginning—you know, when we started sharing what we learned in our most recent life. Remember?"

"Yeah, when you and Murphy insulted me!" Jolly said, pretending to pout. Ivan and Murphy tightened. Jolly laughed and said, "But I know now you weren't *trying* to hurt my feelings. Sorry, guys. Sorry I took it so personally."

"I tink we was all on edge den," said Stealth.

"I sure was," said Beauregard. "I never had to hang out with the likes of you before." He grinned. "I'd always been around prim and proper show Poodles. What a snob I was. Gosh, I've learned so much and feel so much better about myself."

"We love who you really are," said Murphy.

"Thanks, Murphy," he chuckled. "I do too!"

"Oh, this is good," said Ivan. "And I think Beauregard is right. We should probably go back to discussing what we've learned and what we still *need* to learn. Anyone want to go first?"

"I does," said Stealth. "I tink I'm pretty clear 'bout dis. I was always da good, playful dog in past lives and learnt here in dog heaven—last time—dat I hadn't incorporated da tough, fightin' side a dogs, an' dat's why I chose ta be a fightin' pit bull. Dat's why I musta chose Judd as my owner, cuz he needed a champion fightin' dog, an' I did dat fer 'im."

"Excuse me, Stealth," said Ivan, "but I just realized you never did tell us why you were shot."

"Ohhhh, yeah," he said and hung his head for a moment. Then he lifted it. "Dere was two reasons. One is dat I lost a fight. First time ever. Some new pup. Was only twelve months old, but dey'd been workin' wid 'im from da time he was jus' seven weeks. He beat me in da fight, and Judd lost a lotta money. He was furious wit me. I tought he was gonna shoot me right den, cuz dat's what dey did wit dogs dat didn't win. Dey'd shoot 'em an' stuff 'em in da trash. I saw it a million times.

"But I tink Judd was gonna give me anudder chance. He said it was a fluke dat I lost. He still believed in me, dough I heard his buddies tell 'im ta just shoot me. I knowed Judd loved me, cuz he didn't shoot me right away.

"An' den Judd had dis lady an' her kid move inta da house wid us. Da boy was always whinin' and causin' trouble. Judd smacked 'im a buncha times, but da kid jus' kep' it up. Da mudder didn't do much wid 'im neider. She smoked a lot and took a buncha pills an' gave herself shots all da time.

"Judd had started lettin' me come in da house a lot. Sometimes he chained me to da tree in da back yard, but like I says, I was kinda special to 'im. So's one day he an' dis lady was yellin' at each udder, an' da kid was cryin' and carryin' on. Da lady bursts outa da house, an' Judd follows her, leavin' da kid behind. Dey was gone da longest time, an' da kid was pullin' stuff outa da kitchen cabnets and outa his ma's dresser. Den he discovers my toys in da wooden box wit da lid. Some of 'em was my chew toys and udders was da ones Judd used to rile me up fer a fight. So da kid opens da lid an' gets inta my stuff, starts pullin' my stuff out. I had ta investigate an' make sure he wasn't hurtin' none o' my tings. And den he finds da pull toy Judd used ta get me ta latch on an' fight. Da kid starts wavin' it at me, so I grabbed da udder end. An' we was tuggin' and pullin' on dat ting, an' I felt myself gettin' riled, an' den da kid started makin' shriekin' noises, an' I don' know what happened. It was like I was in da ring, my fightin' juices jus' took over, an' I grabbed dat kid round da' neck. It felt so damned good, I couldn't let go.

"I don' know how long I had 'im by da neck, but I know I wasn't usin' my noodle at all. My fightin' instinc' took over, an' it jus' felt right. Da kid stopped fightin' an' was limp 'n' quiet, so I finally let go an' took a nap. He was all bloody, but dat was what I was used to. I kinda knew sumptin' was wrong, but at da same time it felt real normal, too. Ya know what I mean?

"An' den Judd an' da lady come back. All Hell broke loose, an' Judd took me out in da back wid his gun an' shot me in da head. I knew it would happen some day, cuz dat's how most of us went. I jus' figured he'd shoot me one day cuz I was losin' fights. But, I know it's cuz I killed dat boy. I didn't mean ta kill him. I didn't tink ta myself, 'Oh, I tink I'll kill da boy now.' Sumptin' else took over, like I said. It's dat instinc' ting we was talkin' 'bout, Ivan. I couldn't help myself.

"I felt so guilty 'bout dat boy when I first comes here. But now, after bein' wit Garmr and you talkin' to me, Ivan, I unnerstan' why I did what I did. I do feels bad 'bout dat boy, dough. Yet, I unnerstan' now dat Man made me do it. Well, Judd 'specially." Stealth held his head up and looked from one to the other.

"That's quite a story," said Jolly with somberness. "Ivan

helped me remember when I was an attack dog, too." She glanced shyly at Ivan. "But I never told him what I did."

"You sure scared me, Jolly," said Ivan. "I couldn't believe how you growled and came after me. What was going on?" He turned to the others and added, "She was in a meditation to remember some past lives."

"Well," she said, "I was a Schutzhund-trained German Shepherd. I worked for a police force in a big city. One day I was on a beat with my policeman. The other cops called him Gazpacho, I don't know why. He was a sweet man and not very tall. Not very hefty either, so I felt like I needed to protect him. Someone else had trained me in Schutzhund, not him. One day, he was called to a convenience store burglary. I was with him. We barely got into the store when one of the burglars—there were three of them—punched Gazpacho right in the face. So, I attacked the guy. I really mangled his face and arms. His friend tried to kick me away, so I attacked him too and did a lot of damage, enough that I thought maybe both these guys were dying, and I felt some guilt about that. At the same time, though, it also felt right, and it made me feel worthwhile. The third burglar had a pit bull like you, Stealth. The guy tried to shoot me but missed, because I was jumping around so much, and I managed to knock his gun out of his hand and push him through the front window. When his dog growled at me, I went after him, too, and I believe I killed him. By the time more cops came, Gazpacho and I had it all under control.

"I did some thinking afterward about all the damage I'd done to those men and killing their dog. I was torn between feeling guilty and feeling proud. It was strange, and

I can't say I was comfortable with those opposing feelings. Other than that, my life was pretty quiet, and I just sniffed for drugs. That was my only attack episode aside from the training when I attacked the trainer. And I do know what you're saying, Stealth, about how good it feels to chomp on someone. But once I'd done it, I didn't want to be that kind of dog any more."

"I don't recall ever being an attack dog," said Beauregard earnestly.

"Me neither," said Murphy.

"I don't recall such a life, either," said Ivan.

"But, I don't want to be one in my next life," Murphy quickly added. "I mean, I'd like to be able to protect Helga if she needs me to, but I don't want to be the kind of dog that Man breeds to fight."

"Me neither," said Beauregard. "I think I'd like to be a real retriever next time."

"I just want to be with Helga," Murphy said, looking around at each dog to make sure they understood his intentions.

"I think I need to have that ability—to fight—within me," said Ivan, "but don't want it as my total focus. I need to choose something extraordinary to help humans." The others nodded.

"I think I'd like to be with Jane, the oldest of my four children," said Jolly. "I'd like to be her companion and protector while she's in college and after that when she gets a job or gets married."

"I'd like to be someone's special pet, one wit lotsa talent," said Stealth. "Maybe compete in Agility or Obedience. I would still have da protective instincts in me, too, in case my owner needed dat—but not as my total focus, like you jus' said, Ivan."

"Wow," said Ivan. "That was quick. I thought there'd be more to it."

"You know what I'd like?" said Stealth. "Fer all us ta live in da same neighborhood, maybe where da back yards all comes together, so's we c'n talk to each udder. Is dat possible?"

"Oh, I'd love that," said Murphy.

"Me too," Beauregard and Jolly said, grinning at the others.

Ivan smiled. "That would be nice. But I don't know if we can plan it that way. I guess we'll find out in the Room of Knowledge, wherever that is." He listened from within his head for some directions from Surri, but nothing was there. However, he did feel a strong nudge from the other four meerkats to talk further about aggression. He didn't want to go back to that topic, but the meerkats nudged harder, so he obeyed.

"I hate to divert us from this charming idea, but I think we should talk more about aggression." He paused, then Carl's image came to his mind. He said, "Funny, just this moment as I said that, I wished Carl were here. I think he'd have something important to say."

"I agree we should do that—talk about aggression," said Jolly. "But what better expert could you want than Stealth? And I've told you what it was like for me."

"Maybe, . . . maybe you needs to explore it in yerself," said Stealth. "Remember, we was gonna do dat, you and me? You asked me to help you."

Mia spoke inside Ivan's head. "Just because you're the

leader doesn't mean you can't explore some of your own issues. We think you've been avoiding this. Go ahead and talk with them about your own fears."

"Fears?" Ivan said aloud. The others looked at him quizzically. He shook his head and said, "Sorry. One of my meerkats was just telling me I have a fear about aggression."

The others all nodded their heads hard, and Jolly said, "That's obvious."

"Yeah, you seem really uncomfortable when the subject comes up," said Murphy.

"Yeah, I senses dat, too," said Stealth. "I tought so when you and me talked about me. But don't gets me wrong. You did a great job helpin' me. I just tinks you got some buried issues of yer own." Stealth looked kindly at Ivan.

At that moment, Ivan spotted a clump of brown bear fur clinging to the edge of the rug and knew Humphrey was telling him this was truth, and he should be open to it. He looked at the others, was aware of fear sitting like a big, ugly hole in his gut, and felt pushed so strongly by Humphrey, he said, "Okay. Let's take a look at this. Will you help me?"

"Yes! Of course!" they all said in unison.

"Ivan, remember back in the pit-bull garage when we were waiting for Beauregard in the back room?" Murphy asked.

"We saw you, Ivan," said Jolly. "We saw you listening to that fight and getting all pumped up. What were you thinking about?"

Ivan forced himself to relax. He took a deep breath. "Okay," he said, hesitating. "I was listening to that fight and imagining myself in it. I imagined what it must feel like to dig my teeth into muscle—so far in that my teeth would slide on the bones." He looked at them and could feel the fear on his own face. He took another deep breath. "And . . . and . . . and I imagined what it must feel like to latch on even harder with my back teeth and jerk backwards and sideways with all my power, feeling the flesh rip." He felt his heart pound and his eyes widen as he looked from Jolly to Murphy to Stealth, and then to Beauregard. They didn't look upset but listened with compassion on their faces.

"And so what's wrong wid dat? It's all part o' bein' a dog," said Stealth.

"Well, . . . I suppose so. But I don't like it. It doesn't sit right with me."

"You just think," said Murphy, "that, because you're at this higher level of evolution, you're above all that. I think it's part of being a whole dog."

"Wow," said Ivan, grinning. "I guess we don't really need Carl."

"Yeah, Murphy," said Beauregard. "You sounded just like Carl there,"

"I agree," said Jolly, getting back to the subject at hand. "I think it's part of being a whole dog,"

"Then why do I fear it?" Ivan asked.

"Maybe it's cuz it's da one part o' bein' a whole dog dat you's missin'," said Stealth.

"Wow," said Ivan softly, thinking back through what he knew of his past lives. "You may be right." He surveyed the parade of selves he'd seen with Boy, and he couldn't find any attack dogs. "But, what on Earth could I possibly be next time that would both serve humans in an extraordinary way and fulfill this aggression void at the same time?" The others looked upwards and this way and that, thinking hard, then finally just looked at Ivan with blank faces. "Great," he said. "I don't have a clue either."

"Maybe if we go back to talking about what it means to be a whole dog, something will surface," Jolly suggested. "Personally, I'd like to understand what we mean by 'whole dog.' I know I've said it, but I'm not sure of its true meaning. Are you?"

"Well," said Ivan. "'Whole' to me means we've learned all there is to learn about being a dog on Earth, about serving humans in some way, . . . and . . . um . . . ." Ivan searched his brain for more. He knew there was more. He glanced at Jolly, whose question hung in the air like an innocent cloud, and searched his mind for his own understanding of "whole." He realized that through all his different lives as so many different kinds of dogs, his basic essence lay beneath the various personalities. It was the core nature of being a dog. He felt it and knew it was there, but he couldn't find words to define it.

He looked at Jolly. Her eyes met his with hopeful expectation. Ivan felt pressure to give her a clear answer full of wisdom, but one wouldn't come to him. He stammered, "Well, it's about what it means to be a dog . . . any dog . . . all dogs."

Jolly asked, "You mean compared to being a cat or a goose?"

"No, no," said Ivan. "Well, yes, maybe. Do you guys know?" he asked the three male dogs.

"Seems t' me," said Stealth, "dat you's tryin' ta define da basic canine nature—what it is we all shares as who we is—as opposed to a cat or a goose."

"And just what is that?" asked Beauregard.

"Maybe that we all care about human beings," suggested Murphy, "that we all can hear high-pitched noises, can smell really well, and know when our person is almost home. I always knew when my Helga was nearly back from being taken to the doctor's."

"Me too, me too!" exclaimed Jolly. "I could always feel when any of my children were nearly home from school. And I was always right there at the door."

Ivan recalled his discussion with his spirit guides about intuition but didn't want to change the subject. He glanced at Stealth. "Can you think of anything else, Stealth?"

Stealth sat weaving back and forth. "Yeah, well I was just tinkin' about what yous all said 'bout wantin' to serve human bein's. I tink dat's true. But what my owner wanted me to do fer him, I just didn't tink was right. But I knew deep down I was s'posed to do it. An' I really wanted ta please him. An' I felt fulfilled when I did it. Dat's a tough one—pleasin' da human when what da human's doin' ain't right." He shook his head sadly and looked at the floor.

"Okay, that aspect might be difficult, but we have a good start on the rest," said Ivan. "So we have, first, caring about humans and wanting to serve them; second, knowing when they're on their way home; third, that we can smell very well and hear high-pitched noises . . . . Anything else?"

"Yes," said Beauregard thoughtfully. "How about pride and honor?" The others slowly nodded as they pondered this.

"Can you say more, Beauregard?" Ivan asked.

"Well, didn't you all feel proud to be a dog?" Beauregard asked. "—never ashamed of who you were? I mean, I never wished I were some other type of animal or even a human. I felt very good about being a dog."

Jolly began to wiggle. "Oh, yes," she said. "I never wanted to be anything but who I was. I couldn't have been happier."

Stealth pursed his lips and cocked his head to one side. "Proud ta be a dog . . . proud ta be a dog . . . ," he muttered several times. Then he lifted his head and addressed the group. "Clearly, I never wanted ta be a human, dough I often wished I could carry on conversations wit 'em. But I never wanted ta actually *be* one of 'em. I tink it's much better t' be a dog."

"Oh, no doubt about it," said Beauregard.

"Can you imagine walking around with all your skin exposed?" piped Murphy.

All five dogs shuddered. Ivan said, "So, being proud of what we are. Sounds like we all agree on that. But, Beauregard, you also said 'honor.' What do you mean by that?"

"Well," said Beauregard, concentrating, "I mean that we should always do the right thing. If our people leave us alone in the house to guard it while they go shopping, we shouldn't steal food off the kitchen counter."

At this, the other four hunched down and stared at the ground. Ivan recalled several times, when he was an adolescent, and Sarah had left him alone with ground beef thawing on the kitchen counter and another time when she'd left two freshly-baked custard pies up there. The fragrances of these foods had beckoned him so strongly, he'd had no will power to resist, and he'd jumped up and gobbled them down.

Jolly wiggled immediately after looking guilty. "But . . .

but . . . but what if they leave your very own food up there and go off to work and to school, and you're left alone all day . . . and starving? Then it's okay, don't you think? I mean, it was mine. They just forgot to give it to me. Or . . . or . . . or what if they make seven batches of Christmas cookies—all decorated with icing and sprinkles—and then they suddenly remember they forgot some things at the mall—and the whole family jumps into the car and leaves me behind—forgets to take me along!—but left me there with cookies actually hanging over the edges of the counter—me all alone during the holidays. And the cookies smelled sooooooooo good. All that butter. Just hanging over the edge . . . calling to me . . . 'eat me, eat me.' Sometimes Christmas cookies do talk, you know. And because my humans left me behind and left all those cookies hanging over the edge, don't you think they meant for me to eat some? Huh?" She asked, reverting back to her original personality.

"Weren't they mad at you when they found them missing?" Beauregard scolded.

"Oh, no. I was very careful. I just took the ones from the very edge. And there were so many. They never noticed."

Beauregard frowned. "Definitely not honorable. You knew you were wrong."

"Well . . . well . . . well . . . maybe. But they'd left me home. Usually they took me along for the ride. They forgot me!"

Stealth said, "So ya really figured it was okay? It was da okay ting ta do? It was da honorable ting ta do? Stealin'? I calls it stealin'. Doze cookies wasn't yours. You knew dat, Miss Jolly. But ya took 'em anyways. Now dat's what we's talkin' 'bout here. Honor."

Jolly's face went from playfully innocent to blank. Her body was still. She blinked once at Stealth. Then she looked away from him, off into the air. She seemed deep in thought. When she looked back at the circle of dogs, she glanced at each one while tears welled up in her eyes. She hung her head. Without looking at any of them, she said, "Yes, now I see. It was not honorable of me to take those cookies." She hung her head lower, then looked at Beauregard. In a thin voice, she asked, "Is this what you mean? To be a good dog, you have to have honor? So I wasn't a good dog? I thought I was."

Regret appeared on Beauregard's face. He didn't know what to say.

Ivan glanced around at the others, and Murphy came to the rescue. "Jolly," he said. "Everyone has a dark side. No matter how hard we try to be good and perfect, we all have a part of us that does bad things once in awhile. You weren't a bad dog. I'm sure you were a very good dog who was normal."

Ivan felt his own guilt lift considerably as he said, "You sound like Carl again, Murphy."

Jolly said, "But . . . well . . . I'm confused. I thought you guys just said that to be a whole dog is to have honor. And now you're saying that it's normal to *not* have honor sometimes. I don't get it."

The others pursed their lips and, in unison, said, "Hmmm" or "Hmph" or "Ohhh." They sat, thinking.

Finally, Murphy said, "I agree with Beauregard that to be a whole dog means to have honor. But I also think we have honor most of the time, but once in awhile we make a mistake and steal cookies off the counter. That doesn't make us bad dogs. It makes us normal dogs. Do I have this right?"

"Nicely stated," said Ivan. "Very nice."

"Yeah," said Beauregard. "You really put it all together."

Jolly once again looked happy and began to wiggle. "Whew," she said. "You guys had me worried."

Ivan had been so caught up in the discussion and worrying about his own sense of honor, a lull in the conversation reminded him that he needed to step forward again. He took a deep breath. "That was very interesting. So, let me see, where are we? We've now added to the list having pride in being a dog, and having honor. Is there anything else?"

"How about a hunting instinct?" asked Beauregard.

"You mean," asked Murphy, "as in hunting for food? Or chasing cats?"

"What about other instincts like herding sheep?" asked Ivan

"Or wrastlin' bulls?" asked Stealth.

"Or pulling sleds?" asked Jolly.

"Well, we can't really say all dogs have these same instincts, can we?" asked Ivan. "Those are breed-specific. I think we need to focus on what's common to all dogs."

"Yes, I tinks so," said Stealth. The others nodded.

Jolly asked. "Why can't we just be as good and helpful as possible? Isn't that what it's all about?"

"What about protectin' humans?" asked Stealth.

"Oh, yes, protecting is a key element of being a dog," said Jolly. "That was my primary duty to my family. I barked at suspicious noises, and I stood guard with my children in the back yard."

"I protected Helga by helping her do things she couldn't do," said Murphy.

"I protected Sarah," said Ivan, thinking back on how he'd attacked Don as a visiting spirit dog back on Earth. "Maybe," he said, "protecting goes hand in hand with aggression. What do you think? I would have become a fighter to protect Sarah." He paused, then added, "I did that when my spirit went back to visit her. This guy, Don, a friend of hers, came over. For some reason, I guess because she was all bandaged and had the cast on her leg, I felt protective and chomped on him. Fortunately, he couldn't feel me."

"I think that's all we're talking about here," said Jolly. "Aggression arises out of the need to protect."

The others gave her their full attention.

"I think it's true," she went on. "All my Schutzhund training was for the purpose of protecting."

"But not my kind of aggression," noted Stealth. "I wasn't protectin' nuttin' but myself."

"But, that's breeding—Man's doing," said Murphy. "Man took the basic, protective instinct of all dogs and sculpted it into this heightened, intensified, unnaturally strong trait."

The others looked at him with appreciation.

Ivan kidded Murphy, "Did you steal Carl's brain before we left Garmr's realm?" Murphy grinned. "I think you've nailed it, Murphy." Ivan felt his tension drain away.

"I see it," said Beauregard. "We all have the basic drive to protect our humans, and, as you pointed out Stealth, our food, before we were domesticated. That's a natural, normal part of being a *whole* dog. Aggression beyond that is Man-made."

They all sat and nodded their heads. Ivan felt relieved, pure, relaxed, and at peace with himself. "I think we've reached a conclusion," he said. "We have our definition of 'whole dog.' Does anyone have anything to add?"

"Just one thing," said Jolly. "Playfulness. Don't all dogs like to play?"

They thought about this. "I din't play as an adult," said Stealth, "but I do remembers playin' when I was younger. So, yeah, I tinks yer right."

"Helga never felt like playing," said Murphy. "But, I would have if *she* had."

"Sarah played with me," said Ivan.

"My handler played with me before every show," said Beauregard.

"I played all the time," said Jolly.

"Okay, let's add that to the list," said Ivan. "We now have, I think, six items, right? Good hearing and smelling, knowing when our people are coming home, pride in being a dog, honor, protectiveness, and playfulness."

"An' bein' glad we wears fur," added Stealth, chuckling.

"Yes! We have it," said Ivan. "And you helped me with my concerns about aggression. I was so afraid I'd have to go back my last time as an attack dog. Whew! What a relief. But, I think that I *will* have to tap into my protective tendencies somehow." The others agreed.

Chapter Sixteen

Boy appeared in their living room. "I think you're ready to go to the Room of Knowledge," he said with both warmth and efficiency. The spirit dogs leaped up.

"Where is it?" Ivan asked.

"Come with me, all of you," said Boy.

Ivan followed Boy outside onto the lawn with the others close on their heels. Boy turned to face the group. "Now that you have learned translocation, have become acquainted with your spirit guides, and understand the 'whole dog' concept, it's time to travel to the Room of Knowledge where you can view both yourselves and your prospective humans ahead into the future and back into the past. The Room of Knowledge stores data on every dog and every human lifetime."

"How do we get there?" Murphy asked, then nodded politely at Boy.

"Translocation." Boy nodded politely back. Murphy's ears dropped in reverence. Boy continued. "First, visualize such a room. The image will be different for each of you. Next, ask your guides to help you travel there. Just as you did for your escape from Garmr's realm, you must give your heart energy over to the desire. Your guides will lead you there. Any questions?"

They all shook their heads, eyes wide. Then Jolly changed her mind. "Yes, sir. I have one question. We're all hoping to live in the same neighborhood . . . back on Earth . . . , so we can continue our friendship. Is that possible?" She perked her ears slightly, and only the very tip of her tail wagged.

"Yes, it's possible, though not probable. I hope you can work it out. Best of luck. May you all find love and fulfillment." He vanished.

Ivan realized that both Boy and Garmr were equally adept at instant translocation and wondered if he would ever master the technique. To desire to be someplace and then all of a sudden *be* there was very appealing. He stared at the spot Boy had just left and wondered where he'd gone and how many other groups of dogs he was helping.

"Ivan?" Murphy asked. He cleared his throat, trying to get Ivan's attention.

"Yes?"

"Can we go now?"

"Huh? Where?"

"To the Room of Knowledge, Ivan," said Jolly.

"Oh yes, of course. Sorry to space out there. I was just wondering how Boy and Garmr translocate so easily."

"I don't think it's so hard," said Murphy. "Remember when I tricked you guys in the snow field?"

"Yeah," said Stealth. "How'd you do dat so fast?"

"I just asked my guides to help me. It was easy."

"But, how did you work your heart energy so fast?" Jolly asked.

"I just really, really didn't want to walk in the snow and sort of willed myself to be back on the grass. I asked, and it happened. It surprised me, too."

Ivan waited a moment, then said, "I guess we should do as Boy suggested and imagine the Room of Knowledge. Then, ask our guides for help . . . ."

Murphy continued, "And wish very hard to be there,

and we should all get there about the same time."

"What are we waiting for?" asked Beauregard. "Let's go."

They closed their eyes. Ivan imagined the Room of Knowledge as indigo blue with a dome-shaped ceiling. The air inside was soft, like on a humid day. He imagined a movie theater screen at the front where he could view the information. He thought of Surri first and then Humphrey, Samuel, Isotope, Esmerelda, and the other four meerkats. He felt love in his heart for them, sort of pushed it toward them, imagined the Room of Knowledge, and let go. Instantly, he sat there in the blue, domed room, and beside him sat the other four dogs. They looked at one another with expressions of satisfaction.

"That wasn't very hard," said Beauregard.

"Dat was easy!" said Stealth.

"Wow," said Jolly.

"This is beautiful," Murphy murmured.

Ivan was fascinated with the movie screen as it began to exhibit the lifetimes he'd seen with Boy when he first arrived, only these displayed every detail of every life— each human being he'd known and every activity he'd performed, as well as every emotion he'd felt. He was surprised that so much detail could pass before his eyes in such a short time, yet it all seemed to be there. He was pleased to see that he had, in fact, never been an attack dog.

He glanced at the others to see them equally engrossed and wondered how they could be so fascinated with every detail of *his* life. He felt some pangs of guilt that they had to sit through all this.

"Hey," he said in a soft voice. "Thanks for watching."

"Well, thank you all for watching my lifetimes," said Jolly.

"I didn't see your lifetimes," said Beauregard.

"I only saw my own," said Murphy.

"Me too. Jus' mine," said Stealth. "I din't see yers, Ivan."

"Well, that's interesting," said Ivan. "I only saw my own and thought you were all watching mine on the screen."

"I don't see a screen. What are you talking about?" asked Jolly. "I see a lovely turquoise bubble that has all my lifetimes and all my people in it."

"Mine's like a TV," said Stealth.

"So, we're only seeing our own," said Ivan. "How clever. Murphy, what does the Room look like to you?"

"It's not a room. It's a summertime beach. I saw all my lives and those of my owners on a pretty cloud that hangs over the ocean there. See?"

"No, I don't," said Ivan. "I think the Room looks to each of us like we want it to. How about you, Stealth? What does yours look like?"

"Oh, it's bootiful. Sorta peach-colored an' friendly. Sometin' like our livin' room, only da colors is very cheery. And da TV is huge."

"To me it's Madison Square Garden," said Beauregard. "The stands are full of admiring people, and I'm in the center, having just won Best in Show, and there are several gigantic TV monitors hanging from the ceiling, all playing scenes from my past lives."

"Jolly?" asked Ivan.

"Mine's a screened-in porch overlooking a back yard with children playing, and, like I said, my screen is a big bubble."

They gazed at each other in wonder. "This is so cool," said Beauregard.

"Let's talk about this for a minute," said Ivan. "Did seeing all these details about your lives and your humans make it even clearer what you need for your next life?"

Surri spoke in Ivan's head. "They each need to meet with their guides. Each group of guides will serve as a committee to help them chose who they'll be next. You must do the same."

"Oh, okay," Ivan said.

"What?" asked Stealth.

"Oh, sorry. Surri was just telling me we each need to meet with our own committees—our groups of spirit guides. They'll help us choose a next life."

"Wait," said Jolly. "Do they realize we want to be together?"

"Yes," said Surri to Ivan. "We do. We're trying to work that out, although the primary concern of each committee is to guide the dogs to choose a lifetime that will fulfill that individual dog's needs. We must take care of that first, and then, if possible, we'll help you chose the same neighborhood. No guarantees, though. This won't be easy. And it's impossible for you all to arrive at the same time."

"Oh, please, Surri. We want to be together," Ivan said. "You've done other things that weren't easy, and you were successful, like getting us out of Garmr's realm." The other dogs knew that Ivan was conversing with Surri and sat, heads cocked, listening.

Ivan thought he could hear Surri sigh. "We'll try, Ivan. All we can do is try."

"They're going to try," Ivan said to the dogs. "But no guarantees. Surri said the most important task for each committee is to guide each dog to choose the best experience. All we can do is hope we'll be together. And we wouldn't arrive at the same time." The others nodded with understanding.

Ivan took a deep breath. "Shall we begin?"

"Where do we go?" asked Beauregard.

"Just stay put," said Surri to Ivan. "Each of you can only see your own process. Tell them to sit back and be open to their committees' suggestions. Each one's guides will manifest, and, together, they'll discuss what would be best."

"Okay," said Ivan and explained the process. The dogs understood. They sat back and closed their eyes. Ivan did the same, and instantly, Surri and the others appeared. Ivan felt the familiar flood of love, and they conveyed the same.

Isotope began. "Ivan, we've been very impressed with all you've done here. You're an effective leader for the other dogs and survived not one but two visits to Garmr's realm. That's unheard of. We agree with Boy that your next incarnation will be your most grand, a *grande finale*, so to speak. We know you've been struggling, wondering, trying to figure out what you should do, what you should be . . . ."

"We know you want to be neighbors with the other dogs," said Mia. "They'll most likely choose to live in the western world, and we think you would be most helpful in the Middle East with the terrorism and fighting there." Ivan's heart sank. "Or in Central America with the drug wars."

"Can't I be someone's pet, live in a nice house, and still do something helpful?" Ivan asked, sounding way too much like he was whining.

"Like what?" asked Humphrey. "Do you have some ideas?"

"I'm aware that terrorism is no longer just in the Middle East but all over the globe. It's in the United States. Could I not be helpful in the U.S.? I was aware, before I died, of many of the heroic tasks performed by dogs in New York City when the World Trade Center collapsed. Couldn't I be a dog like that, one who would lead dozens of people to safety or find survivors? That would still allow me to be a hero while living in the same neighborhood with my friends."

Ivan's angels looked at one another. They raised their eyebrows, shrugged, nodded, and turned back to Ivan. Samuel said, "We can look into the future and see what's likely to happen in that regard."

Ivan's hopes rose. "Oh good. How do we do that?"

"Look at your theater screen," said Sunny.

Ivan focused on the screen and saw several scenarios being planned in the United States by terrorists. One was the release of a poisonous gas in a shopping mall in St. Louis, Missouri. Another was the bombing of the Chicago lakeshore from under-water vessels in Lake Michigan. The third was the explosion of a major computer software company in California. The fourth was the flooding of the ventilation system with small pox in the largest postal center in Houston, Texas. The fifth was another airline hijacking and suicide crash into the Pentagon in Washington, DC.

"Geez," said Ivan, grimly. "Are all of these actually going to happen?"

"They're being planned," said Hom. "Planned very well. They could happen, but might not. We never know for sure. What we see here is simply what is most likely to occur. Things can change. There are no guarantees."

"And what would I do in these situations?"

Surri spoke. "Just as you said, Ivan. You would lead people to safety. Without your keen sense of smell and intuitive senses, many people would die. After that, you would be asked to find survivors in the rubble."

"Geez," Ivan said again, feeling very strange about choosing among such gross catastrophes. "What a huge responsibility. Yet, it's what I want to do. I can't think of anything better. Not even herding sheep," he added, grinning slightly.

"Does one of these situations appeal to you?" asked Esmerelda.

"Gosh, I don't know," said Ivan. "Can you tell where the other four dogs will be? Have they chosen yet? Maybe I should wait until they choose, so I can pick a place near them."

Ivan's guides disappeared momentarily, then reappeared. Kit said, "It appears they're all leaning towards the suburbs of Chicago. We'll know soon."

Chicago? thought Ivan. *I'd rather go back to Colorado. I'd like to be with Sarah again.* "Who would I live with? Who's pet would I be?" he asked.

"That comes second," Isotope explained. "First you choose the situation, and secondly you choose the person or family."

"I see," said Ivan. "Why can't I remember doing this before?"

Humphrey said, "There are many things you're meant to forget. If you remembered everything, you wouldn't evolve as quickly. Once you're back on Earth, you'll forget having been here in the Room of Knowledge. It's part of how The Source designed it."

"Ah," said Ivan, not sure he agreed with The Source's way of doing things.

His guides all disappeared and came back again. "They've chosen Deerfield, Illinois, a northwest suburb of Chicago," Samuel announced.

"Can I be with Sarah again?" Ivan asked.

"Welllllll, let's see," said Esmerelda. "Let's look into her future. Watch on your screen there, Ivan."

Ivan watched in awe as he saw Sarah's life fast-forward about five years. She'd healed completely from the car accident. She still had some scars on her neck and face, but they had faded, leaving her face shining and happy. She hadn't acquired another dog yet, but she had married Don. Don had accepted a good job in downtown Chicago, and Sarah taught literature at a private high school right in Deerfield. Sarah was concerned about the terrorism that was occurring throughout the free world and was seriously shopping for a puppy to train in rescue work. She belonged to a local dog training club and taught several classes there. She was torn about breed, though, not wanting to get another Australian Shepherd, because it would remind her too much of Ivan, whom she still mourned.

Ivan couldn't help himself and began jumping up and down. He shouted, "I could be her next puppy! I'll be any breed she wants! Oh, please, please, let me be her dog again!"

Surri said, "My goodness, Ivan. You just might get your wish. I didn't think it was likely, but here it is. Let's look a bit further into the future, though."

Ivan watched as Sarah made a visit to the home of a young couple who had a litter of mixed-breed puppies. The mother was there, still nursing pups that were about six weeks old. She appeared to be part Labrador Retriever, part Border Collie, and probably part Basset Hound, as she was built long and low. Ivan thought, *Heaven only knows who the father is.* Just then, a scene appeared of a handsome Australian Shepherd like himself mating with this mother dog nearly four months earlier. *Awwww. This would be perfect!*

"Oh, Surri! This is it. I want to be one of those puppies. But, how can we guarantee that Sarah will choose me?"

"I think if we select the one that looks most like you when you were a pup, that would help. How old were you when she selected you?"

"Eight weeks."

"Okay, so when these pups are eight weeks old, you can choose the one that most looks like you did. Then, you'll enter that pup's body with its first breath when he's born. When you're eight weeks old, and she comes to select a puppy, make sure you're the one who runs up to her first, licks her the most, and stays by her side. Recall that this whole scene is in the future. It's not that far away, but it hasn't happened yet."

"Okay," said Ivan. "Whatever you say. This is what I want."

Surri turned to the other guides for their opinions, and they all nodded enthusiastically. "This is quite amazing," said Isotope, "It's not so difficult to choose a situation and an owner, but to also achieve a location with your group members is rare."

"Oh, I'm so happy!" said Ivan. "Thank you for your

help. And Stealth, Beauregard, Murphy, and Jolly found what they want too? And we're going to be neighbors?"

The animal spirit guides shook their heads with disbelief, then nodded. "Yes," they said. "Yes."

"So, now what? What happens next?" Ivan asked.

"You wait."

"How long?"

"Time is irrelevant here," said Samuel. "There are no hours, minutes, or days like on Earth. The five of you will not incarnate at the same time. That's asking way too much. Each of you will go when your individual moment is right. In the meantime, you can enjoy Heaven. You've noticed other dogs playing games or simply enjoying being. This period of time also allows you to work with us further to better prepare for your next life. We suggest you meet with us every day to discuss your questions, desires, intentions, etcetera. You'll also meet with Jolly, Murphy, Stealth, and Beauregard to discuss how you'll assist one another on Earth."

"That's great," said Ivan. "And I may go out into those pastures and herd sheep, right?" They nodded. "How lovely."

"I think we're finished for now," said Surri. "The other dogs are done as well, so you may return to your living room."

"Okay!" said Ivan. "Thank you again. But wait! You'll be with me on Earth, right? I'll get to talk with you there, too?"

"You won't see us with your eyes, Ivan, but you'll continue to hear us in your head, listen to us, and perceive our urgings as intuition, and you'll also feel our nudges when we want you to do something."

"I see," said Ivan. "I'll miss seeing you with my eyes."

"You can use your inner eyes, Ivan—your imagination," said Hom.

"Oh." Ivan had to think about that for a moment. "I see. Okay." He smiled at them. "So this is it? We're saying good-bye now?"

"No. As long as you're here, we will continue to materialize for you."

"Oh good. I like seeing you." They smiled.

"Bye now, Ivan. Take care of your group," said Sunny, and they vanished.

Ivan watched them disappear. He looked beside himself, then shook his head as there, still sitting next to him in the Room of Knowledge, were Jolly, Stealth, Beauregard, and Murphy. "Hi," he softly said to them.

"Hi," they responded.

After sitting quietly serene for some time, Ivan suggested, "Let's go back to our living room." He paused, took a breath, and said, "Just relax and imagine being there, and I think that should do it."

They took deep breaths, closed their eyes, and in a flash, they stood together on the lawn just as when they left for the Room of Knowledge. As they looked about at each other, they were too overwhelmed to speak. Finally, Jolly couldn't maintain her silence and said, "It's one wondrous thing after another here."

Ivan thought of suggesting a nap, but sleep would ruin this moment. He decided that "enjoying being," as Samuel had put it, was the appropriate thing right now. He nodded at Jolly. She looked from one to another, expecting someone to talk, and when no one did, she settled back.

Ivan wondered how these dog spirits would be his

best canine friends back on Earth, and he realized they wouldn't look like they do now. He wondered what he himself would look like. He had an image of a mish-mash of all the different breeds of his parents and grandparents to-be. He tried to form them into something handsome. He couldn't decide whether he would get the shorter coat of the Labrador and the Basset or the longer, fluffier coats of the Border Collie and Aussie. Would he have semi-prick ears or flap ears? How long would the flaps be—extra long like the Basset's or moderate like the Lab's? And what color? *Probably, a mixture of the Border Collie and Aussie.* He would have brown watch eyes, those signature brown spots of fur that sit above the actual eyes of many herding breeds. Gradually, a clearer picture began to take shape. He would be Basset-size but leggier, have a longer coat like the Border Collie's but colored like a red merle Aussie. And the ears . . . the ears were still problematic as he tried on, in his mind, different shapes and sizes. Finally, he decided that a cross between the Labrador flaps and the semi-prick ears of the Aussie would produce medium-sized ears that stood partway up, then flopped out to the sides, giving him a comical appearance. He liked that and chuckled at the image. He imagined a nobleness that would shine through the clownish appearance. *Yep,* he thought, *that's it. That'll be me.* Smiling, he turned to the others and wondered what they had chosen to be.

Speaking seemed appropriate now, so he said, "I'd like to hear all about what each of you has chosen to be. Who would like to go first?"

"How about you going first?" Jolly asked.

"Okay," said Ivan and told them the whole story as

well as his dilemma about ear choice. They laughed lightly at the verbal picture he painted.

"I'll go next," said Jolly, obviously excited. "I'm going to be Jane's dog right after she graduates from college. She's going to get a job in Deerfield, Illinois as a computer programmer. I've chosen to be a Samoyed. I like being white, but I want to be a pure-bred dog this time and be in dog shows like Beauregard. Jane will get married and have a couple of children, and I'll be there to take care of them." She grinned.

"I'm very happy for you, Jolly," said Ivan. "It sounds like a perfect life. Do you think Jane will know it's you?"

"Oh, I'll be sure to display some behaviors that were unique to Jolly, and I hope she'll figure it out." She smiled hesitantly. "Do you think it's wrong to let humans know we've come back?"

"Oh, no—no, not at all," the others replied together.

"What about you, Beauregard?" Ivan asked.

"I'm going to be a Flat-Coated Retriever who becomes a champion field trial dog. I found a wonderful man and his wife who have owned Flat-Coats before and field trained all of them. They seem like very nice people who will probably have a child, and the best part is they love to train retrievers! I'll get to carry real birds in my mouth."

"Ohhh, that's so wonderful, Beauregard," said Ivan. "I'm very happy for you." The others wagged their tails.

"Murphy?"

"Oh, you know, I'm going to be with my Helga again. This time, she's going to be an athlete, a long-distance runner—just like you suggested, Ivan, except she'll live in Deerfield, Illinois, too, and I'll be another mixed-breed dog who loves to run with her. I'll be bigger next time so I can keep up with her. I'll have a heavy coat, because Helga will run throughout the winters. I'm very pleased. She'll need me to protect her when she runs at night and if stray dogs ever come after her. Or muggers," he added.

"That sounds perfect, Murphy," Ivan said. "And Stealth?"

"Dis time I'm gonna be da fancy show dog, kinda like Beauregard was, 'cept I'm gonna be a little foo-foo dog. At first I wanted ta be a Bichon Frise or a Miniature Poodle, but den I decided ta be a Papillon. Dey's not quite so foo-foo, ya know? And no one will expect me ta be in fights." He added, "But I'll bark and growl if that's needed."

"Oh, that's great, Stealth," said Beauregard. "It should provide a nice balance after your last life."

"Dat's what I tought," said Stealth, his eyes gleaming.

They shared how their guides helped them plan when to be born, how to be chosen by their new owners, all of whom would live in the same neighborhood near Chicago, and how they would be able to talk to one another through the fences of their back yards.

"What about Carl?" Jolly asked. "Will we ever see him again?" She looked hard at Ivan.

"I'm guessing we'll have to deal with that the next time we're here," said Ivan. "I don't see any alternative. Unless you want to go back now. We can do that."

They all gasped and shook their heads. Murphy said, "I really think he'll be happy there for awhile." The others agreed.

"So, who will leave first?" Ivan asked.

They did some calculations and figured out that Murphy would be leaving first, then Stealth, then Beauregard, then Jolly, and lastly, Ivan. Ivan wondered how he'd feel once they were all gone, and he was left alone. He was eager for time to pass so they could rejoin one another in their new bodies. But, as Samuel had said, Time was different here.

⋯

Ivan went out to the pastures and played games with the other herding dogs, and he sat by the retriever pond and watched Beauregard play retrieving games with Spruce. He strolled past the beach to see Murphy lying in the sun, and he cantered out to the snow field to watch Jolly play with Lars. Stealth remained in the living room, and Ivan spent what seemed like weeks discussing all kinds of things with him. He also spent a good part of every day talking with Murphy, Jolly, and Beauregard, making agreements on how they would help each other in Deerfield. Talking with Surri and the others were especially precious times. He tried to soak his brain with their images, knowing he wouldn't see them with his eyes until he returned here.

One day, after the dogs had come back from their activities, Murphy announced that it was time for him to leave. Helga had already done her work in Heaven, planned her next life, and grown to be a high school senior in a town in Maryland. She had a promising career in track and had earned a full track scholarship to a major university near Chicago, was planning to live in an apartment in Deerfield, and had convinced her parents to let her adopt a dog from the animal shelter. The apartment she'd found was attached to a nice house in the neighborhood where the dogs were all planning to live, and the people had a fenced yard for Murphy. It backed up to the yards where the others' yards would be.

"Do you know what your name will be?" Jolly asked.

"No, I don't. Helga will now be Samantha. That's all I know. She'll probably name me. Hey! Maybe she'll name me Murphy again!" He looked at Ivan. "Is that possible?"

"I would think so," said Ivan. "Does anyone know?"

"I would think it's possible, too" said Beauregard, "but not likely."

"I guess we'll just see," said Murphy. "I'll let you know who I am." He grinned at them. "And Stealth, you're coming next?"

"Dat would be me," said Stealth. "I'm next. When is you leavin', Murph?"

"I think during the night. Tonight."

"Gosh, we're going to miss you," said Jolly.

"We sure are," said Beauregard. The others nodded.

They had trouble sleeping that night, watching for Murphy to disappear. But, at some point, they all did fall asleep, and when they awakened, Murphy was gone. No one said anything, and they left the living room to spend their day doing what they pleased. Ivan stayed inside with Stealth, knowing he'd be leaving next. They conversed easily about life, life after life, death, Garmr, aggression in dogs, their hopes for this next incarnation, and hopes for subsequent incarnations. Stealth wondered how Ivan felt about this being his last lifetime on Earth.

"In some ways I feel sad, because I love Sarah so much and because . . . well, I love life!"

"I can see dat," said Stealth. "But life won't be over.

It'll jus' be here instead, and dis is bootiful."

"You're so right, Stealth. You're very right. And some day you'll do the same. How do you think you'll feel about it?"

Stealth chuckled. "Well, now dat you puts it dat way, I see whatcha means. I likes Earth. I likes people. But in some ways dis is better den dat cuz you's helpin' udder dogs be better *wit* deir people."

"And I suppose if we have a favorite person or two, just like Murphy with Helga, we can go spend time with them."

A voice surprised them, saying "That's exactly how it is." It was Boy. He'd appeared suddenly in the living room. "Dogs and their people evolve at approximately the same rate, so when my people left Earth for good, so did I. It's extremely gratifying to spend time with your people here on the other side. And, although I haven't mentioned it yet, on occasion, once you've reached this stage of evolution, you may reincarnate if you believe it's in your best interest. I have twice since reaching this level. Sometimes we need a refresher, so to speak."

Ivan and Stealth sat in awe of the incredible Collie, whose aura was bigger, brighter, and more shimmering than ever. Ivan felt tremendous appreciation for Boy's guidance, then realized *he'd* have this same effect on other dog spirits some day. Knowing that he could go back to Earth now and then took away the anxiety he just felt. "Thank you for telling us this," said Ivan. "I feel better now about my next step."

"You're welcome," said Boy and vanished.

Stealth and Ivan looked at one another, feeling like two children who'd just been told they'd won new bicycles. They stood up and danced with joy. Ivan couldn't remember dancing before. He'd played with other dogs, bowing, leaping, spinning, and dashing around, but this was different. This was movement for the pure joy of moving. They coordinated their steps like country dancers in a line dance. Filled with this joy, they danced themselves to the outdoors and took a canter through dog heaven. Ivan was happy that Stealth finally felt secure enough to leave the living room. Neither spoke a word as they fell into a comfortable pace side by side and cruised. They enjoyed being. Ivan felt greater appreciation for this place, knowing he would be an important part of it some day.

As they were about to make their next loop, Stealth spoke. "Ivan, my turn to leave is tonight."

At first, Ivan's heart sank, but it recovered spontaneously as he thought about Stealth's new life as a show Papillon. "You know, Stealth, you didn't tell us about your people. Whom did you choose?"

"Ah, ye'r right. I do believes I left dat part out. I chose a middle-aged couple, Harry and Daniella, and dey's got two kids, a boy 8 and a girl 13. Daniella, she always wanted a Papillon. She'll take me inta conformation shows and do 'vanced obedience and 'gility trainin' wit me. I'm so 'xcited I can hardly stand it." Stealth's aura doubled in size and radiated an intense rosy-orange color.

"Gosh, Stealth. You know so much, have been through so many difficulties, I bet you won't have many more lifetimes on Earth, either. There's something very substantive about you. You're so strong."

Stealth's aura turned rosier. "Wow. Dat's so kinda you to say. You really tink so?"

"I do. I think *you're* a hero in the making. Don't you feel it?"

Stealth thought a moment and said, "Yeah, I kinda does feel like I might be gettin' dere. Maybe after my next life, which should be a very sweet life, I'll be ready to be heroic." He grew a bit taller, straightened his shoulders, lifted his head, and Ivan knew he was imagining himself doing something special.

The End and
the Beginning

Stealth was gone by the next morning, Beauregard left not many weeks later, and Jolly said her good-byes several weeks after Beauregard. Ivan continued to meet daily with Surri and the others. One day, as Ivan babbled on and on about the visions he had of the five of them living in the same neighborhood, Surri interrupted him to say, "You must understand that once you inhabit a new body—re-incarnate—back on Earth, a curtain is drawn, so to speak, and you start afresh with no memories of past lives or even of being here. It's part of The Grand Design." Ivan's face fell. Surri saw this and added, "You in particular will get glimmers, feel the hunches we talked about before, and have a sense that someone or some thing is familiar. The more 'highly-evolved,' to put it in human terms, you are—that is, the more lives you've had and the more you've worked toward becoming 'whole,' the more aware you'll be. You will likely become reacquainted with your guides, mainly because of events in your current life on Earth, not because you remember being here. When you and the other dogs encounter one another, you'll feel a familiarity, but you won't know why, although you and perhaps Stealth, and maybe the others, may figure it out. As you all proceed through this next life, you may become aware of a greater purpose. It's up to each of you how much growth you achieve in a lifetime and how much closer you come to reaching the Plane of Xoltl. Some dogs do it in very few lives. For others it can take hundreds."

Ivan's sunken dreams sat heavily. "I'm not always in agreement with how The Grand Design works," he pouted. Surri explained how it's actually more growthful this way, and Ivan regretfully understood. They talked about other important things, too, although most of the topics were ones they'd covered before, and Ivan felt impatient. He wanted to get going and inhabit the new puppy that Sarah would choose.

"How will I know when it's time?" he whined to Surri one day while his guides were discussing the ways in which humans can mistake imagination for intuition. "How much longer?"

Surri sighed deeply. "Oh, Ivan, I'll be glad when you reach the Plane of Xoltl, because then I, too, can move on to my next level, and I will be rejuvenated." Surri looked especially tired today, Ivan thought, so he stopped whining. Surri went on. "Actually, Ivan, you will be happy to know that those puppies will be born during the night tonight, and we better get back to the Room of Knowledge. We must be certain that you choose the right puppy."

Ivan felt some anxiety at this. "You mean we could make a mistake?"

"Not likely, but it's happened."

Ivan felt his heart tighten. "Okay. Should we go soon so we have plenty of time to do it right?"

"Time is not the issue, Ivan. Your heart's deepest intent is what's crucial, and I have no doubt that your heart is in the right place."

Ivan relaxed only slightly. "That would be awful, with all the planning with the other dogs, if I were to do this wrong. They're counting on me."

"We'll help you, Ivan. Now, please . . . relax, close your eyes, visualize the Room of Knowledge again, and allow your heart energy to flow to us so we can lead you there."

Ivan had no trouble doing this and translocated in record time. He felt exhilarated to have mastered the technique, and this, in turn, boosted his sense of his capabilities. The tension he'd felt moments earlier washed away in the glorious indigo light of the domed Room. In front was the theater screen. He settled into a comfortable sitting position, eager to choose his puppy body. A scene of Ivan's mother-to-be appeared. She was lying in a wooden whelping box filled with clean newspapers. A heat lamp had been clamped to a nearby chair to warm the puppies after they were born. A middle-aged man named Alex and his wife, Maria, kneeled at the mother's head, stroking her and talking in soothing voices.

"We need to flash ahead about two weeks in order to identify the puppy that will be you," said Surri, and the scene changed to one of squirmy puppies adeptly moving along their bellies to find their mother's teats. One had the exact coloring that Ivan had imagined but with greater detail. This pup was red merle, had a broad white collar, white belly, three white legs and one brown one, a white blaze that saddled his snout with a white path that led to his forehead. His body was longer than most of the others, and his ears, although barely developed, were longer than those of his litter mates. "There you are," said Surri. "Any doubts?"

Ivan felt great warmth for the image of this physical body. He felt a strong pull to be inside of it and to nurture it as the vehicle for his spirit. "Oh, gosh," said Ivan. "I love that puppy. I do want to be him. I'm one hundred percent sure. I feel it so strongly in my heart."

"That's what we need. Okay, then, let's go back to the whelping box." The scene went back to show the whelping of this very pup. They watched as the translucent, wet sack containing a new-born pup oozed out. The mother dog carefully bit through it and began licking at the puppy's face and belly with vigor. Surri's voice was barely audible to Ivan as he felt himself uncontrollably vacuumed into the little body with its first breath. "So long, Ivan," Surri said. "We'll be with you."

Ivan felt panic as he gasped for breath. He felt fluid in his lungs and nose spew out in little bursts with each forceful stroke of something moving across him over and over. There was no light. There was no sound. There was only the sensation of cold air, wet skin, a sense of struggle, and the loving, warm lash of each stroke of his mother's tongue.

About the Author

Susan Kelleher is the pen name of Susan L. Metzger, adopted when her short story *Spirit Dogs: Heroes In Heaven* was published in 1998 and retained for the sake of consistency.

She recalls beginning to write her first novel at age nine and has written numerous short stories and other novels since. She grew up with dogs, cats, horses, and her brother's pet crows and chickens in a rural setting near Elgin, Illinois. She was the assistant editor of her high school literary magazine and graduated from Iowa State University in 1970 with a BS in Sociology and minors in Psychology and English. Writing was her best subject, but she craved a more active life. She became very involved in the Civil Rights movement of the 1960s and decided to become a psychologist. She earned an MS in Counseling Psychology and an MBA in Management & Organizational Behavior from George Williams College. She returned to her first love in 1987 and earned an MFA in Creative Writing at Western Michigan University. Her never-published first novel, *Two Boys*, is the based-on-fact story of a Satanic child sexual abuse case. Her second novel, *Berengei: A Modern Fairy Tale*, is about a mountain gorilla.

The sequel to *Spirit Dogs: Life Between Lives* is a work in progress and portrays the dogs back on Earth. "These books have the potential to be a never-ending series," says Kelleher, "as the dogs experience recurrent cycles of death and renewal." She is also at work on *Jolene*, a post-Civil

War story and *Bertie and Pip*, both novels with humans as central characters.

Her childhood menagerie of dogs, cats, horses, pet crows, and chickens, and her creation of Snowdown Kennels, were a clear foreshadowing of her use of non-human characters to portray universal themes. She has been breeding, raising, and training Flat-Coated Retrievers since 1982. Ivan is a real dog who, at this writing, has crept into old age but is alive and well.

Susan lives 9000 ft. up in the mountains of Colorado where she has a private psychotherapy practice, teaches Reiki, runs a spiritual exploration group, writes novels, plays violin with the community orchestra, and hikes, skis, and snowshoes with Fiji the Flat-Coated Retriever. She has one son, Alex, who is a pianist and medical student at the University of Pittsburgh.

Susan Kelleher

First Spirit Dogs Book

Spirit Dogs: Heroes In Heaven
The first Spirit Dogs book
by Susan Kelleher
illustrated by Rod Lawrence
$12.95

An illustrated short story that serves as a thoughtful gift for those whose dogs have passed away.

70 pages, including 9 illustrations. Hardcover with jacket.

Spirit Dogs: Heroes In Heaven is the story of a woman and her dog, Ivan, who are in a car crash and experience a near-death experience. The woman is invited to visit dog heaven where she learns how deceased dogs continue to send love to their humans, even after the dog has passed away.

Visit **www.spiritdogs.com** to order both books and to email us with any questions.